Understanding Thinking

Maps Models Meanings Values
Goals Motivation &
Neural Networks

Fluffbuster Books

Fluffbuster Books

First Edition

Printed on demand by www.createspace.com
Published by Custom Books Publishing

Summary of contents

Chapters

1 A Brief History of Thinking 1
2 Neural Networks 35
3 Evolutionary Thinking Levels 94
4 Systems Thinking for Systemic Problems 121
5 The Possibility of Self-Managed Personal Change 184

Full-scale coloured versions of the
diagrams in this book
are available at
www.fluffbuster.co.uk

Full Contents

Acknowledgements x
Introduction xi

Chapter 1 A Brief History of Thinking

The Search for the Truth 1
The Importance of Agriculture 2
Remote Causation and Troublesome Gods 4
Agreed Explanations 7
Illuminating the Darkness 8
Two early beams of Light 9
Plato – the Pure Light of Reason 9
The Liberal Arts 10
Aristotle's approach to the Truth 12
Science and Technology 14
Bringing down the Curtain 16
Back into the Light 17
Towards the Enlightenment 18
The Scientific Method 18
The Romantics 19
Grand Narratives 19
Beyond Modernism 21
What is Postmodernism? 21
An Unholy Alliance 22
The Attempted Murder of Meaning 24
Babies in the Bathwater 26
The Decline of Wisdom 29
Group -Think 31
Systemic Literacy 32
The Tree of Knowledge has Biological Roots 33

Chapter 2 Neural Networks

(The Biological Basis of Thought and Perception)

The Fundamentals 35
Excitation and Inhibition 36

Chemical Soup

Neuromodulators and Hormones 39
Amines 39

Peptides 40
Hormones 40

What is going on in the Brain?

Is the Brain like a General-Purpose Computer? 42
Plasticity in Neural Networks 44
Grouping things Together 44
Things with Common Properties 45
Classification, Generalisation and Abstraction 45
Non-Equal Membership 48
Metaphor, Simile & Analogy 49
Sequence Sensitivity 50

How do Neural Networks register Associations?

Post-Synaptic Changes 51
Pre-Synaptic Changes 52
Sensitisation 52
Habituation 53
Experience Trapping 53
Factors in Brain Development 53
Summary of Plasticity 54
General Purpose vs. Task Specific 55
Selective Sensitivity 56
Relative Speed 57
Size and Efficiency 57
Emergent Properties vs. Explicit Rules 58
Top-Down vs. Bottom-Up 59
Precision vs. Ambiguity 60
The Tip of the Iceberg 61
Time 62
Attention 63

Making Meaning

Natural Learning Machines – Experience vs. Rules 63
Spatial Mapping - Attaching Meaning to Places 64
The Leaning Curve 65
Black Swans 66
Stability, Reliability, Memory, Change and Learning 66
Neural Networks Make Meaning; GP Computers Do Not 67
English Spelling 68
The Educational Value of Rules and Organising Concepts 71
Hard and Fluffy Standards 72
Consolidating Experience 74

Isolated vs. Associative Memory 75
The Pleasure of Learning 76
The Modern Urban Landscape 77
Relative Duality 78
The Social Construction of Reality 79
Social Groups 81
Cultural Transmission 82

Back to Basics

Framing - a question of context 83
Evolved Innate Framing 84
Essence and Substance 85
Our Historical Prison and the Great Escape 89
The Moral 90
Freewill and Destiny 90
Submit or Do Your Own Thing 91

Chapter 3 Evolutionary Thinking Levels

Attention Management and Priority Juggling 94
Too Much Information 95
Attention Control 95
Making Sense 95
Social Meaning 95
Multiple Models 96
Competing Packages 96
Managing the Options 96
Self-Awareness 97
Back to Basics - the Frame Problem 98
Intelligences 98
Threats and Emotions 102
The Autopilot 102
Goal Setting 103
The Multi-Headed Egos 104
The Possibility of Change 106
Mind and Body 107
The Conscious Thinker 109
Games 112
Conscious Conscience 115
The Role of the Conscience 116

Chapter 4 Systems Thinking for Systemic Problems

Modern Problems 121
Thinking is a Natural Activity 122
Conscious Observation and Testing 123
Understanding vs. Memory 123
Static Linear Association 124
Understanding 125
Model Making 126
Diagramming 127

Graphical Thinking System

Relationships 131
Conditional Properties 135
What about Concepts and Ideas 136
Graphical Thinking (GT) diagramming - general 138
From the Big Picture to the Detail 139
Representing Systems 142
GT is to Thinking what Topology is to Geometry 145
GT and Neural Networks 146

Wider uses

For Students 146
For News Hounds and Journalists 149
From Text to Understanding 150
For Policy Officers 151

Model Making, Problems Solving and Thinking

Models 152
Building Blocks 153
School-Type Problem Solving 154
The Goals 155
Proof 155
The Euclidian Method 156
There are Several Other Approaches to Proof 159
- Trial and Error
- Counter Examples
- Double Contradiction
- Persuasion
- The Legal (and Theological) Model

Analysing Arguments vs. Exploring Deep Structures 159
Strategy 161
School Tools 162

School Strategies 163
Experience 166
Real-World Problem Solving 167
A Generalised Problem-Solving Model 169
How does this Contrast with the Usual Critical Thinking Model? 173
Problems with Language
Is and Are 174
Direction of Causation 174
Causes (and is the only cause) 175
We Over-Generalise 177
We Leave Out the Quantifiers and Qualifiers 177
False Opposites 177
We Leave out Crucial Elements of an Idea 177
We Misuse what Linguists call Modal Operators 178
Model Mismatch - a hasty generalisation 178
Common Manipulative Forms of Argument
False Dichotomy 179
Causation Errors 179
Slippery Slope 180
Begging the Question and Circular Argument 180
Popularity 180
Appeal to Traditional Models 180
Discredit the Person 181
Guilt by Association 181
Knocking down Straw Men 181
Linear Language vs. Diagrams 182
Hidden Agendas 183

Chapter 5 The Possibility of Self-Managed Personal Change

The functions of the Pre-conscious Mind 184
1) It Looks After the Body and its Fundamental Survival Responses 184
2) It Gives Us our Experience of Space and Time 184
3) It Handles our Basic Emotional and Motivational Systems 184
4) It Manages our Attention, 185
5) It Managers our Identity 186
6) It Traps and Accumulates Experience 186
Models Meaning and Motivation 187

Passive Perception 187
Active Perception 188
Updating Old Models 188
7) It Manages Multiple Emotional Vectors 189
Parts Integration 190
Goal Setting 191
Values Tell Us Why
Models Tell Us How
Emotional Associations
Successful People 192
Successful Projects 192
Vector Mapping 194
Groups 198
Do We Create our Own Universe? 199
Internal or External Causes 199
So 200

Word List 202

Acknowledgements

Special thanks to Paul, Kamran, Vesna, George, Roxy, John and John,
some Russians, some prisoners, some NEET dyslexics,
Marsha, Krysha, Jeannie, Jamie,
Paul, Gina and Ms Stone.

Introduction

The idea to create FluffBuster Books came into being during an experimental project to teach systems diagramming tools to a group of illiterate/dyslexic prisoners. They responded magnificently. The fact that someone has difficulty extracting meaning from text does not mean that they are incapable of enjoying the world of ideas, and does not justify their exclusion from the world of work.

The author is dyslexic and the book is written in a dyslexia-friendly Fluffbuster style. This can result in longer (but less convoluted and less memory intensive) sentences than you may be used to. Sometimes particularly important words are emphasised so that they don't get **lost** in the crowd. Sometimes, simply naming things, ideas and relationships, does not convey the desired meaning with sufficient precision, and it is necessary to draw **attention** to a list of **specific properties.** This can result in longer strings of adjectives and adverbs than you may be used to. This is not done to be annoying; it is done to enhance the meaning of the text. The ':' is used to introduce a list, or to mark a transition between the general and the detail, or vice versa.

Sometimes the text in chapter 1 is supported with gratuitous diagrams. They are intended to be a gentle introduction to the use of this style of diagram as a tool for explaining complex ideas, and to prepare the reader for Chapter 4, where Graphical Thinking is explained in more detail.

Chapter 1

A Brief History of Thinking

The Search for the Truth

We humans (*Homo sapiens*)[1] have an anxiety that drives us to build believable models of the world around us. We feel uncomfortable when we don't have a socially agreed story that explains what is happening, why it's happening, and what we have to do to make things go the way we want.

This is why we are so concerned with the idea of **truth,** why we are driven to achieve an ever greater degree of certainty in our understanding of what **exists** out there in **reality,** and the mechanisms, laws and causes that control the way things interact. We get anxious because we know from our own personal and cultural history, that our understanding of reality very often turns out to be flawed, and that things are not always quite as they appear to our sometimes unreliable senses.

This has been a long-running problem for our species. Most of the words we use to discuss our ideas about truth and reality are at least 2000 years old.

> How can we be sure what actually **exists** (Latin) out there in **reality** (from Latin for *thing*)?
>
> How does reality differ from the **phenomena** (from the Greek for *show*), the way things *appear* to our senses?
>
> The study of how, and what, we can know about reality is called **epistemology**, (from the Greek for *knowledge + study*).

The study of neural networks can now shed some new light on the question of what we can and cannot know about reality. After reading Chapter 2 (on neural networks), you will hopefully understand some of the reasons why we cannot know reality directly.

For example, our senses can only detect a tiny portion of the information that is bouncing around the universe. We are like a radio

[1] H*omo sapiens*, Latin for *wise / knowing / conscious / discerning* man.

receiver that can only tune into five radio stations even though there are thousands of radio transmitters actively broadcasting in our area. So at best, we only experience little snippets of information about reality. These snippets are trapped and organised by our neural networks, and assembled into very limited, but very convincing working-models of reality. What we know and interact with is our internal, personal, pre-consciously formed, mental model of reality. We cannot know reality directly.

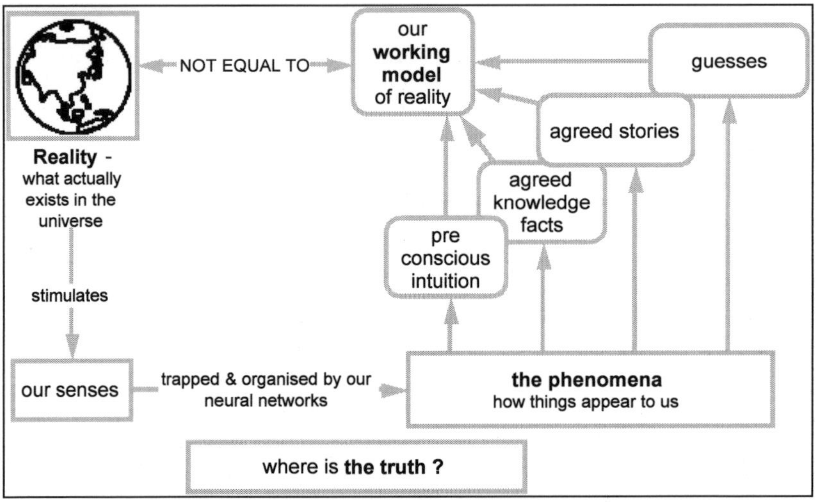

Figure 1.1 We cannot know reality directly.

This is a new concept, a new understanding, which was not available to our ancient ancestors. They **felt** as if they were dealing directly with reality, but often found that their impressions and conclusions about reality turned out to be very inaccurate. So they invented reasons and mechanisms to explain these recurring mismatches between their sensory impressions and hard-edged reality. Some of their ancient explanations are still influencing our ideas about thinking and knowledge, and need to be rethought, updated, to take account of what we now know about our neural networks - and that is the purpose of this book.

The Importance of Agricultural Dependence

Around 10,000 years ago, the climate stabilised, which allowed humans to begin to develop a new agricultural lifestyle. Instead of relying on hunting and gathering the animals and plants that nature provided, these people started to actively manage their own food crops, and domesticated their own herds of animals. When circumstances were favourable and the harvests were good, there was plenty of food. As their knowledge and skills increased, they were able to sustain larger populations and to group together in urban centres, which themselves grew larger and more numerous.

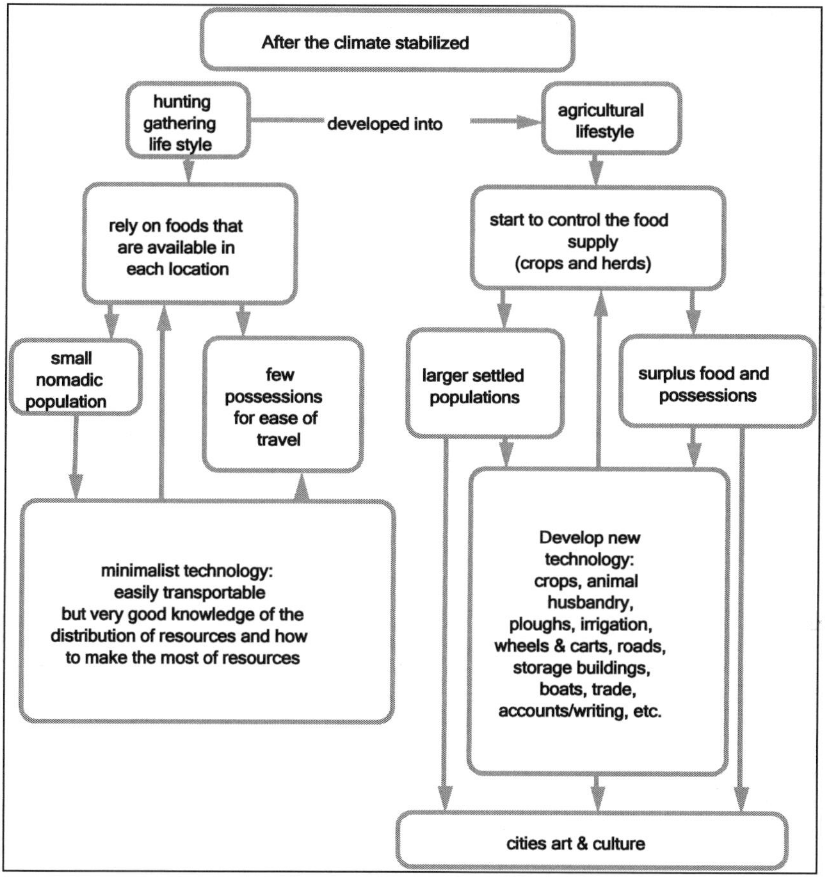

Figure 1.2 The changes that came with agriculture.

Early human civilisations grew up along the banks of major rivers such as the Indus, the Tigris, the Euphrates, the Nile, the Ganges and the Yellow River[2]. These people applied their considerable practical thinking skills to build up knowledge about farming and animal

[2] Chinese cultural development took a rather different path from the one described here, based on the wisdom given by three Cultural Heroes and three Sage Kings.

husbandry, food preparation and storage. They quickly developed supporting technologies to prepare and irrigate the soil, to preserve, store and transport their produce, to build roads, buildings, boats and carts. All this deliberate intelligent activity produced a massive improvement in living standards, and the spare time and resources to explore art and culture.

This new life style brought new problems. By settling in one place and giving up their nomadic hunter-gatherer lifestyles, these people had become very dependent on the weather, the state of their river, and the fertility of their particular piece of land. If the harvest failed, it was a very serious matter for these densely populated urban areas, as they had no other food supply capable of supporting such a large population.

When the harvest was good, the stored food surplus attracted raiders. The cities became centres of trade, but bandits attacked the goods in transit. Government became necessary, to organise an army to fight off the raiders, or to negotiate with one band of raiders to get them to take up residence and live off the fat of the land in exchange for fighting off the others. Productive land became a valuable resource, and laws became necessary to handle disputes over property rights, inheritance and taxation.

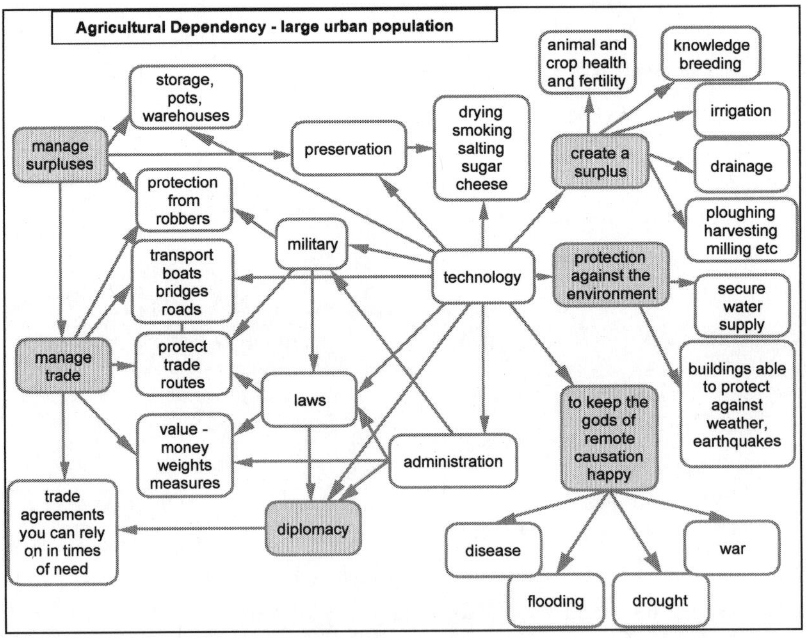

Figure 1.3 The problems of wealth.

Remote Causation & Troublesome Gods

But many of the dangers of this new settled lifestyle could not be controlled by laws, armies or governments. Floods, droughts, diseases, plagues of insects, etc., came periodically, and for no apparent reason. Why did these sometimes cataclysmic events happen, and what could people do to control them?

Belief in the interconnectedness of things seems to be a common human experience. All over the world it gives rise to feelings that there is some kind of god, a higher or absolute being that is responsible for creation, the weather, fertility, etc. So, in the absence of any other apparent local, visible, touchable cause, a common explanation for these disasters was to attribute them to the changeable moods of remote and troublesome gods who, if annoyed, could unleash these punishments on their people.

These gods were assumed to have personalities rather like humans, and all the unpredictable events in the natural world (both beneficial and disastrous) were thought to be the result of petty squabbles or even outright wars between the gods, or between the gods and mankind, motivated by familiar human causes such as: temper, jealousy, pride, revenge, insults, thefts, gifts not given, customs not observed, and rewards for good obedient and respectful behaviour.

The rivers were an essential element in the development of all these ancient human civilisations, providing food, water, energy, transportation and defence, but the different rivers had very different characteristics, which gave rise to gods with different assumed personalities. The Nile was very reliable, so the Eqyptian gods had reasonably friendly relations with their local people. The Tigris and the Euphrates were very troublesome rivers, prone to disastrous flooding, which was explained in terms of rather more angry, jealous and revengeful gods who kept getting annoyed with the bad behaviour of the local peoples.

So, in their model, their understanding of the universe, there was a great benefit in trying to keep their gods happy as this would make life more pleasant and predictable for humans here on earth. All our ancient communities tried to control their circumstances by creating and investing in a class of specialists - priests - who acted as intermediaries to intercede with the gods, to try and keep them happy. The farmers gave valuable things to the priests (animals, foodstuffs, incense, statues and other artefacts), who would pass some of them on to the gods as sacrifices (sacred gifts), in the hope that these would keep the gods in a good mood, or placate them if they were already annoyed (as evidenced by some meteorological, geological or biological havoc).

The priests studied the stars for clues about the gods' moods. They noticed that some of the objects in the sky, (the **planets**, from Greek for *wanderer*), move in irregular patterns. They thought that since the celestial bodies were also under the control of the gods, then these irregular planetary movements might be indications of the state of mind of the gods, and therefore indicators of imminent events here on earth. They were particularly alarmed by solar or lunar eclipses. The priests studied the movements of the heavenly bodies and began to be able to predict some of these astronomical events, but they kept the knowledge of how they did it a closely guarded professional secret, thus reinforcing the illusion that they were indeed in private communication with, and knowledgeable about, the will of the gods. This gave them great psychological, political and economic power.

If the river or the weather failed, then the priests would invent reasons - explanations - that conformed to this angry god model. In very extreme circumstances, the priestly representatives might be accused of incompetence and blamed for their failure to keep the gods happy, but more probably the blame would fall on the ordinary people for their failure to properly observe the culture's current sacred rituals, and serious sacrifices would be prescribed to remedy the situation.

Within this way of thinking, it follows that the thoughts and words of the gods have total creative power, as they can manifest creation, archetypes, forms, laws, causes and effects. As above, so below. Therefore, the thoughts, words and ritual deeds of the priests and magicians were also assumed to have significant creative power. Written words and symbols had a special sacred place in these cultures as they were assumed to be carriers of the same potent forces that manifested creation.

These ancient peoples were not hopelessly irrational. They were extremely competent human beings, who created very practical ways of improving their quality of life. They were good at inventing machines and technologies, and applying their understanding of cause and effect, particularly when the causes and effects were closely coupled, obvious to the senses and therefore easily understood.

They developed wheels, carts, ploughs, clay storage vessels, stone and brick buildings, irrigation canals, casting and shaping metals, sickles, axes, swords, music, theatre, governments, laws, writing, money, trade, boats, weapons, etc. They must have been very pleased with what they had achieved through the exercise of their personal will and inventive intelligence, but very concerned and confused about the hidden and seemingly unstoppable forces of fate that periodically afflicted them.

This brings us to the issue of the limitations of our illusory senses. Even though we splash about in a sea of false assumptions much of the time, we know that we can understand and interact very effectively with **local**, observable causes and effects. Unsupported objects fall to the ground, liquids flow to find their own level, smoke and flames rise up into the heavens, wood floats on water, push a boat and it moves. But we also have to accept that there is a huge realm of other more **remote** causes which have powerful effects on our lives, but about which our earthly senses can tell us nothing.

When the ancient thinkers thought about the illusory and incomplete nature of our sensory perception they came to the conclusion, that this perceptual trickery was, as usual, the result of interference by the accepted agents of remote causation - those playful gods, or demons working on behalf of the devil.

Agreed Explanations - to relieve the disabling anxiety of uncertainty.

So it seems that we humans are really quite comfortable with **local chains of cause and effect.** If we put a pan of water on a fire, we are not surprised when it begins to boil. Most of us don't really know what **heat** is or why the bubbles form in the water, but we can see what the immediate cause was, we have come to expect that it will always happen, and that is good enough. Flick a switch and the electric light comes on. We don't really know what **electricity** is, but we know quite a lot about how it behaves. As long as the behaviour matches our expectations we are satisfied. But we get very anxious about **remote, invisible causations**, and desperately want answers to relieve our anxiety. The problem is that, in these domains, we have very little sensory information to stop us dreaming up very poor-quality explanations.

Science and technology has come up with comprehensible local, microscopic or macroscopic explanations for **most** of these previously troubling events. Newton came up with a form a mathematics that very accurately explained and predicted the behaviour of the wandering planets. Recent improvements in our ability to measure, predict and sometimes even explain the causes of hurricanes, earthquakes, volcanoes, droughts and diseases, have removed so much of our group anxiety that it is very hard for us to understand what it must have been like to live within the total conviction that these overpowering phenomena are the result of a god's response to the bad behaviour of our tribal group. But occasionally we get reminders. The eruption of Mount St Helen in 1980 and the tsunami on Boxing Day, 2004, caused most of us to wonder, briefly, privately, if there might be some higher level reasons for these events.

In modern scientific cultures, we have put a huge effort into assembling a set of agreed explanations for almost all the significant events and processes that affect our lives. To make this system of explanations appear reassuringly all embracing, we have agreed not to notice that a lot of unexpected things do still happen and that a lot of things still can't be explained. We have all signed up to an unspoken pact **not** to ask ourselves the sorts of questions that science can't answer, certainly not in public, but we are still driven to resolve the many remaining gaps in our scientific understanding and spend a fortune smashing up hadrons in the hope of glimpsing illusive species of subatomic particles, and the assumed carriers of fundamental forces such as gravitons. We are not going to stop looking until we find the grand unified field theory of everything, and it's a sure bet that we will keep looking for something even when we have found it, because it is in our nature to try to make sense of our surroundings.

At a more mundane level we crave reliable socio-economic / market data: what is available, how much does it cost, what do people want, how much are they prepared to pay for it, will we sell more or less 'product' if we change the packaging or the logo?

Illuminating the Darkness

So what is the truth about reality, and how can we uncover it? What are the causes behind the events that happen?

Modern science has found anxiety reducing, material level, explanations for many of the events which were previously thought to be *transcendental* (from Latin for *above or beyond experience*), yet most people still have a vague intermittent feeling that the cause of all the interconnected events and phenomena here on earth is to be found in some universal and absolute source that is, largely inscrutable and often beyond our power to influence or evade. We feel, suspect, imagine, the influence of this super-material source even though we can't experience it with our senses, and don't understand the mechanisms by which it holds sway over all our lives, believers and non-believers alike.

We are aware of the inherently dualistic and relativistic nature of our experience of the universe, that we perceive and describe things in terms of opposites, that we can only feel and understand darkness by contrasting it with the experience of light, that warmth is the relative absence of cold, that plus and minus are inextricably linked - and yet we yearn for absolute certainty, an overarching, unequivocal **truth.**

Two Early Beams of Light

There have traditionally been two western approaches to finding the truth. One is attributed to **Plato** (428-348 BC) and the other to **Aristotle** (384-322 BC). These approaches are often presented as being in opposition to each other, but really they are very similar.

Imagine a pyramid representing human perception. At the base of the pyramid is a vast assortment of illusory and confusing sensory impressions and experiences of the material universe. At the top of the pyramid is the goal of human understanding, the truth – a condensed, refined, purified and de-fluffed unity of laws and principles, idealised categories with life cycles of probability and possibility, coherently organised into a cross-indexed matrix listing all their possible interrelationships.

Plato – the pure light of reason.

Plato preferred to spend his time at the top of this pyramid. He was an educator and wanted to develop a training programme which would produce high quality philosopher-kings, with the necessary wisdom, character and self-discipline to enable them to build balanced communities of balanced individuals. He thought that the task of a philosopher (Greek for *friend* or *lover of wisdom*) was to rise up, from the world of phenomena (Greek for *appearances*) to the **noumena** (Greek for *realities*), by which he meant such intangible qualities as: greatness, goodness, beauty, wisdom, the idea of man, the idea of hope, etc.

For him the **real** world is the world of **ideas**, a world which can only be reached through intuitive contemplation (a state of mind we would probably call mystical meditation). He thought that the reason we spend so much of our time adrift on a sea of false assumptions and tricky illusions is because we mistakenly pursue the truth through our senses. He urged us to turn our attention away from the constant changes and illusions of the material world, away from the confusion and ignorance of the senses, and to direct our energies to raising our consciousness, pursuing the truth through **reason and intellect**, and engaging directly with the archetypal ideals and the sources of creation.

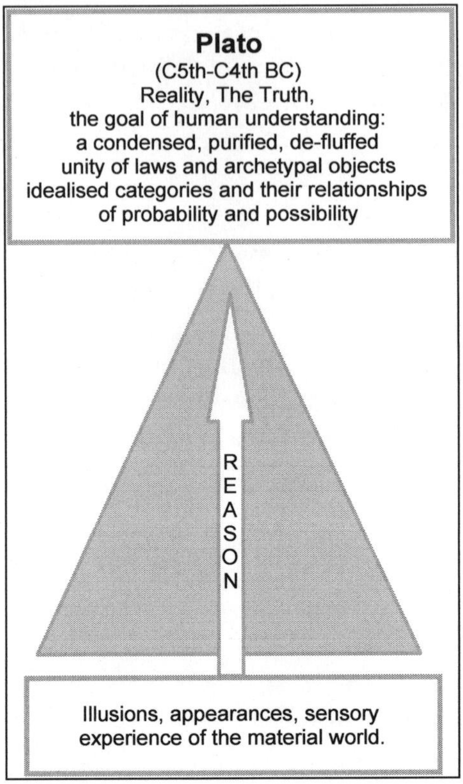

Figure 1.4 Plato's transcendental pyramid.

Plato gave us this **transcendental** model, in which we climb above physical experience, to engage with the highest truths, the highest reality, at the top of the pyramid. For Plato, the truth can only be approached through the pure light of reason, through the intellect. To know the truth is to become acquainted with absolute reality and pure beingness, rather than with existence - things - the multiplicity of illusory shadows projected down into the phenomena of matter. For him, the pursuit of truth is a journey which advances upwards, from these lowly shadows, to the clear light of reality, via conjecture and opinion, to the final destination - knowledge and truth.

The Liberal Arts

His reason for pursuing the absolute truth was the assumption that it would lead to the greatest good for all concerned. This was the thinking behind the 'liberal arts' style of education that was common across Europe for 2000 years or more. This was the liberating work of the pursuit of true knowledge - the **truth that will set us free** (liberate us) from the illusions of the material world and from our slavery to earthly desires and senses. There was also an idea that we should all have access to the best ideas and wisdom that humanity had so far constructed, and then, if we are worthy, a chance to add our own contribution.

In Middle Ages Europe there were four phases to a liberal arts education.

In phase 1 they studied **grammar, rhetoric** and **logic**. The aim was to enable students to use language precisely, so that they could understand and criticise faults in other people's arguments, and construct convincing arguments of their own.

In phase 2 the students concentrated on **Arithmetic** (numbers and measurement), **Geometry** (numbers space and shape), **Music** (numbers and ratio in rhythm, pitch and frequency) and **Astronomy** (numbers and the heavenly bodies).

In phase 3 they learnt **Latin** and or **Greek**, so that they could read the great accumulated works of human achievement in the original languages, and reflect on how appropriately they had been translated. This gave them access to a vast store of accumulated concepts, and observations about human nature, experience and existence.

So, 'liberal arts' students learnt how to use language with beauty and precision, and how to structure and criticise an argument, a play, a myth or a poem. They learnt the best available set of **analytical** (Greek for *unravelling*) tools and read the greatest available works from the past in their original languages.

Then, if they were good enough, the students passed on to phase 4, in which they were considered ready to start on their own personal work, to see if they could add anything to the accumulated store of human understanding.

Some people think that the word **education** probably comes from a Latin word, meaning 'to draw out' or 'to lead out'. The idea being that education should take us out of our usual frame of reference, so that we can see the world, and our position in it, from different points of view.

This enables us to get a sense of perspective and proportion on our current sea of assumptions, illusions, prejudices, values, desires, etc.

These ancient Greek ideas shaped the European approach to education for over 2000 years, even in communist Russia, but it began to fall out of favour in postwar England. The emphasis began to shift from quality to equality as education became a tool for social re-engineering. The aim was to redress social inequalities, and to put an end to any physically or emotionally abusive teaching methods, but education soon became caught up in the postwar postmodern battle for hearts and minds.

Aristotle's Approach to Truth

Aristotle was also interested in the organisation of society and the training of good citizens, but he took a rather more pragmatic approach than Plato. He had observed that even when people do know 'the truth' or the 'right' thing to do, they very often don't act on it. He attributed this to a **lack of will power**, a lack of **self-control**, and to personalities controlled by their **desires and appetites** rather than by their rational will. So he argued that we need to **practice the fundamentals**, repeatedly, to develop good **habits** and strength of **will** so that we can act on the truth and do the right thing.

As regards the pursuit of the truth, Aristotle did not seem to disagree with the general idea that the universe is the result of the ongoing contemplation of a supreme being, and that the highest truths and reality were to be found at the top of the pyramid. But whereas Plato thought that observing material manifestations of reality was a distracting waste of time, Aristotle had a burning passion for **observation** (Latin for *watching*) and **examination** (Latin for *balancing*). He thought that these two intellectual techniques are a very good place to begin our search for the truth, provided we are fully aware of the imperfections of our sensory perception and do everything we can to compensate for these weaknesses whilst we make our observations and examinations (watching and balancing).

So, whereas Plato's attention was directed on the apex of the pyramid, Aristotle's efforts were focussed on extracting as much high quality knowledge and experience as he could from the bottom of the pyramid, and in so doing he gave us **empiricism** (from Greek for *experience*), the other great theme in western approaches to the truth.

Where Plato emphasised only one route to the truth, Aristotle thought it was worth considering many different approaches, and he distinguished between the **method** of observation and thinking, and the **content**.

Some key features that distinguish Aristotle's approach include the following:

- he was not averse to metaphysical analysis;
- he thought we should take account of the traditional skills and knowledge built up over the centuries by ordinary practical people;
- he advocated discussion as a way of refining our understanding, and clarifying the deep meaning behind the vague and confused words and phrases we often use to communicate;
- he particularly encouraged the careful examination of what he called 'first principles' (*a priori* knowledge), those things which seem to us to be obviously true but which we can't really demonstrate and which don't seem to be based on experience.

He tried to look at each field of study from many different points of view in order to build up a broad superstructure of **experiential knowledge**. He then sought to classify things into natural groupings, on the basis of their **essential and variable properties**, and on the **possibilities and probabilities** of their life cycles. He was aware that we have some innate predispositions that influence the way we categorise things – as if the categories had somehow been predetermined by the universe (Chapter 2, on neural networks, offers an explanation for this innate bias.)

Having thus established the classes - the categories of things, he then looked for the **relationships** between them, the **causes**, the **reasons** why things relate in the way they do. He was a **systems** thinker.

His ultimate aim was to formulate **theories** (Greek for *look at, a way of looking at things*) that gave a broad, coherent and workable explanation, consistent with the examined observations.

Aristotle's main tools for climbing the pyramid were, **generalisation:** identifying and extracting the important recurring commonalities to be found in a lot of detailed observations, and **abstraction:** discarding the irrelevant fluff.

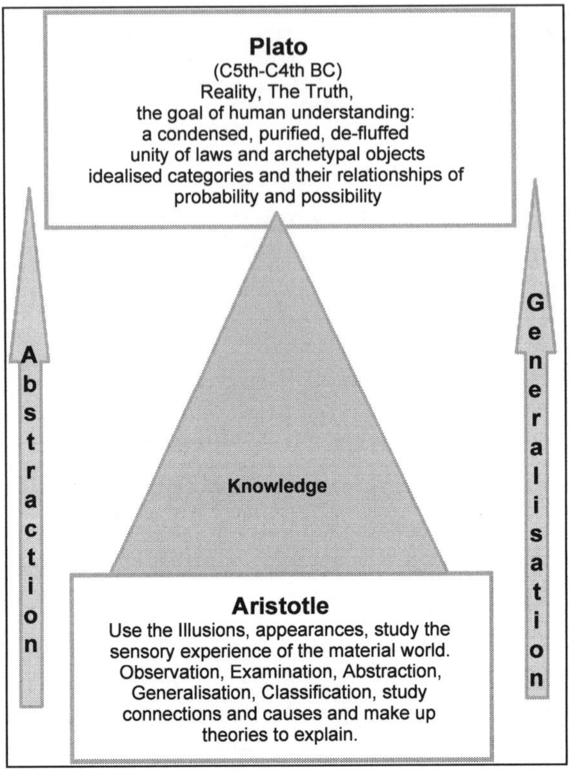

Figure 1.5 Plato's pinnacle on Aristotle's base.

Science and Technology

This process of going **from** lots of detail **to** generalised principles is called **induction** (Latin for *lead to*). This is how we climb the pyramid, level by level, from sensory experience to reality. This is the job of science. Level by level, we build up generalised knowledge, theories, that can explain the behaviour of the material world at the level above. As we improve our knowledge of the nature and interactions of the fundamental physical particles, we begin to be able to understand (explain) chemistry. As our knowledge of chemistry grows, it helps us to understand biology, etc. To understand is to stand under the next level.

Technology works in the opposite direction. It works from the generalised knowledge built up by science or tradition and applies it (20 or so years later) to make inventions, physical and practical manifestations of the ideas, usually in the hope of financial gain. Working in this direction, exploring ways of **applying** the generalised knowledge, is called **deduction** (Latin for *lead from*).

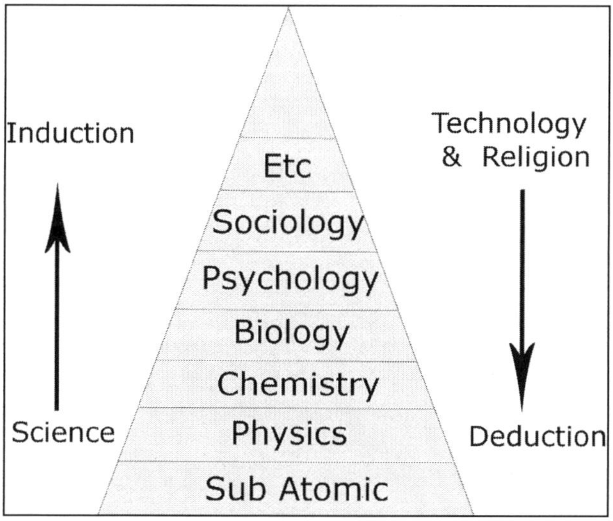

Figure 1.6 Layers of Enlightenment - Science and Technology.

Was Aristotle sure of his truths? Not entirely. He particularly liked to use demonstrations as a way of communicating the practical truth of an idea, but he also used the notion of probability/possibility as a tool for dealing with uncertainty. He was aware that this whole process is a kind of game, in which we do our best to approach the truth.

Bringing Down the Curtain

Plato and Aristotle have usually been portrayed as holding opposite opinions in these matters. This is a false distinction which was created, like so many others, for political, religious and financial reward. Their two positions are very similar and complementary; there is just a slight difference in the emphasis. For Plato, the proper exercise of the power of understanding is in discovering the **essence** of each thing. Clearly this process must begin with a wealth of sensory observations, but the higher truth is in the purified, abstracted, de-fluffed, generalised essences. This is the same process that Aristotle is pursuing, but Aristotle goes into much more detail about how to make good observations (given the limitations of our senses), and how to extract the essence from those observations. Both Plato and Aristotle agree that the quality of the truth gets better as you climb the pyramid from sensory observation to generalised essence.

The difference between them was exaggerated for political reasons. There were elements in Aristotle's work - a natural order in the universe - which the Christian church preferred and promoted, and there were elements in Plato's ideas - particularly the transmigration of eternal pre-existing human souls - which the Christian church wanted to squash. The concept of transmigrating pre-existing souls, or reincarnation, as we might call it today, was popular with many Greeks and early (Greek) Christians, but it became a big problem for Christian theologians after the Roman Emperor Constantine's reshaping of church theology in the 4th century. Their 'marketing team' had decided to distance themselves from the popular Greek and Vedic notions of reincarnation, and to promote the idea that we have only one material life, at the end of which we will be judged once and for all, and the only way to be sure of saving yourself from eternal hell and damnation was through exclusive membership of the Christian Church. In Plato's view (which was widely held at the time) a human soul enjoys many material lives during which we gradually refine our awareness and expression, on a journey to eventual perfection and reunion with God (theosis), so there is no need to be saved by a church. Aristotle's observations and speculations about the nature and working of the soul were, in the main, less incompatible with the views of the later Christian church, which may explain why Aristotle's approach to thinking and the truth was promoted, and Plato's was not.

Back into the Light

Although neglected in western Europe, Plato's ideas remained very influential in the Greek-speaking East. Very few of us (in the modern West) seem to have been taught anything about the Greek-speaking Eastern Roman/Byzantine Empire, which did not collapse in 410 A.D., but continued uninterrupted until it was consumed by the expansion of the Islamic Ottoman Empire in the 1400s. The religion of the Byzantine Empire was (Eastern) Orthodox Christianity, whose traditions had stayed much closer to those of the early Greek speaking Christian Church. During the Renaissance - a period at the end of the Middle Ages when there was a great rediscovery in western Europe of the ideas of ancient Rome and Greece - Plato's ideas were formally rediscovered (in the West). These rediscoveries (not just Plato) began a process which freed up European thinking, gradually reducing the power of the Church (although Christianity continued to be a central organising principle in European life) and softening its influence on our understanding of external reality.

This led to the **reformation** of the church in northern Europe and the division of the western Christian Church into Catholicism (the evolved original) and Protestantism (the reformed, back to the Bible version).

In north western Protestant Europe things began to change. The Middle Ages were coming to a close, and the new **modern** period was beginning, bringing with it great changes in the way people approached the truth. The modern period saw a huge shift in the focus for human endeavours, characterised by a sustained period of exploration, colonisation and empire building. The change was driven by improved boatbuilding technology and navigational techniques. Attention turned to the international race to sequester and exploit the natural resources and products (precious metals, timber, rubber, fabrics, dyes, furs, food crops, spices, etc.) produced by the newly contacted peoples in the Americas, Asia, the West and East Indies, West Africa, Russia and China. As a result of this sustained contact between different cultures it gradually became clear that there are many different ways to organise human society and to make sense of the world.

Towards The Enlightenment

The scholars of the Middle Ages, brought up on Aristotelian ideas, believed that everything could be discovered through the process of clever educated men arguing from what was already known. They had huge respect for the great authorities of the past, but had difficulty moving forward because they had lost sight of Aristotle's emphasis on observation. **Francis Bacon** (1561- 1626) successfully reintroduced the idea of careful observation, examination, and practical experimentation (contracting a fatal pneumonia in the process). He pioneered a new, scientific, way of approaching the truth. This became very influential and created an intellectual movement which we now call the **Enlightenment**, because its advocates hoped that their new way of thinking was going to illuminate the underlying secrets of the universe, or God's creation, as they still thought of it. Bacon also drew attention to common mistakes in human thinking, such as tribalism, personal prejudice, and the tyranny of words and received systems of thought. Political correctness and group-think are not new phenomena.

The new Protestant flavour of Christianity thought that our personal access to Heaven depended either, on our inner faith alone, or that the matter had already been predetermined by God and was therefore beyond our personal control. So, in both the Protestant views of salvation there was no longer any reason to spend our personal wealth building fine public buildings as thanks to God, or as recompense for our sins.

Consequently, the cities of northern Europe were pretty bland in comparison with those of southern Europe and the Byzantine empire, and there was an accumulation of personal rather than municipal wealth in the north, which paved the way for scientific research, investment, and for **capitalism**, which used **science** and **technology** to better exploit the resources of the newly discovered territories, and used aggregated **personal savings** to bankroll investment in trading expeditions and industrial processes.

There followed a great **positivism**, driven by the rising popularity and success of the new ways of thinking: rationally, empirically, scientifically, and objectively. The new thinkers had freed themselves from the power of the papacy and tamed the power of the monarchy. Modern science was on the rise, resulting in technical achievements that brought a great increase in financial wealth. People began to hope that this new scientific thinking would enable them to overcome all practical problems, and improve their quality of life, whilst exploring the wonders of God's creation, and thus getting closer to God as well.

The new thinkers were on a roll. Their approach was going to facilitate the triumph of reason over ignorance, order over disorder, science over superstition, and the **rule of law** over the **divine right of kings (**to rule**)**. They also wanted a new ethical framework, less dependent on historical religious revelation or intuition, and more scientific, objective and quantitative. With the ending of the divine right of kings, they needed a new social order to replace the old f**eudal** system. So they looked for new ways of organising society, with the aim of emancipating humanity from ignorance, poverty, insecurity, violence, oppression, etc. They thought about new ways to justify and legitimise government, but instead of looking back to the Golden Ages of ancient Greece and Rome, as they had in the Renaissance, they looked forward to the new and infinite possibilities that might now be available.

The Scientific Method

But how were these new advances to be made, how were these new ambitions for the human species to be realised? The new scientists were keenly aware of the fundamental fallibility of human knowledge, the incomplete and sometimes illusory nature of our sensory perception, and our difficulty in being objective when evaluating evidence. They thought that the best way forward was to carry on refining the new scientific methodology: make lots of observations, measure, quantify and classify as carefully as possible, invent a hypothesis that might explain the observed facts and which makes precise quantifiable predictions that could be tested by experiments. These new searchers after truth realised the importance of **testing** their ideas, so they set up their experiments in such a way that they try to find faults and expose weaknesses in the hypothesis. They also thought it was important that the experiments should be capable of being replicated by anyone else who might want to check the results for themselves.

Where the subject matter was not so amenable to measurement (art and literature, theology and history), the new methodology focused on the evaluation of the evidence, getting access to the original authenticated documents where possible, studying the language and social context of those primary sources, considering the reliability of witnesses (checking for hidden agendas, self-interest, etc.), and being scrupulously accurate in making quotations and citations.

The Romantics -

reacted against all this cold dispassionate analysis, and emphasised the unique importance and value of human feelings. This didn't have much influence on science and technology but it deeply affected thinking in music, literature and politics. In Britain, there had been huge and disruptive social adjustments brought about by changes in agriculture and industrialisation. The new romantic sentimentality coincided with a wave of social reforms which attempted to address the poverty, difficult living conditions and political under-representation of the new urban workers (at home), and to abolish slavery across the British Empire.

Grand Narratives

There was also, as there has probably always been, a tendency to believe that there are some divine hidden laws and forces guiding the progress of human civilisation towards either perfection or destruction - our old friend remote causation again.

As usual, people dreamed up less than rigorously scientific explanations, and imagined the hidden mechanisms that must be driving this progress. More often than not, these were based either on a fundamentally flawed theory of human nature, or, on a theory about the fundamental flaws in human nature. Recently, people have taken to calling those ideas about the hidden forces driving human history - **'grand narratives'**.

These ideas had very serious consequences. They shaped the way humans decided to organise their societies. Some grand narratives suggested that because human nature is so awful, we must have a strong state to prevent us killing each other and generally behaving badly. Others thought that human nature was basically good and that we should have a weak state that would enable individuals to flourish. People proposed democratic states, states limited and legitimised by constitutions, states orientated around the goal of maximising the quantity or quality of human happiness, states led by supermen, or philosophers, or economic theories, or by the most successful, or by the church, etc.

Unfortunately, this tendency to be influenced by grand narratives led to a series of horrific revolutions. Many approaches were proposed, a handful were tried and a few stood out to dominate the 20th century: **communism, capitalism** with a touch of democracy, and **fascism**. Nice simple names to describe very complex and continuously evolving ideas.

Amazingly, and despite the constant stream of horrors that have accompanied the Enlightenment and the Modern Period, most people still held strongly to the positive idea that scientific thinking and technology, under the direction of one or other of these Grand Narratives, was going to lead us to a better place.

In the 1960s and 1970s, both in Europe and America, there evolved a heady political mix, still based on the positive modern idea that it must be possible to improve the situation. This was not an unreasonable idea, especially when set against a background of the Cold War, nuclear arms proliferation, the Vietnam War, the chaos following the collapse of empires, the growth in the power of multinational companies, the end of national capitalism and increasing globalisation, civil rights, the unions, militant socialists, liberal communists and student riots.

For a while it looked as if some broad-left social alliance might actually come to power, but it was not to be. Global capitalism won. The left was disillusioned, and many of its sympathisers concluded that they would never be able to gain power or influence through the democratic process (particularly in America) and so they disengaged from politics and focused their attention on influencing the direction of social development through academia, education and the arts.

Beyond Modernism

In the 1970s a group of French philosophers and social commentators began to question the Modernist assumption of 'social progress'. They initiated a distrust, which grew into strong opposition to the whole idea of the Grand Narrative. They refuted the existence of any force shaping the progress of human society, since all the major grand narratives which had been tried, had failed to describe or predict the reality of social evolution, and more importantly, had failed to lead society in their preferred direction.

They argued that the modern positive scientific enlightenment project, combined with the political power and value systems of the erroneous grand narratives, had been a very dangerous combination and was directly responsible for a long series of massive human disasters. They declared that modernism should be killed off once and for all, and that we must enter a new period of history to be called **postmodernism.**

What is Postmodernism?

This atmosphere of social and political disillusionment was already showing itself in a new kind of art, characterised by:

- a lack of depth;
- a lack of meaning;
- a break with traditional forms, materials, methods and content;
- a break with harmony – there was no longer a requirement for coherence or integrity; 'anything goes' with anything, buildings didn't have to fit into their surroundings any more;
- art became a game, with very flexible rules:
    - sequence, continuity, meaning and integrity were smashed & fragmented into collage and pastiche;
    - words became disconnected from their meanings;
    - words and images could be used in any way you liked to represent whatever you wanted;
    - the reader's impression was at least as important as the writer's intention;
    - the critic/commentator was as important as the creator;
    - the old distinction between high and popular culture was denied – so we got opera stars singing at football matches.

The intellectual creators of postmodernism absorbed these ideas from the world of art and literature, and also incorporated a superficial interpretation of Einstein's ideas of **relativity**. They regrouped in the universities, colleges and the media, and set about undermining modern absolutist traditional values and methodologies. They wanted to free humanity from the shackles of deluded authoritarian ideologies and coercive notions of truth and reality. They taught that there are no underlying laws of social progress, no absolute truths, and that knowledge is uncertain, relative, and contextual. Nothing has, nor needs to have, any specific or durable meaning. There is no such thing as human nature. Life is just a fun fluffy relativistic game. The truth is whatever anyone says it is.

Their simplistic political objective of a free, fair, open and equal society, expressed itself in an openly authoritarian and prescriptive control of language and ideas. They deconstructed literature and historical accounts, and found them to be racist, sexist, elitist, imperialist, etc. Despite their dislike of censorship, they reinvented a highly overt form of **political correctness**, banning particular words and expressions and replacing them with compulsory 'new & improved' ones. They openly undermined long established values from the past which did not directly support their objectives and replaced them with a small set of approved new values. In true tribal fashion, they had no qualms about evicting heretics and dissenters from their jobs. Cultural relativity theory proclaimed that our individual values are all equally valuable - but in practice, it turned out that our individual truths could still be trumped by their group-truths whenever they wanted. So, nothing new there then.

An Unholy Alliance - Global Capitalism, Postmodernism and the Public Sector.

The postmodern intellectual experiment might not have survived very long on its own, but it happened to coincide with huge changes in the victorious capitalist technology of production and distribution. Thanks to the new computers, and improved transport services, global businesses now had much more flexible, and much cheaper manufacturing, marketing and distribution processes. Physical goods were still relatively expensive to store and distribute, but electronic products and information were rapidly becoming very much cheaper to create, store, organise and disseminate. This broke down many of the old geographical commercial barriers, and had the effect of bringing physically distributed customers and producers together in a new virtual global market place. Capitalists no longer had to make, warehouse and sell large numbers of identical products into huge physically protected mass markets. Now they could produce a much larger variety of more individualised products.

The new postmodern, image-dominated, godless, soulless, value-free, meaning-free, fun-filled, fashionable, anything-goes culture was a godsend to the capitalists. This was a perfect cultural backdrop for the production of thousands of consumer life-style magazines which offered to help us find and express our personal identity in this haystack of new products.

Capitalism has only one real value system – reliable cash flow. It gets into conflict where people have other wiser, more humane value systems, so the capitalists were delighted to see all those problematic traditional values being undermined by someone else. The new unholy trinity was completed (in the UK) by the inclusion of the public sector, which got a new lease of life from the vote winning power of the new political correctness. This new language enabled the public sector to portray itself as a moral hero fighting on behalf of the many newly identified, (newly fragmented), social groups. It created an emotive new slogan, 'meeting the needs'. It carefully avoided any serious debate about exactly what it is that humans really 'need', whilst clearly defining itself as the only morally qualified body to 'meet the needs'. In this way it mobilised more or less reliable groups of customer-voters and worker-voters who would support its postmodern partial-liberal[3] public sector expansion project.

A heady mix indeed. So for the last 30 years, there has been a strange period of human history where many influential people (in the media, academia, literature, the arts, history, politics, etc.) openly admit to having abandoned the pursuit of the truth. They argue that because of the inadequacy of the historical record, and humanity's unavoidable perceptual subjectivity, there is no possibility of objectively knowing reality. Therefore there is no point in pursuing it. These 'movers and shakers' considered all previous over-simplistic attempts at identifying big-picture trends in human affairs to be nothing more than cynical manipulations of public opinion in support of old establishment ideologies and institutions. Instead, they preferred to celebrate and draw attention to: differences, fragmentation, discontinuity, disparity,

---

[3] Partial-liberal in that it values tolerance and compassion, but has lost sight of self-discipline, hard work and high standards.

contradiction, discord, ambiguity, irony, paradox, perversity, opacity, anarchy and chaos - presumably because they think it is a more accurate reflection of the reality they want us to abandon.

They denied the relevance of traditional categories such as **nation** and **class**. Some even question the knowability of logical relationships such as **cause** and **effect**, and structures such as **time** and **sequence**, preferring a fragmented pointillist pastiche, a collage of snippets of images and information, from which the readers can, if they like, assemble any meaning of their choosing. They are committed to affirming nothing, which is perhaps why they have such difficulty finishing their sentences when they talk on radio discussion programmes.

They set up publicly funded bodies of experts to advise society on education, housing, welfare, regeneration, community cohesion, etc. The experts organise conferences and agonise over the purpose of education (or whatever) in a postmodern multicultural world. Group-think wins out over functional-systems-think, resulting in recommendations whose main purpose is to create the appearance of universal group support and cohesion. This is achieved by the avoidance of any specific detail (if you don't actually say anything, then it can't be wrong, offensive or controversial). This intellectual monkey business necessitated the creation of a new vague and content-free style of language, for describing non-prescriptive, flexible, overarching frameworks of continuing professional development, and obligations to, consult, benchmark best practice, agree a strategy, and so forth.

Of course, they are right in many important respects. Human understanding is dualistic and relativistic. We cannot have perfect knowledge of what is out there in reality because it is not possible with our limited sensory and perceptual apparatus (see chapter 2). Knowledge is uncertain and culture is relative.

The Attempted Murder of Meaning

Most of us would agree that naïve and over-optimistic modernism was dangerous, but is this nihilistic postmodern attack on meaning, in pursuit of yet another over-simplistic political agenda, any less dangerous?

Partial-liberals demonstrate their group membership credentials by insisting that we tolerate and celebrate everything in sight. The more provocatively a particular activity undermines old-think, the more brownie points they get for telling us we must tolerate it. Many current teachers have a real problem with the idea that they should pass on anything approaching absolute knowledge or cultural recommendations to 'their' students, although they don't seem to have any qualms about promoting their postmodern perspective as the 'correct' analytical framework.

They consider themselves liberal, but seem to have forgotten that the liberal ideal was based on first providing young people with the best available education and wisdom, and **then** setting them free to explore and question. It was not about handing over responsibility for determining educational content to inexperienced children, or agreeing to turn a group-blind-eye to the existence of blindingly obvious systemic problems.

The postmodern attack on meaning, and its refusal to observe, discriminate, evaluate or comment, is preventing us from learning from our experiences, and from updating and fine-tuning our models of reality. It flies in the face of our basic nature, and of the one undeniable reality we do have, our perceptual system, which gets pleasure from, and survives by, creating useable meaning out of our personal and cultural experiences.

I for one, get a real (neurochemical) buzz out of constructing and fine-tuning my understanding of things, forming and refining categories, spotting patterns of cause and effect in time and space, judging and discriminating, assessing risk and opportunity, building flawed but effective models of the world and applying them. When things go wrong, I try to learn from it and update my maps and models of reality. When I screw up I apologise, offer to make amends, and try to make sure I don't do it again.

I use my understanding to build houses, fix cars, write music, cook meals, spot danger and do all sorts of other fun and useful things. It is a fundamental part of my humanity. It becomes even more interesting as I realise the extent of the sea of my false assumptions and the need to take account of my inherent subjective judgementalism. I enjoy making meaning. I love discriminating. It is crucial to both my survival and my sense of identity.

I create and define myself by consolidating my experiences and then discriminating between what I like and what I don't like, what I respect and what I will not tolerate, what might work and what probably will not work. I do not enjoy living in a culture which is being stripped of its meaning, its wisdom, its balance and its effectiveness.

This postmodern attempt to mass manipulate our cultural meanings is all the more bizarre when it is set against the enormous expansion of individual niche choices rapidly becoming available through the internet.

Babies in the Bathwater - the subtle business of destruction and renewal.

It seems to be the case that everything in the universe is eventually destroyed, recycled and renewed. Nature is much better at this than we are. We get emotionally involved, holding onto things we love or value, and rushing in to destroy things we dislike. So we either leave it too long before we do what has to be done, or we get carried away and start hacking away at things that we don't understand, with disastrous consequences. One day perhaps we will learn to do this more smoothly.

When I was about 7, my older brother (egged on I suspect by his friends) took it upon himself to dismantle my bicycle's 3 speed hub gear. I found the parts in a biscuit tin. It was fascinating, beautifully made, some sort of sun and planets arrangement of gears, springs and circlips. Unfortunately it was much easier to take apart than it was to put it back together. He was the only one who had seen the whole system, the big picture, but he had **not** understood it, so he wasn't able to put it back together. He quickly gave up and saved face by moving on to new and more important projects. So I called in the man who fixed bicycles in our village, and we eventually got it back together, but it was never quite as good as it had been. (I now have one of these hub gears on my desk, as a paper weight, to remind me of humanity's capacity to occasionally make genuinely benign and useful things.)

I am often reminded of that episode when I watch postmodernists dismantling the role of meaning in our lives. In their enthusiasm, they have deconstructed complex systems which they didn't understand. They got into such a frenzy of excitement over flushing away the dirty old bath water that they didn't even think to look for the babies.

Wisdom was one of those babies. Both late modernism and post modernism rejected European religion. Many, perhaps most, would agree that we had accumulated a lot of very dirty holy water which was long overdue for recycling, but there was a lot of wisdom suspended in that water as well, the results of thousands of years of trying to make sense of the human condition, and we did not even try to discriminate between the wisdom and the waste.

All of the world's religious systems have noticed that we get our greatest pleasure, our highest sense of identity, and behave the best morally, when we get a glimpse of what feels like the ultimate meaning, the interconnected oneness of the web of everything at the top of the (Plato's) pyramid. Who cares whether it is objective or subjective, reality or just the neurochemical buzzing of our inherited neural networks (see chapter 2 again) - it is without a doubt the best, the highest experience we can have.

Clearly we created problems for ourselves in the past, by dreaming up flawed explanations for this type of personal experience, and then organising society around those flawed explanations. Now we are making the problem even worse by allowing those past errors to diminish the human significance of these peak and fundamental internal experiences.

Somehow, we have rendered the ultimate human experience, a taboo subject, and removed it from the public agenda (unless you happen to be a cold-hearted modernist scientist, in which case it is still considered acceptable to chase after the grand unified field theory of everything).

Thankfully, postmodernism did not manage to permeate every aspect of life. Most people just get on with the business of surviving by doing practical things, developing and applying skills and knowledge, and creating rich cultures and traditions to add meaning, structure and enjoyment to their daily lives. Sometimes these cultural frames get out of date, or go wrong: imposing undesirable constraints on people, perpetuating ideas that are clearly not true, no longer useful, and sometimes positively dangerous to one and all.

Real world scientists and technologists continue in the modernist tradition. They don't build uncertainty cars, stakeholder consulting wishy-washing machines, non-prescriptively framed aeroplanes or perpetually self-deconstructing buildings. They use what they know, to make stuff that works, but unfortunately, they tend to be overly focused on their local patch of reality and miss the bigger picture as regards cultural and environmental sustainability. As usual, it's the fluffy stuff, the stuff of ungrounded, untestable, remote or invisible causes and effects that has gone relatively crazy (once again).

So today's university students will probably encounter a mishmash of different approaches to 'truth and knowledge' on their university campus (logical, mathematical, scientific, revealed, mystical, dogmatic, practical, relativistic, fashionable, subjective and holistic-systemic).

- Social science and psychology are deeply into the hard empirical scientific model, trying to show that they are real academic subjects. They do this by restricting their field of view to only those things that can be measured, and parading their fancy statistical techniques for isolating variables and quantifying the degree of variation from a random distribution.

- History, literature and the arts are away with the postmodern relativistic deconstructed fairies.

- Science now embraces a wide range of approaches from the counter-intuitive mathematical modelling of quantum physics, through to the massive oversimplification of neuroscience brain imaging.

- Technology, electronics, mechanical and aeronautical engineering and the like, get on with it in a very pragmatic sort of way.

- For the law, accountancy, education and public administration, the truth is the latest fashionable batch of manmade rules and regulations.

- As for religion, some theologians are still painstakingly interpreting authorities from the past, while others are into 'anything goes' postmodern deconstruction and literary criticism.

So we have lots of different truth and knowledge games existing side by side. Each one has a strong tribal element: initiation rituals, behavioural codes, taboos, social sanctions, tests, ceremonies and territorial hierarchies of respect.

The new game on the block is **systems thinking.** Instead of studying small elements in isolation (which is what science does); systems thinking tries to look at the big picture, the interconnectedness, in a **holistic** way. Its methods and ideas are sometimes taken on board by other academic disciplines for occasional one-off applications. Technology and the life sciences employ it more routinely, but most of the older disciplines still use the more linear and isolating, scientific, scholastic and critical styles of thinking.

People who follow the existential-systemic approach to the truth tend to focus on what works and what doesn't work. They are not interested in denying obvious problems and inconsistencies in order to fit in with a group's established view of reality. Consequently they often find themselves in conflict with the social-group-think approach, because groups who are organised around the idea of agreeing to **oversimplify reality** are not always happy to see its interconnected complexity so **clearly described.**

The Decline of Wisdom

Postmodernism was not really saying anything new, but it did serve to remind us of something that humans have known for millennia, but occasionally forget, that knowledge is uncertain, and that human perception is both amazing and flawed.

What is new is the wilful absence of any big picture frameworks of wisdom, of care, of quality, of human nature, of any idea of theosis, of a journey upwards, a unique individual journey of self-expression and self-improvement.

We now have the biggest ever economic machinery of global resource allocation and consumption, coupled, possibly for the first time ever, with the complete absence of any agreed operational values of care and maintenance, or of any sense of a grand plan.

Proponents of the free-market economic model argue that one of the great achievements of the free marketplace is that it enables people to enter into mutually beneficial exchanges without having to first agree on shared goals and methods; all that is required is a basic framework of trust, contract law and property rights. They argue that individual humans are extremely complex, and that human society is incomprehensibly complex. The process of cultural evolution has constructed systems that embed an intricate natural wisdom which we do not fully understand. Therefore, it would be very arrogant for any ideology to claim that it understands society, and very dangerous to attempt to introduce over-simplistic top-down social mechanisms designed to steer or engineer society towards particular targets, as these have always, and inevitably will, cause unpredictable and probably undesirable consequences. They argue that it is much better to trust to the local wisdom of millions of free agents. Local mistakes will be made and corrected but the greatest overall good will emerge.

When these ideas were first formulated, the few people who were likely to play a significant part in shaping the free market, were very well educated in the big picture history of human wisdom and morality, and in its historical successes and failures. Unfortunately, science and technology have made it possible for a few not necessarily wise or well educated individuals to make very small-picture short-term decisions with disastrous consequences on a global scale, and from which very little local good might emerge. The free market must find ways to counteract this tendency towards highly-geared small-picture short-termism, and take much better account of future risks (to the environment for example).

Given the free-marketeers' respect for the emergent wisdom of thousands of years of cultural evolution, they should be quite comfortable with the idea that the current system of global resource allocation could still benefit from some evolutionary adjustments.

Perhaps the fund managers who invest our pensions and savings should once again trust in the wisdom of a million local free agents and give us back the voting rights of the company shares they buy on our behalf. Perhaps we would turn out to have a better understanding of long-term economic, social and environmental risks than they do.

Wise people in many ancient cultures, unhindered by wishy-washy postmodern relativism, observed the way things work and concluded that there definitely is a grand plan, a dynamic process guiding individual and group human development. They called it **karma**, the law of cause and effect, action and reaction. We make decisions, and take actions. The consequences of that way of thinking and behaving build up. If the consequences become unsustainable the system collapses and circumstances change. Those who survive get lessons from which they may or may not choose to learn.

It is beginning to look as if our postmodern reduced value system (where self-image is based mainly on consumption, global resources are orchestrated by the promise of short-term profit, and the public sector needs a steady supply of needy people in order for it to thrive) is environmentally and socially very unsustainable.

Postmodernism was right to draw attention to some specific weaknesses in human thinking, but its response was a disaster. Instead of playing to our strengths and acknowledging our weaknesses, it demanded that we stop thinking altogether: abandoning categories, cause and effect, judgement, observation, discrimination, values, standards, accumulated knowledge and the search for improved truths about reality.

The solution to the problems that our old systems of thought have created is to learn more about the strengths and weaknesses in human thinking, and then apply that self-knowledge. We must learn to think much more effectively, both as **individuals** and as **communities**.

Group - Think

The human brain has evolved an ability to distort and even abandon its own experience based perception of reality, in order to fit in with a significant social group. This ability can be both a strength and a weakness.

Its **strength** is that it enables large groups of people to focus and orchestrate their efforts on a particular project. Its **weakness** is that it often prevents us from doing what the ancient Greeks taught us to do - to think very clearly about our beliefs, statements, assumptions, definitions, categories and models. Group-think stifles argument and debate. It creates over-simplistic and unresponsive thinking. Group-think says, "Either you are with us or you are against us." - demanding that we demonstrate our unquestioning conformity to the group's way of thinking or we will be expelled, and thus lose the benefits and privileges of group membership.

Group-think has been a powerful influence in our lives. Human history is littered with secret societies and mystery cults, which grant their members privileged access to the group's secret knowledge about nature and science, routes to trade, routes to redemption, etc. They provide frameworks for understanding and discovering 'the truth'; obligations regarding morality, virtue and personal balance; and rules for group solidarity and mutual benefit. And finally, they provide a model for understanding death, which has often included guidance on how to die, and specific obligations of martyrdom (illustrated with examples and role models: 'The Lives of the Saints', etc.) when necessary, to promote the group's existence or to protect its secrets.

On its own, our innate tendency to submit to the intellectual distortions of group-think is dangerous enough, but stir in a little deliberate manipulation, coercion, intimidation and short-term financial reward, and groups of humans can behave very stupidly indeed. Group-think is what enabled us to construct and implement all those over-simplistic and unsustainable grand narratives in the past.

There was a lot of research into the psychological mechanisms of group-think after World War II. This was done in an attempt to understand how ordinary humans had been so easily persuaded to perform such sub-human actions. Instead of using this new knowledge to reduce or even outlaw group-think, the knowledge has been exploited by many different political, ideological, commercial and religious groups to strengthen their control, power and effectiveness.

Postmodernism exploited group-think very effectively, to stifle and intimidate challenges or opposition as it forced through redefinitions of our language and fundamental changes to our shared culture.

Group-think is a serious problem. It tends to produce dangerously oversimplified and rigid views of reality. It prevents us building a shared understanding of the deep structures and rich interconnections that make up the vital social, cultural, economic and emotional fabric of our human environment. Consequently, we make bad decisions, and have a reduced quality of life.

Systemic Literacy

In its desire to control the communication of its ideas, group-think makes great use of over simplistic text and emotive slogans. Even at its best, linear text is not capable of communicating the degree of simultaneous complexity that is needed to get to the bottom of many modern issues.

Humans are quite capable of understanding and working with the necessary levels of systemic complexity, but our linear language is not capable of communicating it. Fortunately, for thousands of years, we have had access to another way of communicating simultaneous complexity - **diagramming**.

Many of our new systemic technologies (architecture, software design, etc.) have had to develop new forms of diagramming, to enable groups of humans to work together on complex development projects.

These diagramming tools are easy to learn and very effective. Systems thinking and diagramming is not an elite activity, in fact it is far more natural for the human brain than learning to communicate using text. I have taught systems diagramming to dyslexics in schools, universities and prisons, and have yet to meet anyone who can't get the hang of it. Unfortunately, the educationalists and the media have not yet caught on to the communicative potential of these systemic thinking tools.

If we instituted a 'systems' literacy hour in our schools, there is a real chance that we could significantly improve humanity's (individual and communal) systemic thinking and communication ability, and that would be a great help in overcoming the problems of runaway group-think, and over simplistic grand narratives.

Perhaps we should put an end to the practice of the 'intellectual closed shop' that has dominated party politics and public sector employment for the last 30 years. If we required that the staffing profiles of local authorities reflected the diversity of **views** and **opinions** in the community at large, they could no longer intimidate and exclude people who dare to question, or point out systemic problems with their policies.

Perhaps we should insist that all public policy proposals are accompanied by a systems diagram showing the author's understanding of the map of causes and effects that the policy is supposed to be addressing (see chapter 4). Then they might be able to spot for themselves the flaws, the lack of joined-up thinking, the perverse incentives and the unintended consequences – **before** any damage is done.

Unfortunately, the continued existence of the political parties depends in part on their ability to manipulate group-think dynamics and disguise the real thinking (and sometimes the lack of it) behind their policies. So they are unlikely to encourage the widespread development of independent systemic thinking, or promote the kind of holistic debate which explores the **deep structures of cause and effect** that give rise to our modern challenges, and opportunities.

The education system seems equally reluctant to teach the kind of systemic thinking skills that will be needed if we are to find democratic solutions to the systemic problems we face. So we must teach ourselves.

We must turn our backs on the old and distracting argument about absolute or relative truths, and focus on continually refining our models of reality in the light of what does and does not work; what will and will not get us where we want to go. Remember Aristotle - his ultimate aim was to formulate **theories – models of reality** that gave a broad, coherent and workable explanation, consistent with the examined observations.

The Tree of Knowledge has Biological Roots

Those ancient Greek observations about human perception, truth and knowledge, and their questioning of how best to organise society, have continued to be relevant to subsequent European cultures for over 2000 years. The durability of these issues and ideas suggests that they may reflect a biological level of truth about the way the human brain perceives the world.

In the past 20 or so years, we have made great advances in understanding the biology of human perception. We are beginning to understand how the brain makes sense of the world, how it categorises the world into classes of objects, and how it generalises the relationships of cause and effect that operate between those perceived objects. This new understanding comes from the study of **neural networks**.

The next chapter explores some of what we now know about how the brain's neural networks actually work, how they learn, how they accumulate their experiences of the external world and construct maps, models, meanings and systems of values.

After 2500 years of philosophising, theological gymnastics, and humanistic speculations, it is starting to look as though the tree of knowledge has biological roots.

Chapter 2

Neural Networks

The Biological Basis of Thought and Perception.

The Fundamentals

The brain is made of a vast number of richly interconnected **neurons.** There are two main parts to a neuron. It has a **cell body,** which is much like the body of any other type of cell. This takes care of the housekeeping, manages the genetic material and manufactures the proteins and other chemicals that are needed for its special role in the body. What is unusual about neurons is that they have **projecting nerve fibres.**

There are two kinds of nerve fibres projecting from the neuron cell body - **input** fibres and **output** fibres. The input fibres are called **dendrites** (from the Greek for *tree*), and receive electrochemical messages (both positive and negative) from **many** other neurons. The electrical charges make their way along the input fibres to the main body of the neuron. If a sufficiently strong positive charge builds up, the neuron **fires** and sends an electrical signal out along the output fibres (called **axons**). At the ends of the axons, the electrical signal causes the release of chemicals, which drift across small gaps to the next neuron's input fibres, where they initiate either positive or negative electrical charges, which in turn pass to the cell body where they accumulate until they too are fired. In this way, very subtle and intricate 'domino waves' of nerve impulses are set in motion.

Neurons usually have more than one dendrite (input fibre). Along the length of the dendrites are numerous short spines, and on the ends of the spines are special sites (called **receptors**) which are capable of receiving the chemical messages from the axons of other neurons.

Each neuron usually has only one axon (output fibre) but this typically has many branches. At the end of each branch is a site we call the **axon terminal,** which, shortly after the cell fires, releases **neurotransmitter** chemicals, which drift across the small gap between the axon terminals of the fired neuron and the dendrite spine receptors on **many** connected neurons. This gap is called the **synapse** (from the Greek for *point of contact* or *joint*).

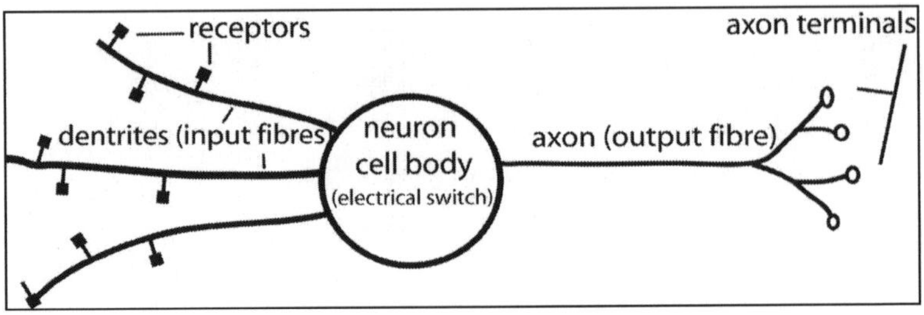

Figure 2.1 Simplified diagram of a neuron – inputs - switch - outputs.

Excitation and Inhibition

There are two main neurotransmitter chemicals - **glutamate,** which causes the receptors in the post-synaptic neuron's dendrite spines to **open**, allowing **positively** charged **ions** to flow through this open channel **into** the neuron dendrite where a positive charge builds up and passes along the dendrite fibre to the cell body. The other neurotransmitter is called **GABA** and it has the reverse effect. It drifts across the synapse and opens **different** receptors, which allow **negatively** charged ions to flow into the neuron. The neuron will only fire when the balance of the many positive and negative charges in the cell body reaches a particular trigger level of positive charge. If it does fire, then the charge passes along the axon to the axon terminals, where it causes special chemical storage sites, called **vesicles,** to release the next cloud of neurotransmitter, which drifts across those synapses and opens channels in the receptors of the next neurons in the network, and so on.

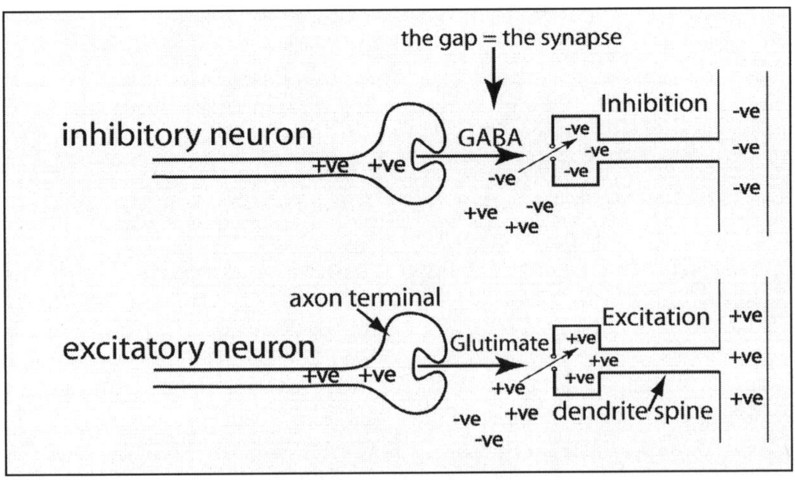

Figure 2.2 GABA and glutamate cross the synaptic gap.

The cells that **excite** their neighbours by releasing glutamate tend to have **long** axons. The cells that **inhibit** cell firing in their neighbours through the release of GABA tend to have **short** axons and they group together into local inhibitory networks. This design principle of **balancing long range excitation** with **local inhibition** has interesting emergent properties. It damps the whole system down, so that an initial stimulus cannot escalate the network into a long drawn-out state of excitement. If that did happen, it would rapidly exhaust its electrochemical reserves and, more importantly, the system would no longer be able to **discriminate** between a really important signal and all the residual excitement and noise. With the GABA damping in place, important excitatory signals stand out clearly against the background. This is very clever. It produces a system which can make reasonably **stable** perceptions and decisions, and resist being thrown into chaos by every little change in circumstance, but which can also **respond** quickly to **important** changes. This micro-level property of neural networks is clearly reflected in our macro-level behaviour.

There are a number of further refinements to this damping system. The receptors that receive the inhibitory signals can be on or **near** the cell body, whereas the receptors that receive the excitatory signals are typically located out on the **extremities** of the dendrites. The networks of inhibitory neurons tend to fire in a continuous background hum, whereas the excitatory projection neurons usually only speak when they have something important to say, and then they talk in loud bursts. As a result, the positive excitatory charges that flow inwards from the extremities have to pass along the dendrite and overcome any **barriers** of neutralising negative charge that have built up there as a result of the background inhibitory humming.

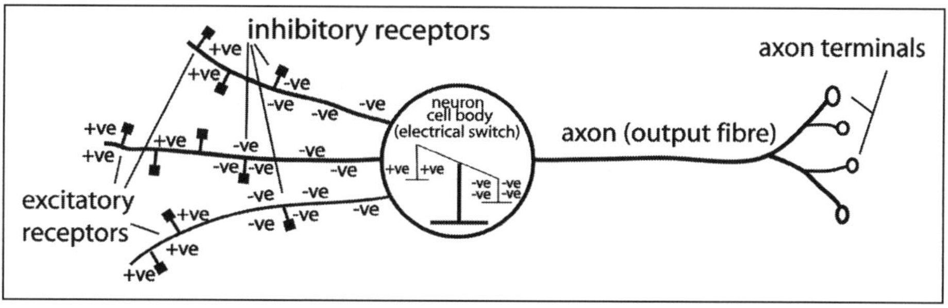

Figure 2.3 Neuron - inhibition and excitation.

It is only when they reach the cell body that the positively charged excitatory signals can cast their electrical vote in the ongoing decision as to whether or not the cell should fire. So it takes a good strong burst of almost simultaneous excitation from a substantial number of excitatory receptor sites to overcome this background inhibition and fire the cell.

In order to further protect the precious excitatory cells from exhaustion there is a process we call **elicited inhibition.** This happens when excitation neurons in an area are wired in such a way that they cause excitation in the local inhibitory cells as well. As a result, a pulse of **excitation** is quickly followed by a wave of increased **inhibition.** Local variations in sensitivities cause local variations in the time delay between the excitation and inhibition cycles. This gives rise to a rich set of **time-based emergent properties,** which we might think of in musical terms such as pitch, amplitude, rhythm, wave shape, attack envelope, etc. These are extremely important, enabling for example, the very sensitive phase shift comparisons that we use to detect the direction of a sound source or the relative movement of two objects.

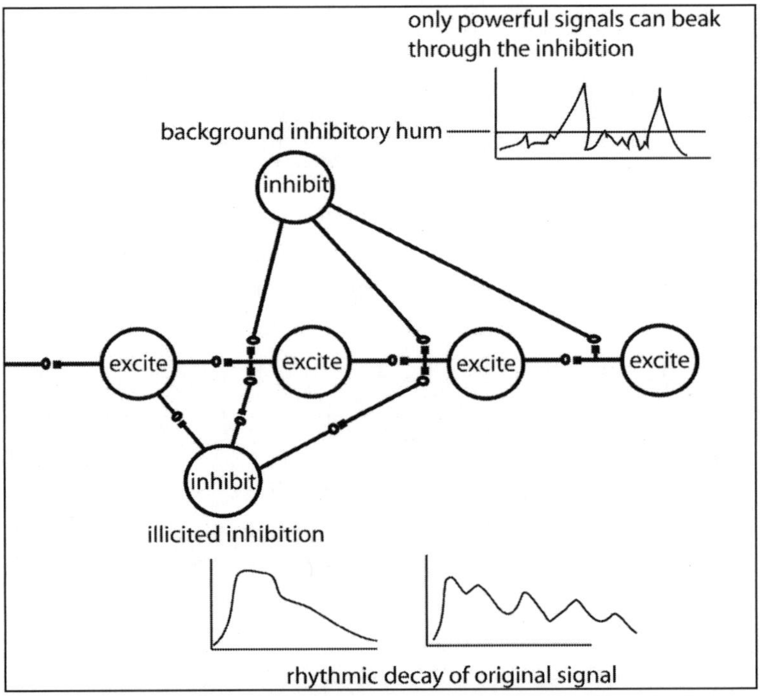

Figure 2.4 Two types of inhibition.

Chemical Soup
Neuromodulators and Hormones

Neuromodulators

are chemicals that are released in the brain by specialist neurons. Their effect is **regional** and they can either excite or inhibit, depending on the local circumstances. There are three main groups - amines, peptides and hormones.

Amines

Amines are a group of chemicals which include serotonin, dopamine, epinephrine, and norepinephrine. These neuromodulators can bring about **non-specific global** changes in many areas of the brain simultaneously. For example, they can initiate general arousal, as in the presence of danger, or they can initiate sleep.

The neurons which manufacture and release these chemicals are only found in a few small areas, mostly in the ancient brain stem, but they have long axons which can deliver the chemicals to many very specific and more recently evolved areas of the brain.

> Have a look at
> www.bbc.co.uk/science/humanbody/body/interactives/organs/brainmap/
> for some basic brain anatomy.

As an example of the effects of this class of neuromodulators, let's look at dopamine and its effect on attention.

The neurons that produce dopamine are located in the old brain stem, but they have very long axons that can release dopamine in other parts of the brain, such as the prefrontal cortex (an area of the brain that is thought to be responsible for the higher and more recently evolved mental functions), where specialist dopamine receptors are located on the dendrites of excitatory neurons. When activated by dopamine they operate to further reduce the movement of excitation from the dendrite to the cell body. The effect of this is to ensure that only the very strongest signals get through to the cell body, and that distracting background signals are blocked. This is thought to be one mechanism by which ancient survival based processes can continue to exert an influence over more recently evolved functions, ensuring, **if necessary,** that we **prioritise our attention** on only the most pressing, high-priority goals and events, and switch off unnecessary luxurious functional areas for the time being.

Peptides

This is a large class of opiate type chemicals (such as endorphins and enkephalins) which are stored separately in the axon terminals of specific cells. They can be released at the same time as excitatory glutamate, or inhibitory GABA, but they are slower to take effect. So the initial signal is passed on unchanged, but subsequent signals are affected by the peptide, which can have a dramatic effect, both positively and negatively, on the cells' sensitivity - their ability to be fired by glutamate.

The effect can be quite **functionally specific** as the peptides can only affect neurons which have specific peptide receptors. So peptides can turn **on** and turn **off specific systems** throughout the brain, but their timing is not very precise as they are slow acting and long lasting. They are known to affect our sensitivity to pain and our general emotional state. Research suggests that they are released during social activities such as laughing, singing, grooming, religious rituals, even public self-flagellation, and that they create a euphoric sense of pleasure, trust and belonging. The actions of this group of neuromodulators have probably played a large role in the evolution and maintenance of complex rituals and social bonds among the higher primates and humans.

Hormones

Hormones are a group of chemicals that are usually produced in and released by organs and glands in the body (as opposed to being produced in the brain / nervous system), and circulate via the blood to the brain and to other organs. In the brain, their effects can be very specific because they can only influence those neural circuits which have the necessary receptors. They bind to specific receptors on specific neurons and work by moderating the efficacy of glutamate and GABA transmission thus influencing both excitation and inhibition in the brain. They can also affect the operation of other body organs, blood supply, muscles, energy levels, etc. So hormones can **orchestrate** very specific effects across the **whole body**.

For example, serotonin is widely distributed throughout the body:

- it constricts blood vessels but dilates capillaries;

- it causes involuntary contraction of the smooth muscles of blood vessels (causing blood pressure to rise) and in the wall of the intestine where it is involved in the wavelike movements that move food through the gut;

- it can stimulate sensory nerve endings causing pain - nettle stings contain serotonin as do many animal and insect venoms;

- it is found in the blood platelets and is released during blood clotting;

- a small amount (1%) is manufactured in the neurons of the mid brain but their axons project into the cerebral cortex, hippocampus, limbic system, and hypothalamus as well as down the spinal cord;

- it seems to be able to affect as many as ten different types of receptors and their precise functions are not yet clear.

Changes in serotonin levels are thought to alter mood: increases have a calming effect, relieving depression, insomnia, and irritability, but high levels are associated with migraine headaches and nausea; decreases are associated with wakefulness and greater sensitivity to pain. When animals are deprived of it (by giving them agents that prevent its synthesis) they show exaggerated responses to many types of sensory stimulus, indicating that it normally has an inhibiting effect on pain and other sensory stimuli.

Adrenaline is released from the adrenal gland into the blood circulation. The release of adrenaline is triggered by the brain's evaluation that the situation is dangerous, and requires a flight, fright, and fight response. It prepares the body to deal with the danger: heart rate and pumping capacity are increased, blood pressure rises, and blood flow to the skeletal and cardiac muscles is increased, while blood flow to the less essential areas (e.g. gut, skin) is decreased. Adrenaline also mobilizes glycogen energy stores from the liver to increase blood glucose. It is also manufactured and released by axon terminals in the brain, when it is called epinephrine.

Hormones can also have a significant role in controlling our attention and prioritisation, by switching neural systems on and off. For example, hungry people are less scared of danger than they are when they are well fed. Stress hormones are known to strengthen the formation of memories of dangerous situations, and temporarily switch off other more luxurious priorities.

The old idea that the mind and the body are separate systems has to be updated. It is quite clear that the brain and the body are intricately interconnected by these neurochemical systems, and they should be considered as a whole system – the body influencing the brain, and vice versa.

What Is Going On In The Brain?

Is The Brain Like a General-Purpose Computer?

The cognitive revolution was influenced by the idea that the brain might be, in some ways, like the general-purpose programmable computers that had started to have such an impact in the second half of the twentieth century. Psychologists studying the brain and its relationship to human behaviour wanted to be scientific in their methodology. But there is a fundamental problem with studying the brain, which is that you can never be sure, objectively, exactly what is going on in someone else's head, and you can never prove to someone else what is going on in yours. Alongside the development of the new computer technologies were new and evolving ideas about the flow and transformation of information. The psychologists adopted this new model and set about the objective study of the way information flows through and is transformed by the brain. Their thinking was strongly influenced by the designs and the seemingly amazing functionality of the new computers.

The general-purpose computer was designed to be a very flexible manipulator of data. It had to be able to hold data permanently and very reliably in long-term memory that could be written to and read from with total accuracy. It was designed to be able to follow programmes, sequences of instructions, telling it how to manipulate the data. It had to be able to follow any programme, provided that the programme only contained valid instructions from a limited set of data-manipulation functions that the computer was already able to perform (add, subtract, move, copy, etc.). These were called **executive functions**. The computer designers came up with the idea of long-term memory stores (slow but cheap to make) and temporary or short-term memory stores (fast but expensive) where the data could be manipulated by the executive functions.

So brain scientists searched the brain looking for long-term and short-term memory, and for the locations of the executive functions that they assumed must be transforming the sensory data. This approach had some successes, but they were limited because the analogy between the brain and the general-purpose computer was never a particularly good fit, and the more we discovered about the brain, the less appropriate that analogy became.

Now we are starting to understand that there are many fundamental ways in which the brain's neural networks are not at all like general-purpose computers. However, unfortunately, many of those mistaken computer/brain analogies have found their way into the general consciousness, so in order to take on board the new discoveries about neural networks, it may be necessary to unlearn previous ideas you may have picked up about the brain.

In a computer the instructions are held separately from the data. Each piece of stored information is held in isolation, and cannot affect any other piece of information unless it is instructed to do so. The hardware of a computer is not changed or restructured by either the data it holds or the programmes it runs. The fact that it ran a spreadsheet yesterday must not affect the way it runs a database today. The results are deterministic. If it runs the same program, using the same data, it will come up with the same predictable results every time.

A neural network is not an accurate data-storage machine and it does not execute programs to manipulate data. It is an **experience machine. Experience flows through it, causing changes to the structure of the network.** This ability to change its structure (its hardware) in response to its experiences is called **plasticity**. If you remember nothing else about neural networks, remember this.

Plasticity

Plasticity in Neural Networks

So how does a neural network achieve this plastic response to experience? As a sensory experience flows through a neural network, many of the neurons receive excitatory and inhibitory influences. For some neurons the balance of excitation and inhibition will cause the cell to fire, passing on a signal to the next cells in the network. For other cells, the balance of inputs will not result in a firing, and that, on this occasion, will be the end of that. The resultant **pattern** of firing and non-firing neurons is the brain's response to the sensory input.

Each neuron may participate in many different patterns. Given the vast number of neurons and connections in the brain, it does not take a mathematical genius to appreciate that this mechanism can create zillions of unique patterns of neural activity to represent very subtle distinctions in our experiences of the world.

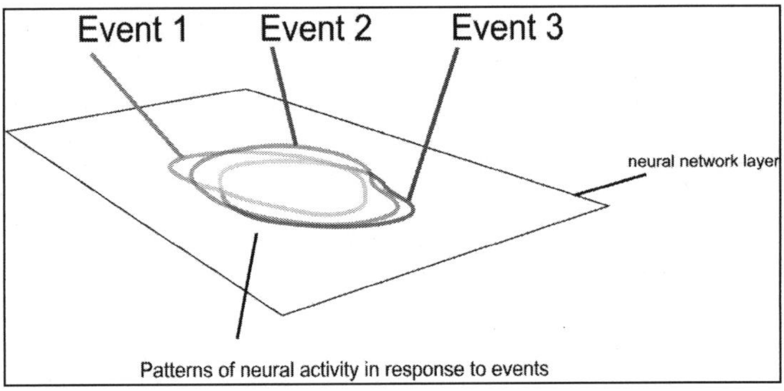

Figure 2.5 Unique patterns of neural activity representing subtle distinctions in our experience of the world.

So this is an immensely versatile mechanism by which the brain can discriminate between very subtle variations in sensory information.

Grouping Things Together

It can also group similar experiences together. It is very useful to be able to recognise that the letter *a,* is the same **kind of thing** as the letter *A,* or that this ginger cat is the same class of thing as that black cat. It is even more useful to be able to realise that this cat is the same cat that I saw a second ago. It looks shorter and fatter now, but that is because it has moved and I am seeing it from a slightly different angle.

Things with Common Properties

This ability, to realise that a lot of slightly different neural patterns have so much in common that they probably represent the same object existing in time and space but showing slightly different appearances, depends on the ability of neural networks to make **associations**. Association is the neural network way of noticing that there may be something important going on when two or more things keep happening at the same **time** or in the same **place**. Association enables a neural network to mark out a special group of cells which fire every time the senses experience an A, an ***A***, or an *A*. The common core of this group of cells comes to represent the general class = letter A. When that common core area is activated, we think 'letter A', irrespective of the font.

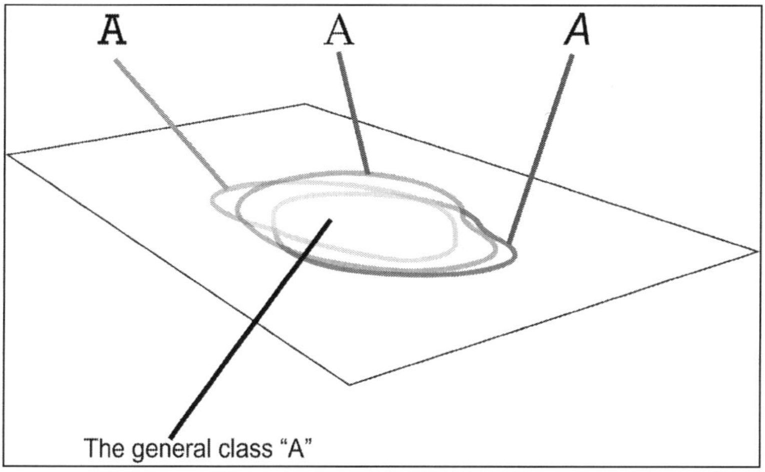

Figure 2.6 Grouping similar things by their common properties.

Classification, Generalisation and Abstraction

Neural networks are often organised into layers. Connections between the layers enable us to analyse or index our primary experiences, forming container ideas. This enables us to recognise that A, B and C ... are letters of the alphabet. 1 and 2 are numbers.

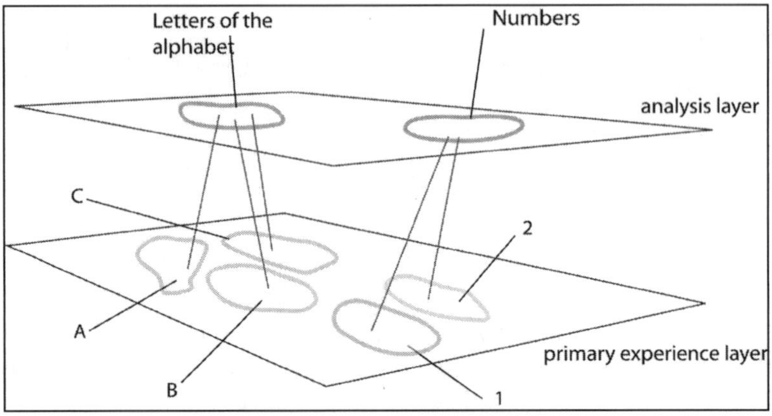

Figure 2.7 Container ideas – analysis layers.

These layer jumping connections give us a very versatile way of grouping the objects we experience into classes, for example the class 'mammals', which connects to the primary neural areas that have come to represent the common essential features of all the dogs, rabbits, donkeys, etc., we have experienced to date. The concept *mammal* may be quite separate from the concept *reptile*, although the primary areas representing *snakes* and *lizards* may overlap slightly (they both have scaly skin).

This neural network mechanism can also index our experiences according to properties within the classes, such as the size of ears. *Big ears* is a concept that connects to primary areas representing the big ears on the *dogs*, *rabbits* and *donkeys* we have known.

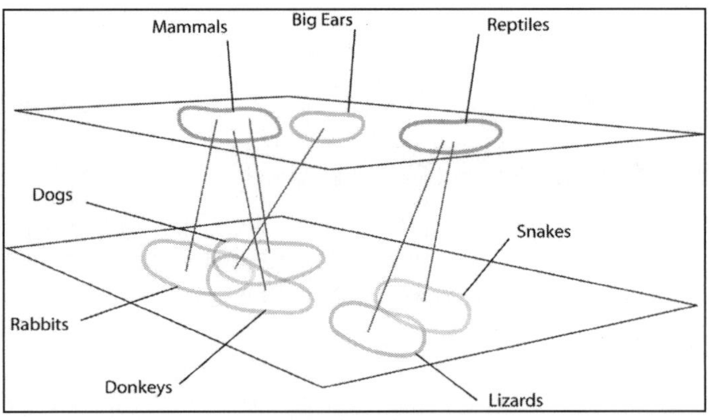

Figure 2.8 Classification, generalisation, abstraction, and property indexing.

These level jumping associations enable us to build up complex experiential categories that transform a continuously changing flow of sensory experiences into hierarchical categories of relatively stable objects. These hierarchies can be multi-themed. Mice can be simultaneously classified as rodents, pests, and pets.

This is how neural networks achieve multiple hierarchical classification, generalisation, abstraction, and property indexing.

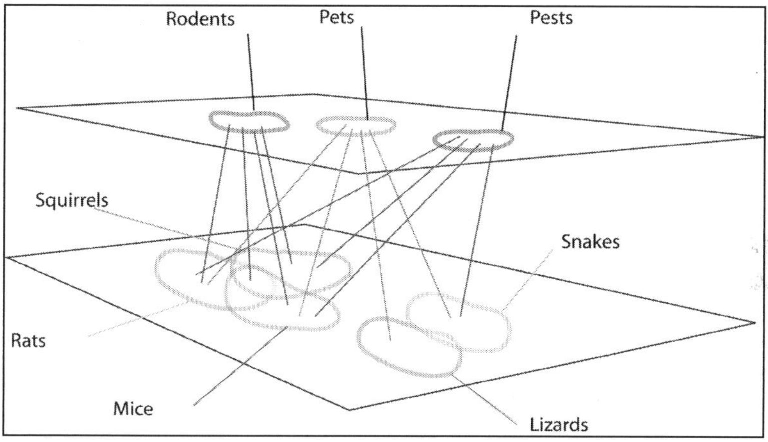

Figure 2.9 The multiple classification of experiences.

The ability to access classes of things by their properties is a particularly important component in everyday practical creative common sense. It enables us to think of temporarily fixing a broken fan belt with a length of hosepipe, a pair of tights, a roll of sticky tape, a length of telephone cable, some wool unravelled from an old jumper, pyjama cords, dressing gown belts, etc. We can follow the property-based neural associations to find any number of things with the necessary properties, in this case: long, thin, strong, flexible, able to be knotted or joined into a loop, and readily available.

A person whose brain had categorised its experiences using only the **names** of things (and has not been trapping its experience of the **properties** of the things), would not be able to make that creative leap. **Name indexes are good for communicating; property indexes are good for solving problems.**

Non-Equal Membership

In the kind of logic we programme into our GP computers, all members of a category are equally good examples of that category. A spade is a spade. This is not usually true in a neural network, where a class of object is represented by a pattern of activity in a region of the network. Class members that are represented at the centre of the pattern, because they are richly connected to all the usual properties associated with that general class, can be perceived as much better members of the category than members that are represented near the edge of the pattern. Cross cultural experiments have shown that we can recognise that a robin is a bird considerably faster than we can recognise that a duck is a bird. A robin is a 'better' bird than a duck. Robins and ducks are not equally representative of birds in general. They have slightly different associations. Ducks live on, in and around water in a way that most birds do not. Some of their watery behaviour (diving and eating underwater) is more fishy than birdie. Ducks don't sound like your average bird, they don't nest in trees like your average bird and they don't hop about like most birds do.

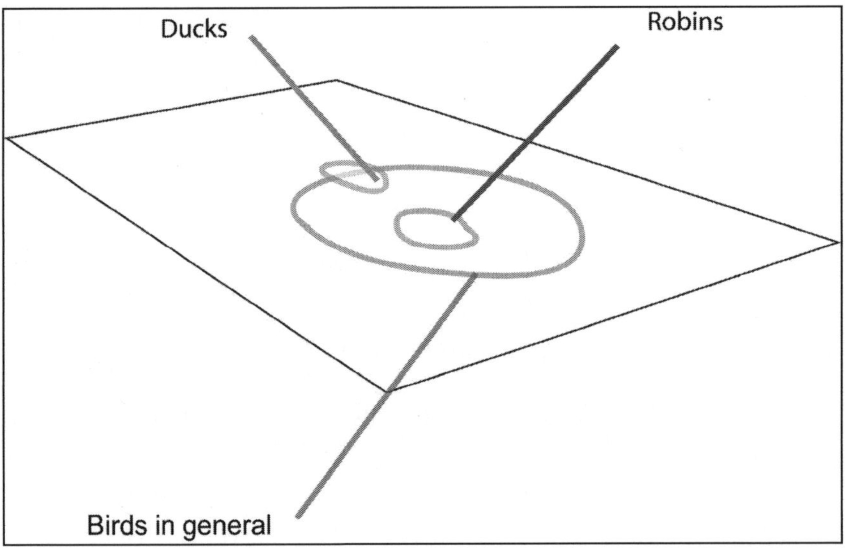

Figure 2.10 Non-equal group membership.

Our rational conscious cultural view of logic usually assumes an equality of membership of categories, but the pre-conscious neural networks which are creating and categorising our internal experience of the external world, are working on a very different, and a much more subtle basis.

Metaphor, Simile & Analogy

Association also gives us the ability to transfer meanings and ideas from one domain to another. Language helps in this process, by giving us the tools of metaphor, simile and analogy. The development of this ability to transfer meaning from one domain to another, seems to be one of the major reasons for the increased problem-solving and socio-cultural creativity that separates modern humans (who have been around for approximately 100,000 years) from our immediate predecessors.

If you think about the language you might hear in a business meeting, it is amazing how many of the words and expressions derive their meaning from older more established domains such as agriculture, building, land transport, sailing or the military.

For example: seed investment, plant an idea, lay the foundation, give it time to grow, ask for a rise, growth, flowering, blossoming, fruits of his labour, reserves, come to fruition, cultivate, past its best, root and branch cuts, pruning, dead wood, fall, drop, collapse, decay, disintegrate, time to bury it, resuscitate it, bounce back, regenerate, pruning, drip feeding, pump priming, dig up a few names, cross fertilisation, graft on a new, milk it for all its worth, bring in some new blood, nip it in the bud, gone rotten, rotten to the core, rotten through and through, a bad apple, gone to seed, out in the cold, frosty reception, stormy meeting, uprooted, reap the rewards, a breath of fresh air, rosy outlook, on the horizon, over the hill, wind in his sails, chocks away, launch, pilot, close to his chest, cards on the table, get the lie of the land, fathom it out, take soundings, sailing close to the wind, into the wind, wallowing, changing tack, shipshape, pissing in the wind, take-over the helm, run with the wind, in a lee shore, calm before the storm, all hands on deck, a loose cannon, tie it down, batten down the hatches, full speed ahead, getting up steam, the eye of the storm, weather the storm, ride out the storm, any port in a storm, (tax) haven, gauge the situation, get him in your sights, on target, going in for the kill, first blood, getting a black eye, loaded, primed and ready to go, take the bait, trapped, get all the ducks in a row, roll out the barrel, blowing your cover, under cover, something in the wind, showing signs of life, on the scent, on the trail, in the bag, got the bit between his teeth, cart before the horse, shutting the stable door, flogging a dead horse, bit of a handful, team, going in with all guns blazing, on a short rein, on the home run, over the first hurdle, don't look a gift horse in the mouth, raise your sights, a bit of a long shot, ram the point home, short fuse, flash point, in your sights, trigger, aim, cut and run, cut and thrust, head for cover, keep your powder dry, set up an observation post, scan the horizon, on the right path, familiar path, slippery path, as the crow flies, cul-de-sac, a road to nowhere, gone off the rails, next junction, next hurdle, crossing the (white) line, get my bearings, sense of direction, destination, enjoying the view, head on collision, out of control, sign posts, follow the signs, he ignored all the signs, etc.

Metaphors and analogies usually only transfer some bits of an idea, some of its properties and some of its relations to the rest of the world. When we talk of seed investment, we don't mean that the money should be buried in the ground. When we describe someone as 'a loose cannon', we don't mean that they weigh a ton and are made of bronze. We mean that they are **behaving as if** they are not properly tied in place and are therefore not moving in harmony with the rest of the ship. They are crashing about the metaphorical gun deck, doing their own thing in a very dangerous and unpredictable fashion.

Sequence Sensitivity

In the world of neural networks, the **sequence** of experiences is very significant. Experience A, followed by experience B, can leave a network in a different condition of learning or knowledge, than it would be in if it had experienced B followed by experience A. The resultant state of the network structure will determine how it responds to the next experience. For example, a person who learns about the operation of compound interest 6 months before getting his first credit card will probably behave quite differently from a person who doesn't find out how it works until 6 months after getting his first credit card.

Our memories are also affected by the sequence of our experiences. They are not held in accurate isolation as they are in a computer. New experiences can affect established memories. When memories (most types) are recalled, they are also rewritten, and can be rewritten to include associations to new experiences, interpretations, meanings and feelings. In some areas of the brain, memories are held very rigidly, because the locally slow rate of plasticity can keep old well-established memories quite separate from new ones. For example, in the amygdala (an area of the brain that specialises in threat recognition), a single exposure to a dangerous experience can be remembered for life, but in other areas of the brain, memories are much more fluid and unstable.

This instability is what allows the brain to learn, and to adjust its structure in response to new experiences. Just as walking is controlled falling, so learning is a controlled balance between forgetting and remembering.

> To walk forward, we must first loose our balance and start to fall forward. To learn, we must be able to forget (delete or amend) old knowledge, and then keep the new knowledge stable, until it is time to update it with something better.

How Do Neural Networks Register Associations?

We are looking for (experience triggered) biological mechanisms that can change the connection between two neurons in such a way that the first neuron comes to have a greater effect on whether or not the second neuron fires. This ability to strengthen connections enables the two neurons to become an associated firing pair. Firing pairs can then be assembled into larger complex firing patterns that can quickly discriminate between many subtle aspects of a particular experience.

The neurons are firing together because they have all been triggered by a collection of **related** stimuli (out there in reality) which all happened at about the same **time, and**, in about the same **place.** Nature is guessing that this spaciotemporal coincidence may carry important and potentially useful information, so our brains evolved to record it as a pattern of neural associations. This is how our pre-conscious brain organises our experience of the world into objects, properties, relations, events and processes in time and space. This explains why we are comfortable with **local** causation but have trouble interpreting **remote** causation. Where a cause and its effects are separated by a significant amount of time or space, our neural networks have great difficulty detecting any significant correlation. It just looks like random activity.

Post-Synaptic Changes

Post-synaptic changes are the changes that happen in the second of a pair of connected neurons as a result of them firing together. One mechanism that can operate to strengthen the connection between two neurons is as follows.

There is a second type of receptor on a (post-synaptic) neuron's dendrites (input fibres). We have already met the first type, which open in response to glutamate or GABA and allow either positive or negative ions to flow into the post-synaptic neuron. The second type of receptor works in a different way. It is initially blocked by magnesium, but once the cell has fired (a bit, or a lot - the amount can vary) this receptor opens and allows calcium to flow into the cell, which leads to the activation of Kinases, which travel to the cell nucleus and trigger changes, including the activation of genes which cause the **growth of new receptors at the site of stimulation**, as marked by the calcium influx. The growth of additional receptors at that site increases the chance of that neural connection influencing the cell to fire in the future. Amazing.

So here is a mechanism that enables a network to restructure itself in response to sensory experience. This ability also enables it to fine tune its sensitivity, so that it can react more quickly to commonly recurring stimuli.

Pre-Synaptic Changes

There is also evidence of **pre-synaptic changes**, that is, changes to the neuron that is sending the message. If the second cell fires, it releases a retrograde messenger, a chemical substance which drifts back across the relevant synapses to the **pre-synaptic** neurons, causing them to **release more** of their neurotransmitters in the future. This has the effect of increasing the chance of them firing the post-synaptic cell, thus strengthening the association.

Other changes can occur which trigger genetic activity causing the axon to grow **new axon branches.** This means that there are more terminals releasing more glutamate, which further strengthens the connection between the two neurons.

There are also some less specific changes which can improve the sensitivity and efficiency of busy neural network sub-systems, such as increased **blood supply** and increased electrical **insulation**, provided by the growth of myelin sheathing around the active nerve fibres.

Sensitisation

These neurochemical processes can combine to produce **sensitisation –** a process which evolution has found beneficial for some brain functions, enabling them to become **temporarily more sensitive** when something important is going on. For example, the neuromodulator **serotonin** is known to be able to bind to specific receptors on pre-synaptic axon terminals, where it activates a protein called PKA. PKA **slows down** the electrical firing process, thus **extending the duration** and therefore the **quantity** of glutamate released into the synapse. This

increases the effect on the post-synaptic receptors, and increases the sensitivity of the system.

Habituation

In some other brain functions, evolution has gone for **habituation.** This process is essentially the opposite of sensitisation, and its function is to stop the network becoming over stimulated and going into a kind of non-stop-firing meltdown. Habituation enables the neurons to adjust themselves so as to react less sensitively to some non-threatening but recurrent event. For example, if you are driving in your car and the silencer suddenly falls off, causing a sudden increase in noise level, your first reaction will be very intense but will quickly calm down. Habituation appears to be caused by a simple depletion in the amount of glutamate released, but no doubt more mechanisms remain to be discovered.

Experience Trapping

All these mechanisms work together to enable the continuous fine-tuning of our neural networks in response to the continuous flow of personal experiences. The brain is an experience trapping machine. **Each new experience is interpreted in the light of all previous experiences, or more accurately, by a network which has been shaped by its previous experiences.**

Factors in Brain Development

So we are beginning to understand some of the mechanisms by which neural networks adjust themselves to trap experiences, but how did the basic neural structures get there in the first place? This is not thoroughly understood yet, but here are some of the mechanisms that have been uncovered, just to give you a flavour.

From the very beginning, **genetic, environmental** and **experiential factors** interact to shape the development of the brain. Genetic factors flood different regions of the developing brain with chemicals which shape its early development by attracting specific neuron axons to grow towards some chemical regions, and away from others. These chemicals also affect the characteristics of the neurons that develop there: the number of connections, the type of receptors, and so on.

Early on in the development of the brain, a structural scaffolding appears to guide the growth of the networks, rather similar to training a rose or a runner bean in your garden. From a very early stage, the sense organs start to fire spontaneously, initiating the experiential/associative structuring mechanisms that we have already seen. This is known to be particularly important in guiding the early development of the visual system.

Throughout the brain's development (all the way to adulthood) different parts of the brain experience periods of rapid growth. These are periods of over production, creating a surplus of neural matter within which experience has a free hand to shape new associations. Then, once experience has done its work and the intense learning phase is over, the neural matter that is not being used dies off and is removed. We call it pruning, to continue the gardening analogy.

Summary of Plasticity

This has been a rather oversimplified description of just some of the key behaviours and properties of neural networks. Hopefully it is enough for you to begin to understand how **the flow of experience** causes fundamental adjustments to the **structure and sensitivity of the brain**, by increasing and decreasing the amount of neurotransmitter released, and forging new connections - growing new axon branches and new receptors. We can see how small, local variations in the properties of particular groups of neurons can produce specialist local networks with very different sensitivities and behaviours.

Clearly the brain is not a deterministic, hardwired, digital yes/no switching mechanism and general-purpose programmable data manipulator. It is a simultaneously sequential, rhythmic pattern-matching and experience-trapping perception machine that is constantly being restructured by a combination of genetic, environmental and experiential factors.

Research into the behaviour of neural networks (both biological and artificial) is still in its infancy, but it is progressing fast. It has already given us many new insights into the way our brains perceive and interact with the world.

In order to take these new ideas on board we must first acknowledge that some of our previous ideas about the brain (driven by the computer analogy) were not quite right. In the past, people talked about the brain encoding, searching, sorting, selecting, deleting, editing and filtering information, in short-term and long-term memory. All these concepts were borrowed from the field of general-purpose computing.

But as we have seen, the brain is not like a general-purpose computer. It is a collection of highly specialised and evolving neural networks, and neural networks don't really do searching, sorting, selecting, etc. In fact it is time to open our minds to the realisation that neural network processes are fundamentally different from anything we have ever thought about before. So, let's explore some of the important emergent properties of neural networks, and contrast them with the more familiar concepts we had mistakenly borrowed from the realm of general-purpose computing.

General-Purpose (GP) vs. Highly Task Specific

The hardware of a general-purpose computer is specifically designed to enable it to process **any** externally provided **data**, according to **any** externally provided **instructions.** Its memory is designed to enable it to accurately remember the data and the instructions. The results are entirely predictable. Every time you run that program, with the same data, you get the same results.

The brain is almost an exact opposite. It is a collection of highly functionally specific neural networks. Each of these neural networks has its own **specialised structure and functionality.** The **structure** of the network **evolves** as it responds to its resonant experiences. When a group of cells fire together, the connections between them may be strengthened or sensitised, making it easier for that group of cells to fire together again in the future. Conversely, synapses may be weakened by lack of use – the 'use it or lose it' idea. The flow of activity through the structure may also trigger the formation of new connections, particularly during phases of brain development. In these ways, **the structures in the brain evolve in response to the experiences flowing through them,** becoming biased towards specific patterns of excitation. This is how we learn. Learning is subtle changes in our neural network structures in response to the flow of experiences passing through them. Neural networks are primarily experience-trapping machines.

In biological neural networks, the processes that emerge from the structures may be very sensitive to the presence of a range of brain chemicals – shutting down some processes and stimulating others.

Out of these fundamental behaviours the brain builds various types of memory capability. It creates, recognises and refines categories and relationships, makes decisions, learns, and creates consciousness.

The important principle here is that it is the **structure** of a neural network that causes it to be **sensitive** to (able to **discriminate** between, and therefore learn about) a particular type of information. A network that is structured in a way that makes it good at recognising vertical lines in the information received from the eye will not be sensitive to the direction and distance of a sound source. Most neural network structures are **highly task specific** and not general-purpose. However, there are many examples of people whose brains have been able to compensate for serious injury by getting other areas to take over some of the functionality of the damaged area, or by developing new ways to achieve the same result, which are not dependent on the damaged area. This illustrates the general ability of neural networks to reorganise their structures and functionality in response to new circumstances, but there are limits.

Selective Sensitivity

Computer designers didn't worry much about the amount of energy our desktop computers used as they pushed to make them more and more powerful. Evolution is not so wasteful. Biological neural network structures have evolved through natural selection, which requires every new development to justify its energy costs. As a result, neural networks tend not to waste effort processing, or even sensing, information unless it has high enough survival value for that species. For example, the human visual system is only sensitive to the few wavelengths of light that are necessary to see in direct sunlight, reflected sunlight and shadow, as experienced on the surface of planet Earth. Evolution did not find it useful for humans to be able to see in any of the other many millions of possible wavelengths on the vast electromagnetic spectrum. Similarly with sound, our hearing neural networks can only respond to a small portion of the available sound frequencies. The blackbird in my garden can detect the sound vibrations of a worm moving underground, but evolution did not find it necessary for us humans to have this ability, as our ancestors did not depend on a diet of worms.

There is a very important point here. Our mental experience of external reality is determined by the highly selective sensitivity of our neural networks and our senses. **We experience a very small, and uniquely human, portion of reality**. Other living organisms have their own small and species-specific view of reality. If we want to know what the rest of the universe 'looks' like, we have to develop instruments that are sensitive to other wavelengths and media, and which can convert that information into signals that our senses can understand. Radar, infrared cameras, X-rays, MRI scanners and radio telescopes are just a few examples of the many devices we have recently developed to look at the universe in other wavelengths.

Relative Speed

GP computers are still relatively very, very slow compared to neural networks. The human brain can interpret the meaning of a visual image in 50 milliseconds (50 thousandths of a second). That image is constructed from information collected by 125 million light-detecting rods and cones in the eye. The stimulation passes through a series of specialised neural networks that are sensitive to motion and rotation, enhance edges, and adjust for brightness, contrast and relative colour in a wide range of lighting conditions, before the really complex work starts, such as picking out a moving object against a moving background. It can do all this, fast enough, to enable us to drive a racing car at over 200 miles an hour. This is possible because the functions being performed are **emergent properties** of the evolved structures. The response is almost instantaneous because the **routes** that the waves of stimulation take as they **switch themselves** through the network **are the interpretation.** The **routes are the result,** and it is achieved in one pass of the 'information/stimulation' through the network. By contrast, a computer is relatively slow because it has to process masses of (often irrelevant) data, bit by bit, (looking at some bits over and over again), following external rules that have the effect of looking for patterns, edges, shapes, etc.

Size and Efficiency

The performance of a GP computer is determined by the speed and power of the hardware, and the design of its instruction programmes. Its efficiency at processing data is not affected by the content of the data.

In a neural network, the performance is determined by how **well tuned** the structure is to the information coming in, and by the **structural richness within the information flow.** The more structure, connectivity, sequence and relevant variety there is in the data, the more the network can respond to it and learn from it. It does not have to be bigger to learn more. The more complex the data available to the neural network, the higher the neural network's performance. **Simplifying the input data reduces the efficiency.** This has profound implications for education. It is easier to learn richly structured, richly connected, well-sequenced material than to learn oversimplified material. This is particularly relevant to the learning of English language spelling, for example, but more of that later.

Emergent Properties vs. Explicit Rules

In a GP computer, the complexity is intentional. The designers strive to direct and limit the computer's behaviour with **explicit rules** built into the hardware and the software. They do everything they can to remove the possibility of anything happening by accident. Sometimes it doesn't feel like it, but there is no mystery and there are no surprises. If a computer occasionally gives the impression of intelligent or erratic behaviour, it is only because that intelligence or error was deliberately designed in at the outset.

Our neural networks exist because of the evolutionary success of their **emergent behaviours**: complex, sensitive and flexible behaviours 'emerging' from the interaction of simple structures. At first this can seem like quite a strange idea, but actually we experience this principle in operation hundreds of times a day. Think of any piece of domestic electrical equipment. There are only five types of components in most electrical equipment:

- capacitors;
- resistors;
- diodes;
- transistors;
- magnets.

They are connected by straight or coiled wires, and switches. Each of these components has simple properties which are determined by their internal structure:

- capacitors have the capacity to hold and release an electrical charge;
- resistors resist the flow of an electrical current;
- diodes allow current to pass through in one direction only;
- transistors are switches in which a small current can turn a large current on or off;
- straight wires transmit current in either direction - depending on the metal the wire is made of, it may get hot, emitting light or charged particles, or it may melt as in a fuse;
- coiled wire generates a magnetic field when a current passes through it, and that field collapses when the current stops

flowing, causing a current to be generated in the opposite direction;
- magnets generate a current in any wire that moves through the magnetic field, and will attract or repulse a wire with an electric current passing through it (depending on the direction of flow).

These simple components can be connected together into quite simple networks from which surprisingly complex behaviours **emerge:** toasters, washing machines, radios, televisions, etc.

Small variations in these structures can produce very different behaviours. A radio receiver is designed to respond very selectively and very sensitively to its electromagnetic environment. By adjusting the tuning control and the volume control you are changing its internal structure to make it more or less sensitive to very particular frequencies of radio signal, and very insensitive to all the other frequencies.

So, from a relatively simple structure made of very simple and predictable components, very complex behaviours can emerge, which are selectively responsive to their environment.

The principle of emergent properties is at work in all systems. In mechanical systems the shape and material properties of the components are very important. A car gearbox does what it does because of the shape and material properties of all those cogs, shafts and bearings. It is just a 3D dynamic jigsaw puzzle.

We are so good at working with this sort of spatial cause and effect that we take the emergent properties of a gearbox or a car engine for granted, but in our social, political or economic life we are frequently caught out by the unexpected consequences of our actions. Our well-meaning adjustments to housing policy, tenancy law, education policy, employment law or taxation, almost always turn out to have unexpected and undesirable consequences.

In the world of neural networks we are seeing the principle of 'emergent properties' on an awe inspiring and previously unimaginable scale. Millions of years of evolution of self-tuning experience-trapping neural networks, has resulted in the flexible environmental response we call intelligence.

Top-Down vs. Bottom-Up

Computer designers can explain in detail, the top-down rules that control everything that happens in a GP computer. No one has yet managed to define a set of rules by which our visual system is able to decide if an animal is, or is not, a rabbit, or how we can recognise a Dalmatian puppy in a shadowy forest. Children naturally learn to speak human languages, and unconsciously use complex grammatical structures that expert linguists are unable to define. A child can achieve this purely by experiencing a language, and without ever having been exposed to any explanation of the linguist's grammatical rules. Neural networks assemble their models of reality from experience, from the bottom-up.

For example, it is common for young children to understand – without being able to articulate it – the 'rule' by which many English verbs add *ed* to form the past tense, and so they will say things like *catched* and *buyed.* What they are doing is perfectly sensible. Their neural networks have detected a commonality in the way many (regular) verbs are conjugated and they are applying this (immature) generalised principle to create new past tenses. As their experience increases their neural networks come to realise that the English language has many irregular verb forms as well, and they learn to discriminate between the regulars and the irregulars.

Our neural networks have survived because they are naturally sensitive to commonality, differences, patterns and structures in our experience of the world. These associations are stored in the wiring of our neural networks and form our evolving understanding of the world, our constantly updating models of reality. If we grow up in a denuded world, we get denuded models of reality. If we grow up in a richly structured world we get richly structured models of reality. Thankfully GP computers do not behave like this. If they did, you would think twice before buying a second hand computer.

Precision vs. Ambiguity

Computers can only deal with precision. Biological neural networks have evolved in a context where, in order to survive, they must be able to function effectively with **incomplete** and **ambiguous** information. Our brains construct an internal representation of the space and objects around us by combining incomplete, noisy and ambiguous information from all our sensory systems. Spend one night camping alone in a forest and you will realise how sensitive we are to fleeting glimpses of movement in the undergrowth, a rustling sound, the crack of a twig. The whole integrated map of our surroundings is constructed from a mixture of little bits of sound, vision, touch, taste, smell, temperature, physical vibration, electrostatic voltage, humidity, wind speed, etc. My computer can't even begin to add an apple and a pear, let alone a glimpse and a whisper.

The Tip of the Iceberg

Language acquisition (particularly the ease of acquisition of inexplicable grammars) clearly demonstrates that our neural networks are pre-consciously processing our experience of the world into many fine and subtle categories that we are not consciously aware of. Our conscious awareness is just the tip of the iceberg in comparison to the vast amount of experiential knowledge, subtle categories and relationships, held pre-consciously in our neural networks. Evolution found that it was a good idea to give us the feeling that we **consciously** make decisions and initiate actions, but it is now pretty much accepted by neuroscientists that, in many situations, our pre-conscious neural network iceberg makes most of our decisions for us, long before we become consciously aware of what is going on. Then, just to boost our egos, the pre-conscious neural network gives us the impression that we consciously initiated that action, made that choice. Maybe evolution found that we are more effective, in those few situations where we do have to make conscious choices, if we are already used to the idea that we are consciously in control, even though we are not.

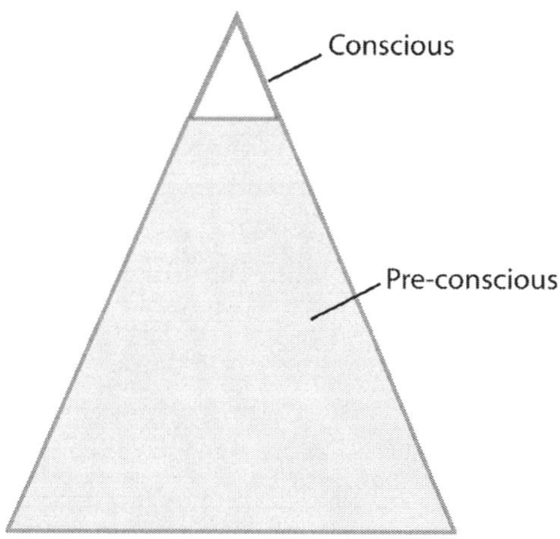

Figure 2.11 The tip of the iceberg.

Our relatively recently evolved language ability is only able to express a small portion of what is actually going on in our pre-conscious iceberg. We are aware of feelings and intuitions, but we often find it difficult to put them into words. We are much better at naming the everyday objects, properties and relations in our conscious awareness, but we still struggle to find a satisfactory way to express and communicate our highest conscious thoughts.

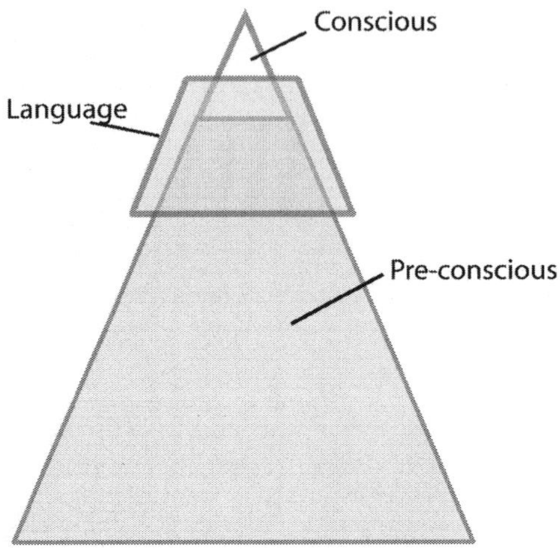

Figure 2.12 The limited reach of language.

Time

Time is just one more precisely measurable variable to a GP computer. In a neural network, time is very distorted. The present is interpreted by networks whose structures were shaped by the totality of their past experiences. In this sense, the past is hugely overrepresented. **The past frames our understanding of the present.** Similarly, consideration of the future is heavily biased towards the present moment. When we have to make a decision between a short-term benefit and a long-term threat, we tend to favour the short-term benefit.

When fund managers invest our savings and pension funds in company shares, their decisions are based on very short-term assessments. Their main concern is whether or not the value of the shares will rise in the near future. As long as they spread the risk, by investing a little in each of a lot of different companies, they do not consider it prudent to make a longer-term assessment of the effect that any particular company's activity might have on the environment in ten years time (or vice versa), or the effect its location, employment and purchasing policies might have on international security or local community cohesion. Only when these issues start to effect short-term prices, will they be taken into account.

Human neural network short-termism is something the global community is going to have to address, sometime soon, particularly if the current concerns about the global effects of rampant human consumerism turn out to be justified.

Attention

A GP computer represents information using digital (on or off) signals. All data looks the same to the computer - it is not selective, it doesn't pay more attention to some bits of data and less to others. Neural networks use digital signals as well, but they are also sensitive to signal strengths and signal frequencies. Learning (restructuring) in neural networks can be enhanced by amplifying a signal, or sending the signal at a particular frequency, that gives it the power or resonance to overwrite or amend previous patterns in the network. Human learning takes place when we pay attention, when we focus in a special way on an experience. Experience, without that special inquisitive, focused, **attention**, may not result in learning. It is clear now that our pre-conscious neural networks have a lot of control (but not complete control) over what we pay attention to, and the study of human learning and development suggests that there are sensitive phases in the development of particular neural network regions, or subject domains, when learning is particularly rapid.

Making Meaning

Natural Learning Machines - Experience vs. Rules

A GP computer is controlled by a single sequential stream of logical rule-based program instructions. Its physical structure must not be affected by the data it processes or the programs it runs. GP computer hardware does not learn from experience.

Neural networks are potent natural learning machines. Their physical structures are continually being transformed by the sequence of the stimulation that flows through them. They are affected (simultaneously) by all the resonant stimuli in their environment. They are purpose built for learning from experience.

There are no programmed rules or logic in a neural network. The natural language of a neural network is one of **continuously evolving categories,** and their **spatial and causal relations.** This is how we capture and reuse our experiences of the world and update our mental models of reality. The current condition (and hence the current behaviour) of a neural network is the result of all its previous experiences and model making.

Spatial Mapping - attaching meaning to places

In comparison with a GP computer, neural networks are extremely efficient at handling spatial information, and at attaching meanings to locations in that space. Most of us can effortlessly recall a vast number of places and routes, and can attach multiple meanings to them all.

Look at a map of your local city. Imagine what a task it would be to write a description of your holistic mental comprehension of that place. You would have to describe each road, one by one: how long it is, which direction it goes in, whether it is straight or curved, what kinds of buildings are on it (houses, apartment blocks, shops, offices, factories, public amenities, etc.). That part is reasonably manageable, but serious problems start when you try to describe how the roads connect with each other. A connects to B, and C and D and E. B connects to F and G and H. But what sequence can you use now? Do you finish describing all the roads connected to B before you start listing C's connections, or do you finish describing all the roads connected directly to A before you start on Bs offshoots (F, G, H)? Whichever way you sequence it, the resultant document would be far too big to carry with you, and it would be completely useless as a tool to help you plan a journey across town. This illustrates our vast mental capacity for internally representing and manipulating our model of our external spatial environment, and for attaching meanings to places. This is a butcher's, that is a baker's, this road is served by a 29 bus, that road is part of a one-way system, and so on.

When it comes to describing and communicating complex spatial information such as how to build a cathedral, the shape of a boat's hull or the dynamic interaction between the components of a car engine, we immediately resort to (simultaneous spatial) diagrams to represent it rather than sequential text, because our brains can handle this type of information so much more effectively in a diagrammatic form.

Some linguists have suggested that our enormous spatial mapping ability may have provided the foundation for the evolution of human language and culture. It is certainly the case that many of the structures found in human language, and human society, have a spatial flavour: inclusion, exclusion, bounded by, intersections with, connections, paths, centre versus periphery, orientation, direction, hierarchy, up, down, on, in, under, over, before, behind, size, length, types of terrain, types of surface, and so on.

The Learning Curve

The **'learning curve'** is an expression that has very real meaning in relation to neural networks. First exposure to a new field of experience may not cause much change to begin with, but as the neural network structure begins to adapt to the new experiences, the rate of learning and development typically increases rapidly. At this stage, the neural network is ripe for learning, and seems able to direct our attention, to search out more experiences with which to resolve areas of ambiguity and perceptual conflict. We typically pay a lot of attention to things that we can't make sense of yet. Gradually, the network settles into a more stable state. It responds less and less to new experiences, and pays little attention, even if it is presented with significant new information. This is the **belief** stage, characterised by fixed interpretations and a lack of sensitivity to new information.

The learning curve has obvious implications for education since not all students will be 'ripe' for learning a particular topic at the same time. The belief phase of the learning curve also has very serious implications. In the West, some belief systems are revered simply for being a belief system, others are outlawed because they are a belief system, and sometimes it's the other way around. If I proclaim a belief, I am basically saying I am no longer able to learn and adapt to new information in that particular area because my neural networks have got locked in a fixed pattern and can't change, no matter what new or contradictory experiences come my way.

I don't think it is very sensible to enforce respect for this state of mind. It is understandable in the elderly, because our neural networks have seen about as much as they can handle by the time we are in our seventies or eighties, but it is rather tragic to see fixed beliefs in young people. Wouldn't it be more sensible to make the gentle, but slightly critical, questioning of all fixed beliefs compulsory rather than illegal? Some have even suggested we should consider a new human right, to protect young children from being indoctrinated into particularly potent and rigid belief systems, until they are old enough and experienced enough to make their own decisions.

Black Swans

Our pre-conscious neural networks build their understanding of the world by detecting and trapping **associations.** Because they can **only** work with what they have **already** experienced, they are very bad at modelling the probability and possibility, the chance and uncertainty, of things they have **not yet experienced.**

Our default setting is to expect and predict more of the same. We don't expect fundamental changes to come out of nowhere. If we have seen a thousand swans and all of them were white, it doesn't cross our minds to wonder if swans come in any other colours. That is because nothing in our past has ever pointed to that possibility. We imagine that things will carry on in the future as they were in the past and we consolidate this perspective by making up definitions, explanations and laws. We settle into a nice comfortable complacency and then bang – a black swan shows up.

Our neural networks are also very bad at spotting associations in irregular, unpatterned, random, chaos. As a result, we oversimplify our own history, as if all the chaos in it had not actually happened, and we extrapolate that forwards into a de-chaosed oversimplified model of the future. That is why we imagine that the world is much more regular than it really is.

We can use our conscious brain to deliberately go and explore the possibility that everything and anything could change overnight, but it's not very efficient to plan your life on the basis that everything might suddenly change, because most of the time it won't. The problem is that some things will suddenly change and it will take us by surprise. The more we didn't expect it, the less likely we are to be looking for it, and the less warning we will get.

> I recommend reading 'The Black Swan' by Nassim Nicholas Taleb, for a very amusing and stimulating exploration of Black Swans.

Stability, Reliability, Memory, Change and Learning

If a GP computer is given the same task on two different occasions, it will give exactly the same results both times. Its memory is accurate. The data and the programs are not affected by whether or not they are used regularly. Neural networks are very different. When new information passes through a neural network, the network may remain in the same condition (which gives it the ability to remember) but it may change in the light of this new experience (which gives it the ability to learn). A neural network probably will not give the same results in two apparently identical situations, because it is so sensitive to the passage of time and experience that there can be no such thing as two identical situations, especially early on in its learning phase.

Another difference is that the memory in a computer is more or less permanent. It can be transferred from one medium to another and from one location to another. The memory of a neural network is not permanent, it can decay if it is not used, and it will be changed by subsequent experiences. It is not transferable. It exists only in the current condition of that specific neural network. The only way to copy it would be to copy the exact structure of the network and to give it exactly the same experiences in the same order and intensity. But by then, the first network may have had some new experiences or decayed a little with under use. This says a lot about the uniqueness of each human's development and experience of the world.

Your experience and understanding of the concepts of democracy, religion, progress, duty, etc., will not be exactly the same as mine. We may use the same words as each other but the meanings and feelings we associate with those words will not be exactly the same. Christians can all recite the Lord's Prayer and enjoy a (neurochemical) sense of community when they do it as a group, but if they explored exactly what the words mean for each of them, the sense of communal agreement might begin to vaporise.

Neural Networks Make Meaning; GP Computers Do Not.

Perhaps the most significant realisation to flow from the new understanding of neural networks is that, for the first time, we can see **the mechanisms by which we construct our own meaning.**

Neural networks start with a genetically inherited and evolved perceptual base which is already predisposed to perceive and categorise the human environment in a particularly human way. To this inherited base is added a stream of personal and cultural experiences which the neural networks use to construct subtle, multi-stranded, hierarchical, generalised and abstracted categories and relationships. All this happens as a consequence (an emergent property) of the ability of neural networks to restructure their internal connections in response to the associations they detect in the limited sensory information they receive.

Early research into artificial neural networks taught us not to assume that our pre-conscious neural networks are detecting the same types of associations, chopping the world up into the same sorts of categories that we use in our conscious cultural explanations.

A military research experiment tried to use an artificial neural network to detect tanks hidden in forests. The artificial neural network was shown pictures of forests with military tanks hidden in them, and pictures of forests without tanks hiding in them. The researchers then asked the neural network if it could see tanks hidden in a third set of pictures. They were delighted and astonished when the neural network interpreted every new picture correctly. They studied the changes that had taken place in the network to find out exactly what it was detecting, and were dismayed to find that all the photographs without tanks were taken on sunny days and all the pictures with tanks were taken on grey days. The neural network wasn't detecting tanks at all; it was just responding to the colour of the sky. **It wasn't chopping the world up into the 'right' kind of chunks.**

English Spelling

This may explain why so many people, all around the world, have problems learning to spell many English words. Because of the rich history of the English language, English spelling is an unreliable and unpredictable mess. Most of it can be understood, but only if you realise at an early stage that English has lots of different sets of spelling 'rules' or patterns operating in parallel, matching its Germanic, Scandinavian, Old English, Early French, Late French, Latin, Greek and assorted other roots. This is further complicated by the fact that English spelling was pretty much fixed by foreign printers, who set up their printing presses here at the end of the Middle Ages, but who did not really understand the language and its many different regional accents and dialects. Since then, of course, the way we pronounce the words has changed a lot, but the way we spell them has stayed much the same. No wonder the over-simplistic explanations given in primary schools confuse a lot of children. People who are able to learn to spell by remembering the visual appearance of the words do OK, but if you are the sort of person who learns by understanding things, you can get into big cognitive trouble with English spelling.

The alphabet was a great invention. Previous writing systems had used stylised pictures to represent the **meaning** of words (pictograms). Abstract ideas could not easily be represented in this way, but the **sound** of an abstract word could be represented by adding together the sounds of existing pictograms, plus an additional sign (a determinative) to tell the reader that this was a phonogram made of sounds and not a pictogram made of meanings.

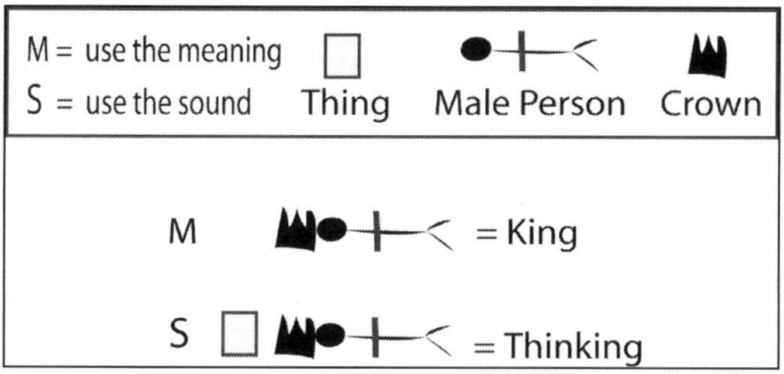

Figure 2.13 Pictograms & phonograms.

The Phoenicians developed this idea of **representing the sounds rather than the meanings** of words. They isolated the different sounds of their language, and allocated a sign to each sound (one sign = one sound, actually they ignored the small number of vowel sounds in their language), thus creating the alphabetic / phonetic system of writing which records the sounds and not the meanings of the words. This was very successful and the idea spread rapidly. An alphabet with about 30 symbols was much easier to learn than a vast array of pictograms, and it was very versatile within each language group. The Greeks found that their language needed the vowel sounds as well, so they borrowed some Aramaic letter signs for sounds which did not exist in Greek, and used them for their Greek vowel sounds, hence: A – alpha, E - epsilon, O - omicron, Y-upsilon, I-iota. The Greek system became the Cyrillic alphabet which spread through Eastern Europe and Russia. The Romans designed new letter shapes that looked better when carved on stone monuments, and Latin sounds and letters came to western Europe. The Indian language scripts are also based on a very structured alphabetic system but the Chinese language stayed with its original pictorial base, with a thousand or so core pictograms and ideograms, supplemented with signs that specify which of many different contextual meanings and pronunciations to use.

The sound-based alphabetic/phonetic system (phonetic, from Greek for *speak*) works really well where there is one letter for one sound. It gets a bit more complicated when you combine two or three letters to try to represent a new sound from another language. In English, the relationship between the sounds, and the various combinations of letters used to represent them, is no longer even close to one-to-one.

I suspect that as our infants start learning the sounds of English, their neural networks chop the sounds up into discrete components, as they would in any other language. This part of the process appears to work well as very few children have problems learning to say the words. But a real problem arises if the sound chunks detected by their neural networks do not match well with the chaotic botched-up written system they then encounter at school.

For example, consider the role of the **letter** 'o' in *on, once, only, woman, women, worry*; or the *ee* **sound** in *leap, people, here, weird, chief, police, me, ski, key*; or the *oo* **sound** in *rude, shrewd, truth, group, move, fruit, tomb, through, blue, shoe.*[4]

There is still a phonetic base, but it is no longer a complete or reliable system. If a child asks for an explanation they are given an oversimplified one, which turns out experientially to be riddled with exceptions, and very soon the child learns that the 'rules' are not rules, the system is unreliable and the teachers can't be trusted.

The problem is compounded by the fact that many of the very common words that we encounter early on in the learning curve, are highly irregular (the, to, you, your, very, many, etc.).

Some experts say that this is not a problem because the brain recognises these small common exceptional words as whole words, as signs, not as words constructed out of alphabetic components.

Well then perhaps we should learn a trick from the ancient Egyptians, and add some determinatives to our early-learning texts, to indicate that these highly irregular words are not like other words. We could underline them, or print them in a different font, so that young children's neural networks have a clear way of discriminating between the regular and the irregular, the 'whole word signs' and the alphabetically constructed words.

We could go a stage further and add some way of indicating which spelling system the words are from, (Celtic, Old English, Scandinavian, Latin, Greek, French, etc.), and whether they are good or bad examples of that system.

We could devise a much richer and more carefully sequenced system of exposure to the written version of the language, which would help the children's neural networks to build up a stable conceptual

[4] Visit www.englishspellingproblems.co.uk or read the book by Marsha Bell, 'English Spelling Problems', for a thorough analysis of the extent of the problem.

pyramid of the whole messy picture without falling into chaos, confusion, distrust and avoidance. And perhaps we should stop discriminating against those students whose pattern matching and cognitive ability is so good that they realise at an early age what a messed-up system it is - a perfectly sensible reaction for a healthy neural network, hungry for order and patterns, but starved of proper nourishment and fed on a diet it is unable to digest.

Some people's neural networks either don't notice, or can tolerate the inconsistent pronunciation of, for example, the 'gh' combination in *through, tough, ghost, night,* etc., Academic society still equates intelligence with the ability to tolerate these fuzzy phonetic inconsistencies, which is strange, because we would not be so comfortable if numbers, arithmetic symbols or road signs frequently changed their meaning without any explanation or justification.

There may well be a new element in this problem in that modern children are exposed to a huge number of different regional and international 'English' accents. Not even the BBC can be relied on for a consistent source of English language sounds. So how is a thinking child supposed to match up all those unreliable sounds with all those unreliable and unexplained spellings?

The Educational Value of Rules and Organising Concepts

The presentation and consumption of conscious rational rules is not, on its own, very useful. They become valuable when they are used to organise and then consolidate a richly structured, well-timed sequence of experiences. Brain scientists have recently discovered the neural mechanism that underlies our top-down ability to restructure previous experience in the light of a new high-level concept or organising principle. There are reverse-projection neurons which can connect the areas representing high-level generalised concepts, back down to the areas representing the mass of relevant primary experience, where they can release neurochemicals which establish and strengthen the relevant level jumping connections. Hence that pleasurable neurochemical 'Eureka' feeling, when confusion suddenly turns into clarity because of the introduction of some new organising idea or principle (force, energy, socialism, capitalism, etc.).

Some of these organising concepts are quite vague (social equality, fairness, justice) and open to personal interpretation because our understanding of them is strongly influenced by our own personal experience. Other approaches to organising our experiences are very precise and measurable, such as sequencing or categorising by weight, number, length, volume, types of shape, destination, date, etc.

Hard and Fluffy Standards

There is currently a bureaucratic fashion for producing written **service standards**, which claim to set out how we can expect to be treated in a range of different situations: if we have to make a complaint, for example. These sound impressive but are actually very fluffy and often bear little or no relationship to reality.

The manufacturing of machines, computers, software, etc., is underpinned by much more rigorous and dependable **standards** that most of us are not aware of, but which have a huge effect on our lives. The nuts and bolts that hold our cars and bicycles together are made according to a set of hard and dependable standards that specify the angle of the thread, the pitch of the thread, the shape of the thread, the tightness of fit and the spanner size. Without these hard dependable standards things would be considerably more chaotic.

In 1948 NATO introduced the Unified National System to overcome the fact that British and American thread sizes were not quite compatible (and had been incompatible all through WW II). This gave us:

UNF - Unified National Fine thread
UNC - Unified National Course thread
which are compatible with
BSF British Standard Fine
BSC British Standard Course
which replaced
BSW British Standard Witworth (55 degree threads which covered fine and course). The Teeth Per Inch for Witworth threads were/are:

Diameter in inches	TPI
1/4	20
5/16	18
3/8	16
7/16	14
1/2	12

We also have the Metric system which specifies:

Metric super fine	1.0 mm pitch
Metric fine	1.25 mm pitch
Metric course	1.50 mm pitch

Also still in use are:
BSCy British Standard Cycle 20 or 26 TPI
British Standard Pipe

(Which explains why my classic Norton racing bike's engine, which was manufactured during the gradual transition between these standards, on some old machinery and some new machinery, has threads from almost every one of these standards.)

The materials, finishes and strength ratings are set by:

ASTM	- American Society for Testing
DIN	- Deutsch Industrial Normals
ISO	- International Standards Organization

Trying to learn these engineering standards without ever having used any nuts and bolts would be a very unenjoyable experience, but if you have already had plenty of experience of messing about with old engines (and have already noticed that some nuts and bolts are interchangeable and others are not) then it can be very interesting to be introduced to these organising principles, and the history of the reasons why they are the way they are - particularly if you can see an immediate use for this knowledge.

So those conscious, rational, high-level rules that we make up to explain and organise things are not in themselves great teaching aids, but can be useful guides for designing **well sequenced educational experiences**, to be followed by a process of **consolidation**, that brings that learning into conscious awareness, where it can be given culturally validated names and stories, making it available to be discussed, shared and communicated with others.

Consolidating Experience

Putting up a tent is a very human experience that most children of an appropriate age really enjoy, but it is also an experience that can be used as a foundation for consciously exploring and naming many of the conceptual building blocks of architecture, mechanics and physics.

For example:

> Structure: foundation, floor, membrane, beam, arch, pillar.
> Force: tension, compression, resistance, balance, gravity, wind pressure, temperature, insulation, condensation, absorption, osmosis.
> Properties of materials: rigid, flexible, elastic, fluid, springy, stiff, tensile strength, compressive strength, cast, spun, moulded, woven, smooth, rough, coloured, transparent, water repellent, water soluble.
> Shape: form, container, boundary, separation, opening, closure, skin, shell.
> Fixings: friction, interlocking tessellations, knots, joining materials, sewing, glues.

Wow, all that from thinking about playing with a tent! But most important of all, is that special learning state that focuses our attention and generates the kind of signal strengths that can restructure our neural networks and so turn experience into learning – that state of mind where we feel an inquisitive fascination and an absence of stress, anxiety, humiliation, boredom, etc. If an educational setting doesn't trigger that special learning state of mind, then it is probably a waste of time.

This new understanding of the functioning of neural networks is clearly going to have implications for many aspects of life. Already we can see that it has implications for education, suggesting that it needs to be based on carefully sequenced, individually tailored, context-rich, content-rich, associative, multi-sensory, pre-conscious experiences, which are then consciously reviewed, analysed, generalised and abstracted into culturally framed and named conceptual building blocks, which can then be assembled, block by block, into a solid socio-cultural conceptual pyramid.

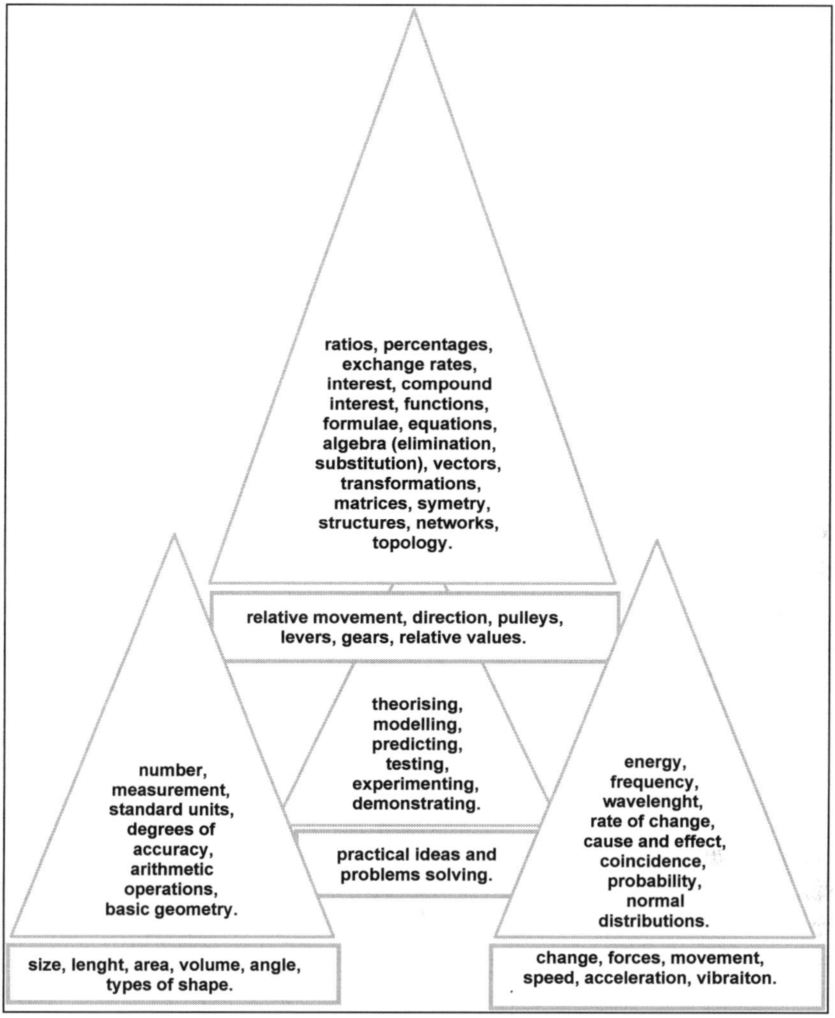

Figure 2.14 A few cultural building blocks growing out of direct experience. There are many more, history, architecture, engineering, music, art, literature, religion, politics, etc.

Isolated vs. Associative and Updatable Memory

In a GP computer, each item of information is accurately remembered in isolation from all other items of information. The memory of a neural network is **associative, expansive and unstable**. This means that the act of remembering one item may trigger the memory of many other associated items.

The ability of neural networks to make associations gives rise to a range of different recall possibilities. The sensing of a small part can trigger, by association, recognition of the whole. Catching a glimpse of a yellow stripe in the undergrowth triggers the possibility that it might be a tiger, a snake, or a banana. This ability to move from the part to the whole is very useful for spotting both dangers and resources, but it is also responsible for us jumping to so many false assumptions.

Neural network memory is stable enough to persist through time, but is also sufficiently unstable to allow it to be changed by subsequent (learning) experiences. Most biological networks rewrite or adjust memories every time they are accessed, allowing old memories to adapt in order to reflect new contexts and experiences.

This can lead to distortions, and inaccuracies. Our memories can be adjusted and reinterpreted to fit in with our current beliefs, or with the expectations of our current social group. Events which were originally imagined, fantasised, embellished to show us in a good light, or exaggerated to make a good story, can come to be remembered as facts. It can also lead to misattribution - I thought I read it in a quality newspaper, but actually I heard it in the pub.

The **good news** is that we can take advantage of this property of our memory systems, to revisit old memories and rewrite them in the light of our current (hopefully greater) experience of the world. We can decide to reinterpret them, changing what they mean for us, and the emotions we associate with them. Because our current models of the world are based on these old memories, a change to the meaning / interpretation of a foundation memory can have a domino effect, causing profound changes to cascade through our models and beliefs, our perception of the world. This is not at all like the memory on your computer's hard disk.

The Pleasure of Learning

So far as we know, computers don't have feelings. They don't care whether their programs play music or search a database. We do care. Neurochemical pleasure is a powerful force, directing attention and learning in our biological neural networks.

If you pay attention to it, you cannot fail to be struck by how very attractive nature is to our perceptual systems, and how fortunate we are that evolution chose to make learning about our environment such a pleasurable experience.

That pleasure makes us want to get out there and immerse our senses in the joys of nature, at the same time feeding our neural networks with exactly the experiences they need to build a valuable understanding of our environment. This pleasure in observation and discovery seems to apply to all areas of learning.

Conversely, we feel anxious in the presence of things we don't understand yet, and we get a real (neurochemical) buzz when we manage to turn that chaos into order. We love to organise things - categorising them, naming them, sorting them into different sequences, spotting patterns, trends, relationships. When we discover some organising principle, concept or filter, that increases our sense of understanding, we may even adopt this new learning as a feature of our social personality, and publicly declare our new view of the world by announcing that we have become Marxist, Thatcherite, Environmentalist, Consumerist, Capitalist, Islamist, Buddhist, Scientist, etc.

So it looks as if evolution has employed the neurochemistry of both pleasure and anxiety as a way of directing our attention towards useful resources. Natural learning begins with an observation, an interest, is followed by a period of fascination and focussed exploration, and ends with a process of consolidation. Each step is enjoyable. Sometimes the process is initiated by anxiety rather than interest, by the need to make sense of something right now, but the subsequent process can still be enjoyable.

Maria Montessori, who developed the Montessori teaching method, noticed that young children learn each new developmental step when they are ready to, when they want to, and not before. So she made sure that each new learning opportunity was available for the children, but she waited until they had mastered the current piece of learning to their own satisfaction, and were showing an interest in taking the next step, before she introduced the next learning experience. If only all formal learning could harness these principles.

The Modern Urban Landscape

What are our ancient neural network structures making of our new man-made environments? They certainly don't appear to offer as rich an experiential environment as the natural environments which our neural networks evolved to deal with. What effect might these denuded homogenised environments be having on the development of our perceptual and cognitive systems? Is it possible for us to learn all our basic model-building concepts in a square-box concrete jungle?

A few years ago, I bought a computer from a man who had grown up in the jungle in West Africa, where he had been trained as a 'witch doctor' (his words not mine). The story he told was that the president's daughter was very ill and western medicine had failed to cure her, so she was taken to the jungle to see if the traditional medicine system could solve the problem. She got better. The president was impressed and intrigued, and arranged for this young jungle medicine practitioner to be sent to study western medicine in London, to get the best of both world views. He had done well and was engaged in cutting-edge medical research. As a sideline, he was selling (second-hand, to avoid VAT) computers which he assembled from imported Chinese components, in the bedroom of his north London council flat. The point of this story is that his early experiences in that rich natural environment gave him the opportunity to develop all the basic and transferable skills he needed to make a significant success of living in both cultures. Would a West African child, growing up in a north London urban 'concrete jungle' and being educated at a local school, develop such an impressive range of transferable skills? The statistics are not encouraging. Maybe the modern urban environment just doesn't offer the sort of rich and stimulating experiences that the human brain has evolved to expect. Whilst city life certainly has its own special challenges, it is definitely a much simpler existence than the ones our ancestors experienced. Energy for heating and cooking comes down pipes or wires. Building materials arrive, ready to use, on the back of a lorry. Rivers have been diverted into underground tunnels. Many modern city children have no idea how their basic foods are grown, harvested, prepared, preserved, etc. Almost all our daily resources come from the corner shop or the supermarket.

From a human neural network point of view, a forest or a country meadow is a more interesting and stimulating environment than a paved city playground.

Relative Duality

Thinking about the way our pre-conscious neural networks construct our meaning for us, brings home the **relative and dualistic nature of our understanding.** The ancients were aware of this. In that classical documentary on human psychology, the *Bible*, the first humans left the world of absolute beingness (Eden) and descended into the dualistic world of relative appearances, to taste the fruits of the tree of the knowledge of Good and Evil (relative duality).

Dithering uncertainty is not on average a great survival strategy, so evolution has arranged that we usually **feel** as though our understanding and knowledge is reasonably absolute. That feeling persists even though in maturity we come to **know** that many of the things we once thought were absolute, turned out subsequently to be relative. We are usually pretty convinced by the truth of our most recent conclusions, but in reality we are constantly surfing that ever-changing, context-framed, learning curve, somewhere between naive ignorance and fixed rigid belief. Although the brain tricks us into feeling that our knowledge and values are definite and absolute, everything turns out to be relative before very long. **Meaning always depends on the context,** on the frame.

The Social Construction of Reality

Within each frame, our constructed understanding is like a wall or a pyramid, with each conceptual layer built block by block on the layers below. For example, to understand maths you have to build up from the foundations. You have first the grasp the ideas of number and length and units of measurement, the rules of arithmetical transformations (+ - x ÷ =), etc. If you leave out, or fail to grasp, any of the low-level building blocks, you are going to have big trouble in the layers above, because the higher-level concepts depend on the lower-level building blocks being in place.

A human culture is a huge, complicated, reasonably integrated, but ever-changing package of these conceptual building blocks. They make reasonable sense within their country or place of origin, but are not necessarily transferable into another cultural setting. A firm handshake is appropriate in some countries, but a weak handshake is expected in others. A thumbs-up sign can get you into deep trouble in some cultures. I have a dear friend from the Balkans who can, in some circumstances, associate my wanting to discuss something with an attack on his intellectual integrity, and therefore, somehow, an attack on his life, which for him justifies a fight to the death, if necessary. Wow. In my (English) culture, to invite someone to engage in a serious discussion about fundamental ideas and values is generally seen as an act of friendship and respect.

Of course, a single swallow does not make a summer. I know other Balkans who do not react this way. I am just illustrating the point that cultural values and interpretations can and do vary. Such differences can give rise to very different ways of understanding and interacting with the world. Discussion = insult to intellectual integrity, is not the same as discussion = friendship and respect. These man-made frameworks of values, equivalences and metaphorical associations, are simultaneously both absolutely meaningless and very important - to human beings. *Meaningless* in that they are man-made, temporary and variable - there is nothing absolutely good or bad about discussion. It all depends on the context. *Very important*, in that they have often caused groups of humans to exclude, persecute, exile and excommunicate non-conformists, and to justify inter-group warfare, especially if there is a prospect of some valuable resources being available to the winner.

Without a cultural framework, our ideas, equivalences and values have very little meaning. We cannot assume that our meanings can be transferred intact into another culture, or vice versa. The reasons I may give to my Balkan friend, to justify the value of discussion in English culture, do not have a similar meaning for him, and vice versa.

We all like to think that our own beliefs and values are reasonably grounded in personal experiences and demonstrable facts, whilst observing that other people's beliefs have a tendency to escape such empirical tests and constraints, and drift off into the realms of wishful thinking, dreams and fantasy. The more remote the causation, the easier it is for the dreams and fantasies to take hold.

Fortunately, thanks to the Greek and Roman Empires, European cultural pyramids (from Russia to Spain) are very similar in most respects. Although Christianity does not play as prominent a cultural role as it once did, it has left a pyramid of shared, spin-off, values that enable a reasonably workable cross-cultural exchange of meaning and understanding. I have no doubt that the great and enduring Eastern cultural groupings have enabled a similar trans-national exchange of meanings, but I don't understand it – yet.

Global capitalism, the new boy on the block, is busily trying to create a worldwide pyramid of shared economic and semi-democratic values. It tries to keep out of other aspects of cultural life but, in so doing, it blinds itself to the holistic, the cultural cognitive big picture, and therefore creates a lot of cultural stresses in the process.

It disrupts traditional patterns of land ownership. Families who used to have independent control of self-sufficient economic resources are enticed into becoming dependent on employment provided by remote (even global) organisations. Broad generalists become focussed specialists. People are separated from natural cycles and their experiences become denuded, atomised, homogenised.

Social Groups

There is no doubt that human survival has been helped by our ability to live in largish cooperative groups. But, in order to benefit from the group's experience, we often have to adjust our perception, our understanding, in order to fit in with the group's expectations.

There is a huge amount of evidence, if any more was needed, that humans can, and do, distort their perceptions, values, opinions, etc., in exchange for the benefits of group participation. Think about our party political system, for example, which requires its members to commit publicly to views and policies even though they strongly disagree with them. While the party is doing well, and it has benefits to bestow on its members, everyone toes the party line, but when it begins to look as if the group's fortunes are in decline, those previously suppressed opinions begin to be expressed.

Recent research suggests that participation in group events, such as singing together or participating in social rituals, releases **endorphins** in the brain which produce a very pleasant sense of comfort, trust, belonging, etc. No wonder human history is so dominated by our tendency to group together into tribes, clans, secret societies, gangs and organisations defined by shared ideology, philosophy, religion, criminal activity, business interests, territorial interest, sports affiliations, etc. This neurochemical inducement to form into non-biological social groups combines with the power of culture, to frame and shape our understanding, and to define the words and concepts we can use to express that understanding.

Belief-gangs usually don't mix very well with contradictory belief-gangs. They often find it very threatening to come into contact with groups who disagree with, and thus undermine, the core organising principles of their world view.

There have been a handful of occasions in human history where great civilisations and empires grew up, which temporarily offered such a compelling and successful cultural system that the lesser belief-gangs were prepared to give up or adapt some of their old ways in order to participate in the benefits of the new super-culture.

Not everyone is equally willing to submit themselves to these major or minor gangs. Some people try to maintain a degree of independence of thought, only to find that independent thought and perception is a very elusive, and a very isolating state of mind, because human thought, perception and communication, can really only exist within (or in opposition to) a pre-existing socio-cultural framework of some sort.

Cultural Transmission

The development of the ability to pass cultural knowledge and ideas from person to person marked an extraordinary change in the mechanisms of evolution.

Before cultural transmission, successful evolutionary adaptations were passed on genetically down through the generations. That is a relatively slow process. The development of cultural transmission meant that successful (and unsuccessful) **ideas** can be passed from person to person within the same generation, and can spread very much faster. This seems to be one of the main reasons for the relatively high speed of *Homo sapiens'* technical and cultural development. Of course, on the downside, stupid and dangerous ideas get passed around too, and good ideas can be widely and rapidly suppressed.

GP computer hardware is much more responsive to cultural transmission than our neural networks. Computers have very little resistance to change. Because of the very clever system of agreed design standards, we can (within limits) simply plug in an upgraded processor or hard drive. We can delete old programmes, old operating systems and install new ones without any complaints from the computer about the erosion of its cultural heritage. They don't have any emotional attachment to their memories - they are very 'here and now'. Our neural networks are not that flexible. Our past has a huge impact on how we experience the present, and we can get very emotionally attached to some aspects of it.

Computer based information and communication technology has had a huge impact on the speed and nature of human cultural transmission. It still takes a few days to drive a truck load of physical goods across a continent, but ideas and information can travel at near the speed of light. Parents and teachers used to filter and amplify the ideas that were passed to the next generation, but recent research found that the average American businessmen spent only 6 minutes a day with his children, and the children spent 5 hours a day on the internet. These internet-wired children are exposed to the same enormous pool of ideas and information whether they live in America or India. So whilst there is still a strong local ingredient in the physical aspects of cultural transmission (local food, local building styles, local customs and rituals) the local ingredient in the transmission of ideas and information has been significantly eroded. Local cultural values will still influence a child's interaction with global internet culture, but this is a very significant change. The internet has taken over from the church/religion as the international carrier of ideas.

This enormous explosion of choice made available by the internet seems initially to have produced a blander more homogenised cultural environment. But now it looks as though this may be just a temporary phenomena associated with the lingering death of the old mass market mentality. As the quality of the available niche options increases, and as we develop better tools for searching that vast new array of choices, we seem to be getting better at discriminating. We are starting to loose interest in fashionable mass market offerings and are pursuing our own personal interests instead. The trend suggests that we are starting to group together in transient online interest-based communities in preference to genetic or geographical communities.

Back to Basics

The old questions remain. How can we know what is out there in reality? What are the threats and what are the opportunities? What might bring pleasure and what might bring pain or disaster? A new but very similar question has recently been added, how can we find the really interesting stuff on the internet?

Planet Earth is awash with a mass of information carried by electromagnetic radiation. Most of it originates in the Sun, but some is released by chemical reactions or the relative movement of charged particles here on Earth. Some of this radiation is absorbed when it collides with matter, but a lot of it bounces off material surfaces such as water, clouds, rocks, soil, plants, buildings, machines, etc., and as it does so the frequencies of the radiation are transformed in ways that carry information about those reflecting surfaces. Some of this information can be detected by our eyes as visible light and is processed by our brain to give us a 3D, coloured, visual impression of our surroundings. Molecules of matter are constantly escaping from every material surface and drifting about in the air or water. They occasionally land on our smell and taste detectors. Pressure waves in the ground, air and water also carry information about what is going on out there in reality.

Framing – a question of context

Evolution has evolved sensory devices which enable us to detect some particularly promising portions of this information, but the really difficult problem is to workout **how to interpret the information**, how to make sense of it in ways that might increase our survivability.

How do we work out that one yellowish beam of light is from something as benign as a Van Gogh painting of sunflowers, whilst another very similar beam of yellow light is from the markings on the back of a poisonous snake? How can we tell the difference between a picture of a poisonous snake and the real thing?

It is all a question of context. The raw data, the beams of light are practically identical. It is only when they are looked at in the larger context that their life-threatening significance emerges. If you are in a famous art gallery, then it is much more likely to be a Van Gogh than a viper. If you are in a forest, it is very unlikely to be a valuable Van Gogh and much more likely to be a viper, or a banana or....

Evolved Innate Framing

So the next question is, **how do we recognise contexts?** This is what has become known as the 'frame problem'. People who struggle to build intelligent robots have encountered this problem head on. Until we tried to teach machines to recognise significant differences in contexts (even in a very simple environment), we had not realised what an enormously difficult task it is, to specify rules for interpreting the relevance of all the different frames the robots might encounter in their cyber life out there on planet Earth, or on the moon. And anyway, we have already worked out that neural networks don't operate on the basis of logical lists of rules, so how (on earth) do they achieve it?

The short and amazing answer seems to be that, over millions of years of living on the surface of Earth, evolution has evolved for us, inheritable neural network platforms which are so well adapted to the recurring problems of our human lifestyle, that they can do almost all of the basic jobs of observing, learning, categorising and framing the world for us, automatically. We then add a touch of individuality, personality and community to the process, trapping and utilising our unique life and shared cultural experiences. As a result we make pretty good decisions most of the time. But we don't make perfect decisions.

Finding high quality resources on the internet is a similar problem in many ways. Like the universe, the internet projects far too much information, so we have to find ways to filter out the really interesting, useful and safe stuff. This is difficult because we don't know what we are looking for until we find it, and we may never know what we missed? Hopefully we will recognise quality when we see it, but until we have seen it, we don't know what to search for. We can't know who will have written it, or when, what genre it will have been classified under or what keywords will have been used to describe it.

Early search engines crawled all over the internet looking at the text in the web pages and building indexed databases of what words were available. We then searched the indexes looking for names, words, categories, places, etc. But the fact that I liked one particular Bob Dylan song doesn't necessarily mean I will like all Bob Dylan Songs. Maybe what I liked was the pattern of the phrasing in that particular song and I would like to find other songs with similar phrasing, but that property of songs, that characteristic, has not been recorded in the database index - so I can't search for it. The framing and categorising doesn't suit my needs.

New generation search techniques are starting to use the principle of association. When you look for a book, the software tells you that people who bought that book also bought these other books. We don't know why they did that, but we can guess that they probably had a reason.

What is happening here is that we are starting to copy the fundamental mechanisms used by our own neural networks to make sense of the world. Trapping experiences and recording associations as a means of learning about subtle indefinable properties and relationships. This method doesn't know or care about the naming of categories. What it does know is that some other human beings found 'something' interesting in this group of books. And in time, when the system has trapped many more associations, it will know a lot more about the structure of what we find interesting in books. But it won't necessarily be able to describe this knowledge in words.

Essence and Substance

Since ancient times (from Pythagoras at least) great thinkers have observed that everything in the created universe seems to have both an *essence* and a *substance.* By substance they meant the physical manifestation, the body, the ever-changing material characteristics of a thing. The essence of a thing is its defining, permanent, unchanging, archetypal properties and relationships.

Ancient thinkers were intrigued by the way that a rabbit, which obviously should have four legs, furry skin, two long ears, etc., is still clearly essentially a rabbit, even if it has lost one of its ears in an accident. How far can you take this? A man who has lost both his legs is still a man. A dog that loses two legs does not become a man, nor does it become some new species of demidog. What defines it as a dog is more than the possession of a full complement of legs. However, the body of a man who is no longer alive, no longer conscious, no longer a thinking, acting, creative agent, is no longer considered to be a man – the essence has left. This gave rise to, or certainly added to, the idea of a soul, an essence, a spirit, inhabiting a material body.

So those ancient thinkers had identified two types of properties – substantial properties and essential properties. A change in the substantial properties of a thing does not change its fundamental identity, but a change to its essential properties does.

This led to the idea that there were very real, possibly even super-real, essences, which were thought to be defined and created by God as a set of archetypes, which were then manifested in the material world as substance, by the word, or thought, or instruction of God.

In more modern terms, we might think of material objects as having two components: an information matrix which fully describes the idea of the thing, which is then dipped in matter to create its physical body. Everyday examples are the collection of ideas and instructions captured in an architect's drawings for a new building, or an engineer's designs for a new model of car. The building can not come into existence (manifest) without there first being this very detailed and comprehensive set of plans. Once the design for the car is completed, a thousand examples of the idea can be manufactured.

The ancient thinkers thought that the **words** that named these essences were very powerful, magical, sacred tools, which were in some way (which is hard for us to understand now) equivalent to the essence of the things they described. They thought that the words had the power to bring that essence into existence as material substance, simply by thinking about them or speaking their name. Hence, "In the beginning there was the *word...*", and God *said*, "Let there be ...", etc. The meaning of words used to be very important to people.

This idea of essence and substance has fascinated western philosophers and theologians for thousands of years, and was a particularly hot topic of debate in the middle ages (see John Duns Scotus, Ockham, Aquinas, etc.).

They were puzzled by the way that humans (for example) are clearly sufficiently similar to each other to be thought of as a valid class or type of being - and yet no two humans are actually identical. There is always uniqueness within the similarity. Similar does not mean identical.

This problem has not gone away. We still have to deal with the difference between the essence and the substance of the categories we use in everyday life, although thankfully it doesn't bother us as much as it seems to have bothered them. When we design computer databases, we create 'records' to record the details of the things we want to keep track of: customers, suppliers, products, students, teachers, etc. There are some essential properties that customers **must** have before they are allowed to be represented on the computer system, and there are some variable (substantial) properties (with values that can vary within limits) that they **may** or **may not** have.

The essential properties will be things like:

- a unique identifier (customer number, account number, or a unique combination of name, address and date of birth);
- a valid delivery address;
- a valid bank account;
- an acceptable credit rating;
- an allocated salesperson;
- a market segment classification.

A customer record is only allowed to exist on the computer system if **all** these essential bits of information are available.

The variable properties will be things like:

- valued customer discount rating;
- credit limit;
- history of purchases;
- history of contacts;
- known interests;
- known dislikes.

The acceptable values that might be recorded against each of these attributes can vary widely, or there may be nothing recorded at all.

The whole package of essential and variable properties is what defines a customer in this system. The values recorded against the variable (substantial) properties can change at any time, without seriously affecting the customer's identity, but if there is no longer a valid bank account, or a satisfactory credit rating, then this is considered a serious change of identity and that customer's continued existence as a member of the class Normal Customer would have to be reviewed. Of course, real customers have many more interesting properties than the few that get selected to represent them in computer systems.

The choice of the *fields* used to describe a customer may seem obvious, but it is not. A lot of thought goes into the design of database records. Well designed systems work well and badly designed ones fail. Although *customer* and *supplier* are fairly simple objects to define, plenty of mistakes have been made. If you want to think about something more challenging, try to define the essential and variable properties of beauty, justice, democracy, your ideal relationship, a song or a perfect chair.

Linguists and logicians have struggled with the inescapable fact than we cannot exhaustively define the thousands of categories we use in everyday life. What we are learning about neural networks cannot resolve for us whether or not a god creates archetypal essences and manifests material substances, but it can offer an explanation of why philosophers have always had so much trouble defining the categories we so effortlessly use every minute of the day.

Our neural networks are **pre-consciously** aware of a huge number of **similarities** between different rabbits; and **differences** between rabbits and dogs - but we are **not consciously** aware of **most** of these subtle discriminations. In order to talk about 'rabbitness', we have to reduce our vast pre-conscious understanding of 'rabbitness' down to the handful (mouthful) of conscious concepts that can be expressed in our common language. We know, pre-consciously, far more than our language can convey.

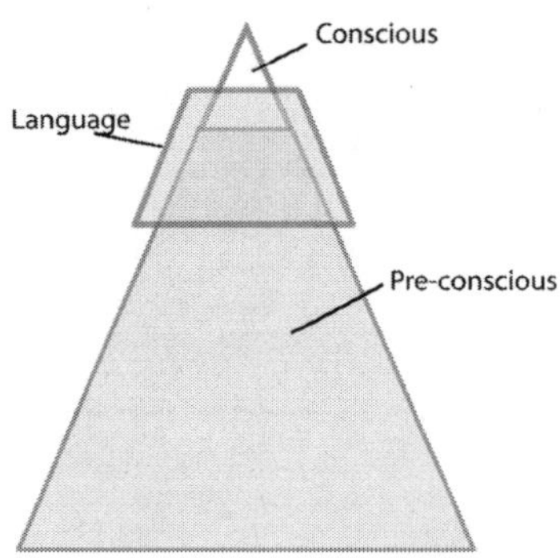

Figure 2.15 We know more than our language can convey.

Our difficulty in expressing essences can also stem from our laziness, or our ignorance of the full range of concepts that are available in our common language. A group of experts in the genetics of rabbit breeding could probably discuss their experience of rabbitness much more precisely then the rest of us.

So neural network research can offer us an explanation of why, for thousands of years, we have been intrigued by this essence / substance / relevant frame puzzle - why we were not able to use language and logic to exhaustively define the properties of the categories and relationships that we use everyday of our lives, or to explain how we arrive at our innate, *a priori* knowledge, and our intuitive gut feelings.

The essence side of the puzzle is the result of the amazingly subtle categorisation capability of our pre-conscious multi-million-year-old inherited neural networks. We are not aware of most of the complex web of subtle associations that work together to categorise our experience of reality, but we have great faith in the resultant conscious categories, even though we can't fully justify them. This gap (between what we **know** and what we can **justify**) needed explaining and the idea of mysterious essences in the mind of a remote creator god fitted the bill nicely.

The variable substance side of the puzzle arises because our neural networks are capable of creating stable classes of objects, despite the fact that those objects may, over time, display very different physical properties. An oak tree begins as an acorn and may be anything from one inch to 100 feet tall. What all the members of the class oak tree share in common, is the oak tree's cycle of possibility and probability. An acorn cannot possibly grow into an ash tree and it is very unlikely to grow to be 1000 feet tall.

Our Historical Prison and the Great Escape

So here we are, as free as a bird, actively constructing our own understanding of the world, enriching our rather limited real-time sensory awareness by adding to it all our accumulated experiences, knowledge and predictive hypotheses. But in another sense, we are trapped in our own private prison, with our perception of reality predetermined by our personal, cultural and evolutionary histories.

Can we escape from that prison? Yes, to some extent. Whilst the past does, in general, have a big influence on our future, we can decide to exercise some control, and change the way we perceive and react to the world. We can't completely wipe the slate clean, but we can deliberately move away from the external influences that frame our experiences and trigger habitual reactions. We can start to build new neural network associations, new interpretations, new understandings. We can exercise some deliberate control over the experiences and ideas we pass through our neural networks. Thanks to those top-down reverse-projection neurons, we can review our old experiences in the light of new conceptual frames, and thanks to the flexibility of our plastic memory systems, we can update our interpretations of old experiences, cascading those changes through our current models of reality.

The Moral

So here is a moral. Our brains are very absorbent, so we should take care what experiences we expose them to. We should bear in mind that as a result of the dualistic nature of our perceptual apparatus, we need quite a range of experiences before we can start making sensible judgements about the many optional fruits available on the tree of the knowledge of this and that. When we are ready, we can start to take some control over what stuff we want to keep in our brain, and what meanings and emotions we want to associate with that stuff.

It sounds simple. It is not. Sometimes we get dragged down by difficult circumstances, but at other times they stimulate us to rise up above them. Sometimes problems arise because of flaws in our internal perception and decision making, and sometimes they are caused by external events and forces over which we seem to have absolutely no influence.

All we can do is try to control what we think about them, what meanings we choose to associate with them, and how we react to them. Sometimes it simply isn't clear what to do, and then our default habitual interpretations and reactions kick in and run our behaviour.

Freewill and Destiny

These are ancient themes in literature. The great Greek tragedies, written in the 5th and 4th centuries BC, explored the never-ending issue of free will verses destiny. A great hero, who appears to be a master of his own life, suddenly falls from grace as a result of a flaw in his personality or through circumstances beyond his control. These external events are variously explained as punishment for his personal failings (or the failings of his parents or society), such as a failure to distinguish between right and wrong, or allowing personal desires to override civic duty, etc. Sometimes the events are not caused by his past actions, but by the jealousy or anger of the gods, engaged either in a conflict with humans or in a war between themselves. Either way, the hero cannot control the situation and in the end he dies in chaos and confusion, or there is a resolution brought about by good luck, or by the hero's adaptive response to the very appropriate nature of the lessons that he brought upon himself.

Despite the fact that we are supposed to be Children of the Enlightenment who don't believe in any unscientific, untestable, unprovable mumbo jumbo, and who base the management of all our public policies on hard facts and evidence, many people still feel, privately, that what happens to us in life is very closely related to our current state of development and awareness, and that our moral and mental states attract to us exactly the lessons we need in order to progress on our journey to some kind of theosis.

Perhaps the persistence of these mystical viewpoints can be explained at a neural network level. We now understand that our state of mind can have a powerful effect on what we pay attention to, which aspects of reality we experience, and therefore what we get involved with (or *attract*, in new age speak).

The ancient mystical religions told us to be aware that we make our own meanings and must inevitably take responsibility for them. That was remarkably perceptive of those ancient philosophers, as it turns out that there is a lot of truth in this idea. We really do make our own meaning, but our culture plays a big part in it as well. So it is not easy to break out of our historical and cultural perceptual prison, but it definitely is possible. The first thing we need is the key - the idea that it is a desirable thing to do.

Submit or Do Your Own Thing

Many cultures have advised their members not to try to create their own understanding, but to accept and submit to the perfect understanding already given to humanity - by prophets, political leaders, party manifestos, philosophical or economic ideologies, etc. In the West, most of us have adopted to some extent the ancient Eastern idea that the benefits of having some degree of free will are balanced against the responsibility for our own mental and moral development. This clashes rather with the idea that we should submit in all such matters to the will of God as prescribed in a book written hundreds or thousands of years ago. These two points of view seem so opposed that we must hope for the arrival of a new, higher, and very attractive cultural frame that can somehow accommodate and integrate both views.

The rest of this book rather assumes that you do want to achieve more personal control over your exploration and understanding of the fruits of the tree of knowledge of this and that.

Chapter 3

Evolutionary Thinking Levels

Please understand that the following ideas about the evolution of human thinking are definitely not true, certainly not with any sense of certainty, and are not proven or provable. It is just a story, or should I say a narrative, which offers a way of structuring our thoughts about thinking with a human brain. I hope you find it useful.

The main point here is that over the last 350 million years of brain development, evolution has exploited gradual improvements in neural hardware, and assembled a range of increasingly complex priority-juggling and thinking strategies. The aim at every stage of development was to keep us alive long enough to raise successful offspring.

Evolution doesn't usually throw away things that work. So any new developments have to work alongside the old and well-established mechanisms. This has resulted in a series of more or less integrated thinking packages, with each new development laid on top of the previous ones.

The oldest layers are very well tried and tested, and deal with the fundamentals of life, survival and reproduction. The newest layers deal with the latest frills and luxuries, but must also add something to the overall survival package, to justify their existence.

As a result, the modern human brain carries within it a repertoire of inherited strategies that have worked well for an unbroken chain of successful ancestors, in a very wide range of very challenging situations. Some of these abilities lie dormant and only kick-in in extreme situations, but many of them are still in everyday use, and play a huge role in the way we think.

The human brain is a special kind of mammalian brain. Mammalian brains have been evolving for 100 million years or so, but they didn't start from scratch. They seem to have evolved from reptile brains, and still have many features derived from that ancient period.

A very important phase in the development of human thinking happened about 350 million years ago when our very distant intellectual ancestors started to leave the **sea** and colonise **dry land.** This was a difficult **transition.** The evolutionary pressure of coping with the threats and opportunities of this hazardous new environment contributed an area of the current human brain called the **limbic system,** which has been performing its fundamental roles pretty much unchanged for about 200 million years.

Life in the sea had been relatively easy. Our marine predecessors were surrounded and supported by water at a nice steady temperature. There was usually an abundance of food. There were predators, but there was not very much that could be done to outwit them, apart from evolving tuned senses, quick reactions, camouflage and shoal/herd mentality. Consequently there was not much advantage to be gained from developing smarter, more intelligent, more independent perception and reaction capabilities. Living on automatic pilot and producing large numbers of offspring was a very satisfactory survival strategy for the genes.

But our discontented ancestors crawled out of the sea and onto dry land, which was too dry, too hot and too cold, primarily two dimensional, dominated by the force of gravity, and dangerous. It is much more complicated for an animal to live on dry land. We have to support our own body weight, we have to avoid falling into holes we can't get out of and we have to avoid things that might fall on our heads. We have to cope with extremes of temperature. In exchange for the benefits of becoming warm blooded, we have to pay attention to maintaining a steady body temperature in an environment that might reach temperatures of 50° C in the day and -40° C at night. In order to cope with intermittent food and water supplies, we had to develop the ability to remember where and when (space and time) the available resources could be found, and we have to get organised about going to find those resources. We also had to develop new reproduction and offspring rearing strategies.

Attention Management and Priority Juggling

So, on dry land, there are a lot more competing priorities to be juggled than there were in the sea. We had to develop new ways of managing our attention that would help us deal with those constantly changing priorities. We had to pay attention to finding food and water at regular intervals, recognising and avoiding numerous dangers, whilst spotting and pursuing resources and opportunities.

Our current limbic system design is the result of that transition. It **juggles** our priorities and **regulates** our body temperature, metabolism, hunger, thirst and weight. It is responsible for **recognising dangers** and **managing** a range of **complex whole-body reactions** to those dangers. This is the 200 million year old basis of our emotional system: packaged whole-body mobilisation in response to perceived external conditions. This ancient organ still plays a huge role in our perception of, and reactions to, the world.

Too Much Information

There is an enormous amount of information available to our senses. Much of it is probably irrelevant to our current number one priority. Not only is there no point wasting mental resources considering all that irrelevant information, but there is also a danger that we might be distracted by something attractive or interesting, and get diverted away from our current number one survival task.

Attention Control

So the brain has evolved amazing, **pre-conscious**, systems of **attention control**, which **focus** our attention onto the most relevant parts of the vast stream of information that the senses are receiving.

Having once evolved these priority-driven mechanisms of attention control and reaction management, it was a relatively simple matter for evolution to start adding **more subtle and luxurious** priorities into the mix, such as **pleasures, wants, desires,** and longer term **goals and plans.**

Making Sense

Initially, priority-juggling was managed on a real-time stimulus/response basis. But on dry land, there was a big advantage to be gained from the development of a conceptual sort of intelligence that can **make sense** of its spatial environment, by trapping its **fleeting experiences** and building them into **durable mental maps and models** of the world, which can then be integrated into the priority-juggling system - and thus improve survivability.

Social Meaning

Being able to function as a group has improved our ability to survive in difficult circumstances, and has been a very important driver in human evolution. But in order to take advantage of our group's shared knowledge, we had to evolve the ability to adjust or override our own experience-based perception and models of reality, in order to fit in with, take advantage of, the group's agreed cumulative understanding.

Multiple Models

So we have **personal models**, embedded in our neural networks as a result of our personal sensory experience of the world, and we have **external models** communicated to us through our language and culture. Most of the cultural models are absorbed pre-consciously, but some (for example, maths or quantum physics) are processed more consciously. As a result, we have many models to choose from, many ways to make sense of, and organise, our perceptions and reactions. But this **choice** has to be managed.

Competing Packages

Evolutionary progress is usually achieved by building more complex and effective systems out of tried and tested sub-units.

The priority-driven, attention-controlling, whole-body-reaction-managing, experience-trapping and model-making system was working well, but it did not have much capacity for the consideration of **optional strategies.** So - make more copies of it. Have **competing packages**, each with a different style of reaction, a different model of the world, access to slightly different mental and physical resources. That way we get an opportunity to choose from a **range of different options** for understanding and reacting to a range of different circumstances.

For example, one reaction package might enable us to share food with close family and group members in a friendly way, while another leads us on occasions to steal resources from non-group people in a threatening way. We can be gentle and patient in pursuing goals with a child, cooperative with some adults, and competitive with others. One package might focus on cooperating with other people to solve a problem, whilst another might focus on solving it alone.

Managing the Options

So we needed a system for managing these options, deciding which package to use in each situation.

Observe yourself for an hour or two, and you will find that our personality is made up of many different perceptual and behavioural packages.

Each package is typically associated with quite a strong sense of self-awareness (I, me, my), but there is usually very little sense of conscious reflexive awareness, or conscious control, whilst each of these packages is temporarily in control of our brain and body resources.

Self-Awareness

A higher mechanism evolved, for choosing between and managing (in a very loose sense) these lower-level transient sub-personality packages. This new self-management mechanism slowly developed into our current sense of self-awareness, a sense of our own enduring personality.

But this fledgling self-awareness highlighted the variability of our perceptions and reactions. This tension, between our internal sense of a permanent self-identity, and the contradictory everyday evidence of a procession of different powerful, but temporary, sub-personalities, has been the focus of much observation and comment for thousands of years. The 'know yourself' motto of ancient Greece originates in this problem of maintaining a durable self-identity in the face of these many different temporary sub-personalities.

Later, as the brain's **self-awareness** became more **conscious**, that consciousness was harnessed and put to work in the research and development section of the priority-juggling department. We began to develop some limited, occasional, **conscious awareness** of our **priorities**, **needs**, **goals**, etc., and a little bit of **conscious control** over our **perceptions** and **reactions** (what the Greeks called **will power).**

The introduction of some conscious deliberate control over our thinking meant that we were able to begin to formulate and agree **communal plans, goals, ideas, and sets of rules** to guide our conscious thinking, and our reactions to particular situations. We became **thinkers** (occasionally) - able to consciously direct our thinking in accordance with some external social rules and guidelines.

This enabled religion, science and technology, reading and writing systems, philosophy and game playing (chess for example), laws, military discipline, strategies, etc.

But this is a very new additional layer, loosely grafted onto a 200-million-year-old system which had been running the show very effectively. So it is not surprising that the old, automatic, habitual, pre-conscious, and very fast systems, often override the new, conscious, rational, and very slow systems, particularly in an emergency.

For example, most of the injuries associated with hot air ballooning happen to the people who handle the mooring ropes shortly before take off. Sometimes a balloon gets caught by a gust of wind and rises up into the air. The automatic reaction of the rope handlers is to grasp tightly onto the rope with the tragic consequence that they get carried up into the air as well, and eventually fall to the ground. The slower conscious rational reaction, to let go of the rope, sacrifice the balloon but save your own life, can be just a bit too slow for this context.

Back to Basics - the Frame Problem

How does the brain decide which is the important information and the appropriate reaction in any particular context? The answer seems to be that our framing ability is the result of millions of years of genetic evolution, which has provided us with a neural network platform which makes available (almost all of) the resources (skills and sensitivities) that were used by our unbroken line of successful ancestors. We inherit the capability to detect and model the same critical features of our earth surface environment that enabled our ancestors to survive similar situations and circumstances. This basic platform is then enhanced by our own unique personal life history experiences, which shape and tune our current neural network connections. So most of our crucial "framing" decisions, what to pay attention to and what to ignore, are happening deep in the ancient, pre-conscious, pre-rational, parts of the brain.

These amazing and yet deceptively simple, everyday framing tasks, seem to have escaped the attention of our academics and philosophers. They had trained themselves for more than 2000 years with the ideas of logic and reasoning, based on consciously defined categories. Until the recent discovery of the extraordinary properties of pre-conscious neural networks, we could not begin to imagine that the process of deciding what information is, and is not relevant, could possibly be achieved without some conscious, logical, reasoned, criteria-based categorisation and conditional filtering.

Now we are beginning to realise that it is well within the ability of neural network evolution to work out ways to pre-consciously direct and focus our attention on resources and opportunities that might help us satisfy our current priority needs.

Intelligences

At the same time as evolving this range of strategies for priority-juggling, attention control, and managing alternative conceptual maps and models of what is out there, the brain was also evolving different 'intelligences' - different sensitivities and capabilities that might be brought to bear on a particular type of problem or situation. Categorising these abilities and identifying the sequence of their development is problematic, but here is a brief list.

Spatial intelligence - the ability to maintain a vast map of the environment, attaching meanings to places and to multiple routes between those places. What resources are available where? What are the properties of the routes? Are they steep, level, fast but dangerous, slow but good if you have a heavy load to carry, snowy and icy in winter, etc?

Social intelligence - all those interpersonal abilities such as: communication (not yet language necessarily), empathy, co-operation, submission to and exercise of group authority, a sense of goals and tactics in oneself and others, group politics, deceit, disguising our real motivation - that support successful group living in a harsh environment. Also perhaps the intra-personal ability to maintain a stable sense of self whilst playing so many different social roles.

Predictive and planning skills - we have very early evidence that our ancestors planned and organised distributed caches of tools and tool-making materials, so that they didn't have to carry their heavy tools with them on long trips to remote hunting grounds.

Technical intelligence - for interacting with tools and materials. A developing awareness of the properties of materials, and of ways to manipulate and combine them, using shape, heat, glue, knotting, weaving, sewing, colour, etc., in pursuit of a desired functionality.

Natural history - the versatile framing and categorising intelligence that enabled us to understand and predict the life cycles of plants and animals, and thus made it possible for our ancestors to adapt so quickly to so many new ecological environments as they migrated around the world.

Language and culture - a new and non-genetic means of transmitting and accumulating ideas, concepts, models, problem-solving skills and strategies. The evolution of human cultures has been an intricate process. Some combinations of cultural features brought durable benefits that worked well in a particular terrain, others did not. This has resulted in a diversity of intricately interwoven cultural elements.

It affects us deeply but its subtle mechanisms are beyond our ability to fully understand and predict.

Metaphor and meaning transfer abilities - enabling the transfer of fundamental units of meaning from one life experience domain to another.

Emotional intelligence – the ability to consciously observe, reflect on, and to some extent influence mental and emotional states in ourselves and in others.

External rules intelligence – the ability to consciously decide to set up, and then follow an external set of rules for addressing particular types of problems. We build approved strategies and frameworks, policies and instruction manuals, to guide our attention, our search, our conceptualisation, our evaluation, our decisions and our choice of behaviours. This intelligence has a strong social group element, giving rise to rituals and traditions in many aspects of life. It has enabled the very important transition from genetic, tribal, clan-based, social and cultural structures to much wider and more inclusive systems of social organisation based on a disciplined acceptance of externally, consciously, intellectually defined rules. This has brought numerous benefits and significant disasters.

For example, we moved away from old beliefs in the patronage of tribal gods and malevolent demons, and replaced them with belief in monarchy, democracy, science, commerce, freedom, socialism, communism, capitalism, etc. Instead of continual intertribal skirmishing over resources, we are able to organise ourselves into much larger multi-ethnic inter-regional ideological units: nations, empires, alliances and trading blocks - enabling occasional but gigantic wars over resources. Instead of intertribal slavery we exploit voluntary economic migrants on a global scale.

So here we are, juggling our priorities on a raft of ancient, tried and tested, automatic and habitual reactions, overlaid with the more recently evolved ability to simultaneously hold a number of different personal and social models of the world, and equipped with a range of different skills and intelligences. This is thinking.

Who is in Control of Your Brain?

Here is a diagram which may help you to reflect on the role these evolutionary levels can play in human thinking.

It shows our senses working away, continuously collecting and presenting information to our pre-conscious neural networks, but much of it is effectively ignored. The focus of our attention is being controlled by the different characters (representing the different evolutionary thinking levels).

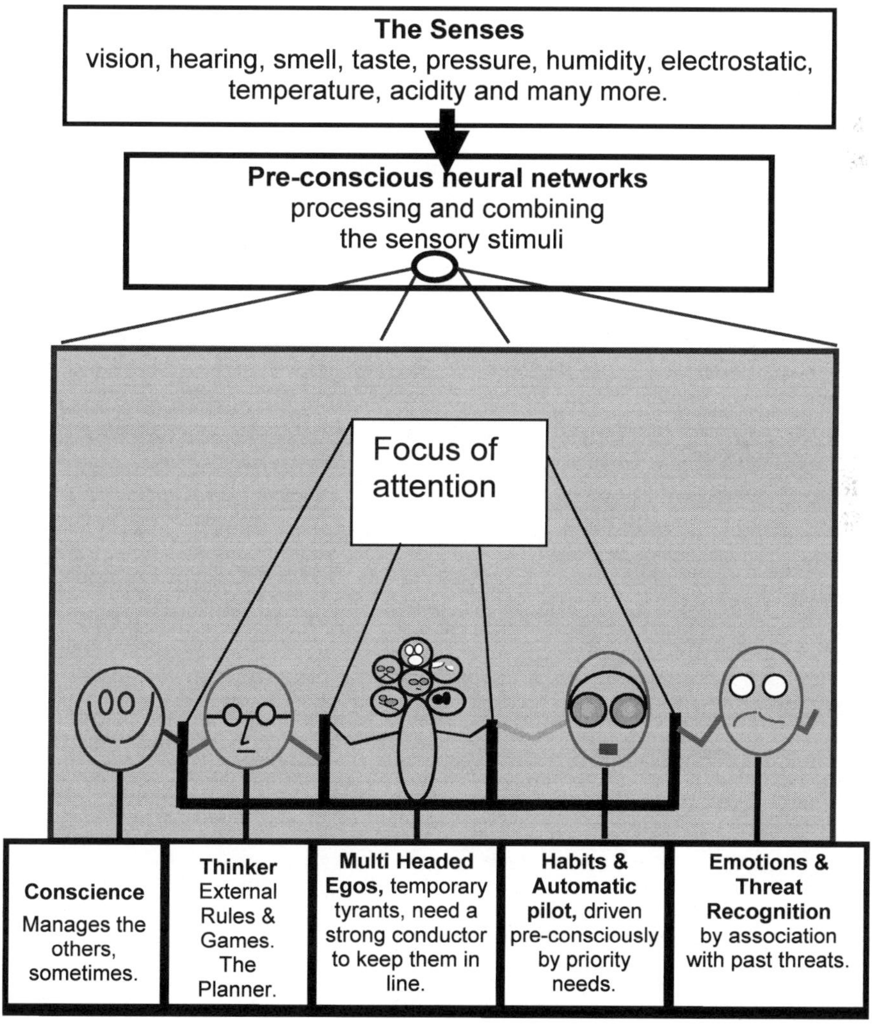

Threats and Emotions

This character started out as a hair-trigger durable-memory threat-recognition and whole-body response mechanism. The aim was to focus all our relevant resources on dealing with perceived physical threats. It moves us quickly to focused action and has been very successful. The system is ancient, very fast, and entirely pre-conscious. We can, some time later, consciously reflect on what we found ourselves thinking, feeling and doing. With maturity, we may learn to, delay, guide, re-direct, possibly even reinterpret, reconceptualise and override the impulses, but only master thinkers can control the initiation of these impulses.

The Autopilot

This amazing system has been taking care of our bodies for millions of years. It regulates thirst, temperature control, electrolyte levels, heart rate, breathing, blood pressure, nutrition, response to injury, healing, balancing rest, work and play, etc. The list is enormous and the various automatic systems manage to maintain our bodies in a huge variety of challenging environments and situations. Although for many in the 'developed' world, these ancient systems do seem to be struggling to regulate our body weight in the face of an explosion of desire-manipulation advertising and the easy availability of high-energy foods.

The autopilot's package of genetic neurochemical pleasures plays a huge role in defining our humanity. We find pleasure in: food, friends and family, sex, nature, activity, novelty, travel and exploration, learning, problem solving, making things, building, competition, the attention of others, approval, self-expression, discipline and self-control, leisure, comfort, luxury, rituals, spiritual transcendence, etc.

It is also a great opportunist. If I am only loosely engaged on some non-essential task, and it catches sight of something that reminds it of a more interesting / pleasurable activity, one of the ongoing projects that litter my work room perhaps, then it has the power to hijack my resources and divert **me** down some path of **its** choosing. I find it is best to keep those other projects out of sight if I want to focus on one task for a sustained period.

It is also very talented. Complex learned motor skills such as riding a bicycle, driving a car, playing sports or musical instruments, can be managed very effectively by the auto pilot. From my own experience as a musician, and motor cycle racer, I know that my best performances were always the ones where I kept my self-aware conscious mind out of the way, and handed over control to my autopilot, leaving it free to do its amazing work. This is part of the idea behind 'Zen in the Art of Archery', a recommended read, from the point of view of training the autopilot and then letting it do its thing. However, I am always alarmed when I find that I have been driving on a motorway in autopilot mode. But I am still alive, so I must have been paying attention, I just wasn't consciously aware of it.

The autopilot's systems evolved before we had any conscious awareness and therefore they do not require any conscious input. But its attention-control mechanisms have been integrated into our more recent and more conscious pursuit of non-essential goals and desires. If you are thinking about buying (or campaigning against) a particular model or colour of car, your autopilot will start to notice them everywhere you go. They were there before, but now your autopilot is paying special attention to them.

Goal Setting

There is a popular new age style idea (actually it was very old age as well) that God, and or the universe, will send us the resources we need if we form precise integrated focused goals. Most of us have experienced situations which we could easily take to be evidence of this principle in action, and many people now consciously use it in everyday problem solving, and claim that it works. I recently met a fascinating man who goes to very difficult parts of the world, advising rural communities on the appropriate uses of modern agricultural equipment. His work sometimes gets him into difficult situations, in remote and hostile places, where he is caught between powerful economic, political and cultural forces. He told me that when things get tough, he always consciously asks – 'What is the best thing that could possibly happen now?' and that this has always been followed by extraordinarily good fortune, new opportunities and new insights into how to handle the situation. Try it.

Now it could be that God or the universe will always meet our highest (or deepest) clearest, consciously expressed needs (your wish is my command), or it could be that clear deliberate conscious goal-setting tells our autopilot to start to pay attention to resources that were there all along, but which we were not aware of. Either way - try it for yourselves. If it works, use it.

Autopilot does a lot of things **habitually**. If they work, it uses them again. It handles most of our daily routine, and enjoys copying and imitating the actions and values of those around us (a major component of cultural, social, cohesion). This is what makes most young humans so very absorbent of peer-group norms, and many adults so inclined to fit in with whatever their significant group requires of them.

It also gets pleasure from playing, from explorative trial and error, and gets a special dose of pleasure when these games produce 'the right results' = a win. But here is that frame problem again. How do we know to get a neurochemical buzz about one particular outcome (a win) and not from all other outcomes? In a technical or scientific experimental context, all results should really be regarded as equally interesting and useful; whether they suggest your idea was right, wrong or inconclusive, it is still useful information. Yet some results will, in human reality, trigger euphoric pleasure and others will trigger frustration, annoyance or disappointment. We intuitively know what constitutes winning, victory, success, etc. It's just another aspect of our inherited system of pleasures and values.

My guess is that between them, autopilot, habit and copycat, are in control of our brains resources for at least 75% of a typical waking day.

The Multi-Headed Egos

Having got the idea of packaging together a focused and coordinated selection of mental and physical resources, evolution decided to repeat and adjust the idea. It developed a range of different specialised reaction packages, to group and focus resources suitable for a range of different problems: technical, commercial, social, parental, gang membership, etc. That way we can have access to a range of different context-sensitive packages of attention control, experiential models, physical resources and behaviours. Each package can be king of all resources, whilst it is in control. A temporary ego tyrant.

Observe yourself, and you will discover that your personality is made up of many of these temporary brain management rulers - many temporary sub-personalities.

In one situation I am selfish and mean, in another I am generous to a fault (particularly if I want something in return). If my car breaks down I go into technical fix-it mode and get great results. If my society/culture breaks down I become an indignant frustrated ineffectual irritant, writing letters to newspapers who don't print them.

Each of these temporary personality packages thinks that 'it' is 'me' 'for all eternity' - whilst it is in control, and it is quite unaware that it shares me with many other temporary egos that also get control of my resources from time to time.

It can appear as if these temporary little egos are engaged in a struggle for supremacy, each of them wanting exclusive control of my:

- attention;
- values and beliefs;
- models, myths, metaphors and understanding;
- application of basic intelligences, resources and skills;
- emotions and motivation (move to, move away from);
- thoughts, actions, words (internal and external dialogue), and behaviours.

Historically, many people have believed that these rapidly changing states of mind were the work of the gods, the devil, or possession by spirits. Now that we are starting to understand the extraordinary properties of neural networks we can see that these different ego packages are not so sinister or mysterious after all. They are just packages of associated reactions, pre-consciously selected and triggered in response to our brain's perception of events. These little egos are not consciously fighting for supremacy, or obeying the will of gods or demons. Fortunately, you don't need to be a trained psychologist, or a theologian, to observe this procession of temporary little egos - so you can form your own opinion.

The ancient Greek motto, 'Know Yourself', should more accurately have been, 'Know Yourselves'. To know ourselves, we must get into the habit of observing the procession of mini-personality packages that take control of our everyday interactions with the world. What are their characteristics? What features of the world do they pay particular (selective) attention to? What meanings and interpretations, values and beliefs, do these egos use to justify themselves? What models of the world, what metaphors and myths, what heroes, role models and life narratives do they adopt? What language and vocabulary do they use, internally and externally, to express themselves? What behavioural choices do they prefer, and what events trigger their rise to power?

As you start to observe them, you may, initially, be a little overwhelmed by their less than perfect morality or intelligence. But remember - 'they' are not 'you'. They are small temporary parts of you. The very fact that 'you' are observing 'them', and that they seem to be incapable of observing you, or the others, is all the proof you need that 'they' are not 'your' highest sense of self - just one of many packages of perception and reaction.

They are a very useful mechanism that evolution came up with to take advantage of the developing connectivity of your neural networks - but they are not your permanent sense of self.

Don't be surprised if these temporary egos come rushing to their own defence, to justify their existence. They will probably argue that their behaviour was an absolutely essential reaction to that insult, obstruction, danger, opportunity, etc. That's OK. They wouldn't be much use to you if they didn't have this ability to hijack your brain's resources with that self-confident sense of certainty.

'Listen to your inner voice,' say the new-age gurus. But which inner voice? There are hundreds of different ones. Listen to the highest one of course, the only one that is aware of the existence of all the others.

The Possibility of Change

Once you become familiar with the difference between your permanent personality, and the parade of temporary, self-confident, (but not very self-aware) sub-personalities, you will begin to realise that the goal of significant, self-managed, personal change and development, is a very real possibility. For there is nothing fixed about these temporary personalities. They come and go all the time. At first you may be surprised by the number and range of personal 'defects' you can now allow yourself to acknowledge, but it can also be a great relief to realise that these are not flaws in your true permanent personality. They cannot be, for if they were, you would not be able to recognise them as defects in the first place.

Mind and Body

At the level of the multi-headed egos, the mind and the body can seem to be inseparably linked. Especially in those situations that involve physical sensation, desire and emotion. '**I** was so hungry', 'Of course **I** was annoyed!' 'Obviously **I** need that new dress, and that new car!' Harvest time for the advertisers.

But we can also access a sense of self that is above and independent of all these states of mind, a sense of self that is separate from the body, which can sit in amiable amused judgement over this procession of temporary egos, deciding to promote some of them, because they are more representative of who we really are, and demoting others, because they no longer fit well with our accumulating experience of our real self. We can consciously decide to reshape the existing ones and create new packages of responses.

But it is not easy. All these temporary sub-personalities are in the habit of saying 'I', and masquerading as me, when actually they are not the source of my sense of 'I'. They are totally egocentric and cannot see the bigger picture.

Each sub-personality has its own frame, models and explanations, emotions and motivations, attention control, and intelligence application strategy. Some of them engage in carefully considered categorisation, while others operate huge overgeneralisations or get lost in an obsessive attention to detail. Each has its own characteristic internal dialogue, which can be a good way to get a handle on them, a way to recognise them. I once met a doctor, who had been plagued by the internal dialogue of one of these temporary egos, which screamed 'It's a disaster, it's a disaster,' every time he had a tricky clinical procedure to perform. This was clearly less than ideal, and didn't leave a lot of space in his head for all those years of training and experience to do their work. Happily, 'he' was able to **create** a **new** response, which reacted much more constructively when it, very usefully, sensed that a serious situation was approaching. (The old 'demon' soon faded away because of a lack of attention.)

Some systems of thought have encouraged the view that these petty egos are bad in some absolute sense, and consequently embark on a futile attempt to suppress them - an activity which (in the world of neural networks) strengthens the neural associations and very often makes the problem worse. It is much more effective to **discriminate**, and **observe** that some of them can be your best friends, when applied appropriately, initiating many fascinating and timely life adventures, whilst others can be your worst enemy, particularly in certain situations, and **are no longer required**.

It is possible to manage your multi-headed egos, through observation and acceptance, combined with the conscious design and promotion of new favourites. Death by disinterest (another neural network law) is the best way to get rid of the redundant ones. Focussing on them only makes them stronger. That is why 'giving up' smoking (or any other addiction) never works, but deciding to make healthy choices does. For the Ancient Greeks, this was the way to a good life - to achieve conscious mastery over the procession of temporary egos, rather than unconscious slavery to them.

With the passage of time and the accumulation of experience, the multi-headed egos naturally mature a little. The overall personality package evolves as its models about the world evolve. It learns that things are not quite as simple, and that consequences are not always as predictable, as it had once expected.

Still later, maybe, it learns that things are indeed quite simple and predictable in the bigger picture of the recurring cycles of possibility and probability.

Shakespeare wrote of the seven ages of man in "As You Like It".

All the world's a stage,
And all the men and women merely players:
They have their exits and their entrances;
And one man in his time plays many parts,
His acts being seven ages. At first the infant,
Mewling and puking in the nurse's arms.
And then the whining school-boy, with his satchel
And shining morning face, creeping like snail
Unwillingly to school. And then the lover,
Sighing like furnace, with a woeful ballad
Made to his mistress' eyebrow. Then a soldier,
Full of strange oaths and bearded like the bard,

Jealous in honour, sudden and quick in quarrel,
Seeking the bubble reputation
Even in the cannon's mouth. And then the justice,
In fair round belly with good capon lined,
With eyes severe and beard of formal cut,
Full of wise saws and modern instances;
And so he plays his part. The sixth age shifts
Into the lean and slipper'd pantaloon,
With spectacles on nose and pouch on side,
His youthful hose, well saved, a world too wide
For his shrunk shank; and his big manly voice,
Turning again toward childish treble, pipes
And whistles in his sound. Last scene of all,
That ends this strange eventful history,
Is second childishness and mere oblivion,
Sans teeth, sans eyes, sans taste, sans everything.

There has recently been a fashion in the social sciences, to deny that there is any such thing as human nature, which seems to me to be a shameful abuse of their academic privileges. But this cultural omission has been more than compensated for by the attention of the marketing profession, which has studied in depth, in theory, and in practice, how to trigger, stimulate and cajole these pre-conscious temporary egos into buying their products. We need a balance here.

The Conscious Thinker

The planner, the predictor, the game player - the deliberate follower of externally constructed rules and approved models, held and maintained as a shared cultural intelligence.

Ever since the ancient Mesopotamian priest astronomers, serious quantifiable prediction has been big business. When someone made a creative leap that produced good results, those skills and techniques were formalised and passed on, within the group. Some spin-offs might have been made publicly available, but usually these developments would have been securely protected as trade secrets within the court or temple.

This was a major development. Here we have humans inventing, formalising and passing on professional rules and methods for observing and predicting particular classes of events. These rules tell us what to pay attention to, how to evaluate what we see, the kind of models to use to make sense of those observations, the kind of explanations to use between those who are in the know, and the explanations to use to communicate with the uninitiated. The rules will be passed on to others in the profession, who will apply them, protect them, pass them on, and occasionally possibly add to them in some way.

This intelligence is no longer internal. Evolution has enabled us to step beyond the immediate control of the autopilot, triggering our behaviour in response to perceived events and circumstances, and the tyranny of the multi-headed egos. We became able to deliberately, consciously and socially, agree on idealised plans which encapsulate the cultural group's accumulated experiences of the best way to react to particular situations. Everyday we submit to external plans that tell us what to pay attention to, what things mean, what models to adopt, how to interpret events, and how to behave.

This development has obvious advantages, but it requires that we leave behind the comfort, the immediacy and certainty of real-time reactions, and move into a rather more confusing mental world where we have no choice but to base our current decisions and actions on assumptions, models, goals, and predictions which will almost certainly turn out to be seriously flawed, before very long.

There is a danger that this new awareness of the uncertainty of our relationship with the universe could be very destabilising for individuals and for social groups. Perhaps this is why we evolved our rather irrational capacity for believing very strongly in our current view of the world.

There is a psychological phenomenon, identified in the 1960s, called 'cognitive dissonance,' which recognises that people initially resist information that suggests that their current models may be wrong. Not until there is overwhelming evidence, does the brain suddenly flip to a new understanding. This rather lumpy response to new information has great benefits in that it provides a more stable platform from which to deal with the world than would be the case if we continually rewrote all our plans to suit every little piece of noisy incomplete or inconsistent information that comes our way.

Social and cultural forces have a powerful influence on this character's view of the world. Depending on the context, this external intelligence may act as a gentle guiding framework, or as a set of rigid rules requiring strict disciplined adherence. We can, and do, pre-consciously adapt our views, in order to conform with significant socially validated views, values, assumptions, etc.

So, once this style of thinking had evolved, socially and culturally transmitted thinking rules became a very significant evolutionary force, affecting everything from technology to morality. Each cultural group developed its own elaborate set of rules, evolved and adapted to its particular historical environmental circumstances. When circumstances change, or cultures collide, the adaptability/rigidity of those rules can have a significant effect on the outcomes for the group members.

This character is so prevalent in modern life that it can be hard to spot its influence. The craftsman, the economist, the priest, the politician, the street mugger and the graffiti artist are all following, and developing, the collective external intelligence of their chosen professional group. This ability to build up shared external intelligences enabled the great religious architecture of medieval and renaissance Europe[5], the technology of global trade, and the development of shared tools such as language, maths, and computers. It underpins every political, economic and religious ideology of human history - for better or for worse.

The **planner** aspect of this character is good at holding on to long-term desires/goals/targets, aims and objectives – despite the constant fluctuations in our short-term priorities. It can take advantage of external long-term memory tools to do this. It has used writing on wax, stone, paper, magnetic tape, optical discs and silicon chips. We record plans, designs, maps, trade accounts, orders, instructions, contracts, vision statements, rules and laws.

Open any public sector or private sector policy document and you will find there, a super-elevated **thinker's** language of visions, mission statements, goals, aims, objectives, priorities, values, principles, strategies, action plans, tasks, targets, monitoring and reviews. Sometimes, the language is so elevated it barely touches the ground, and you may be left wondering precisely which aspect of the real world it is that they are managing.

This character is a great game player. It can accept, and play within, the limitations of any number of different games. When we play chess,

---

[5] Of course Eastern cultures have many similar achievements.

we accept the shape and layout of the board, we accept the definition of the different pieces, and the rules that specify the way they can move and interact with each other. We accept that the idea is to win, and how that is defined. Then we settle down to play, to wind the handle, and to explore the millions of different games that can be played within each set of limitations.

It is easy to see the similarities and differences between chess, golf or tennis. But the same kind of game-play thinking is going on when we accept the rules and limitations of capitalism or communism, democracy, religion, science, finance, technology, maths, art, design, manufacturing, politics, journalism, etc.

This character can flit effortlessly from game to game, barely aware that it is moving from one arbitrary universe to another as it crosses the street from the day-job office block to the creative writing evening class.

The **thinker** can consciously decide to get into role, and adopt a particular frame of mind, to engage a particular package of mental maps, models, attitudes, taboos, values and resources. We are fairly familiar with this idea in relation to activities such as science, technology, art, religion, politics, or business, but we are only just beginning to realise that we could use this ability to consciously select more appropriate maps, models and values in our personal life as well.

We could use it to change our default interpretations of external reality, to design new ways of making sense of the world. Our personalities, our understanding, our expectations and our perceived limitations do not have to be as fixed and rigid as we habitually assume. But the **thinker** is a fairly passive character and is usually content to accept and play the games on offer. It is not often to be found designing its own games and states of mind. Perhaps this is because of the enormous perceptual momentum (and associated benefits) created by a large number of people who are in the habit of playing a particular game in a particular way.

Games

Our culture has a great many games on offer. Think for a moment about the different external rules in operation in each of these different activities: sport, art, business, education, political ideology, the media, old religion, established religion, new spirituality, medicine, alternative therapies, social worker, detective, civil servant, judge, anthropologist, explorer, artist, engineer, architect, film director, etc.

Each of these games has its own set of rules that tell us what to pay attention to, what ideas and concepts to apply, which ones cannot be applied, what types of conclusions and predictions are acceptable, what language can be used to discuss them, and much more.

Old-style thinking about thinking tends to focus on just a few isolated aspects, such as logical forms of argument, evaluating evidence, classes of problem, framing, induction, deduction and analysis, but **thinker** enjoys a much richer life than that. It gets great pleasure from being able to really understand, and immerse itself in the rules of many different games. It enjoys building up a pool of experience of the complex dynamics that can emerge from the interaction of these simple sets of rules. It enjoys:

Modelling Systems - identifying the properties of objects and their relationships of cause and effect.

Modelling Change - recognising and quantifying patterns in the emergent behaviour of these dynamic systems. Identifying trends, probabilities, possibilities, limits, frameworks, ratios, laws, filters, attractors, etc.

Prioritising Goals, Strategies and Tactics - creating, juggling, maintaining, refining, and eventually discarding goals and strategies. Guessing, and testing the other players' goals and strategies.

Flexible Framing - constantly reviewing what is important in the current situation and what is not.

Generating Options - creative searching, collecting information, considering multiple perspectives, testing alternatives, evaluating the consequences of multiple options.

Negative Searching - selecting, rejecting, excluding, refining, defining, simplifying, fault finding, awareness of risks and obstructions, checking for omissions, checking for integrity.

Evaluating - evidence, goals, models, options, behaviour, consequences, effort, risk.

Planning - strategies, tactics, action plans, complex sequencing, reviewing.

Making Decisions - committing (for now) to a stable course of action, playing down contradictory indications if necessary.

Review - checking assumptions, re-evaluation of goals, models, opponent's actions and strategies, admitting to and analysing error, retreating, reverting, retracing, redoing - and learning from events.

Thinker gets great **pleasure** from using all of the tools in its problem-solving toolbox. Thinking is one of the best kinds of neurochemical fun the brain knows.

We all have these skills, but we don't always use them as well as we might. We can definitely learn to use them more effectively, and more frequently, instead of relying on automatic pilot and the multi-headed egos.

Great as **thinker's** abilities are, there are dangers, traps and flaws that we frequently fall into. For example, it is very difficult for us to **avoid** being influenced by socio-cultural rules, models and prescriptions which limit our observations and perceptions, and restrict our search for ideas and information.

These social forces can also distort our perceptions of the goals, intentions and methods of other social groups. This can distort our behaviour towards them, and thus lead them to form a distorted view of our intentions and strategies. And so it goes.

This social group dimension affects us through two mechanisms: the absorbency of our primitive autopilot habitual copycat, and our more evolved ability to submit to external social rules. Both of these mechanisms can be very useful, but they can also be very dangerous. They can hijack our mental resources, separating us from 'reality', and leading us blindly into abandoning our own personal judgement and submitting to the will of the group.

The **thinker's** skills are transferable and versatile. It has the capacity for a **more creative** and **expansive** kind of thinking: ignoring traditional constraints, experimenting with new, wider, grander, less egocentric perspectives, adjusting the framing, generating new options, challenging assumptions, brainstorming without constraint, and without the need for rational/social justification. Under normal circumstances, this kind of thinking is usually frowned upon, but in significant crises it may become more acceptable. If you work in the product design world, these thinking skills will be more welcome (as long as you don't interfere with an established brand's image).

Design thinking focuses on repeatedly refining the desirable features of an idea. Consciously identifying its attractive qualities, and refining them again and again 'to make it more like itself'. My graphics design teacher told us to go round that loop (analyse / describe / refine) at least six times - to 'give an idea's essence a chance to emerge'. It's a very Platonic idea, trying to uncover the essential properties of a pre-existing archetypal form. It's great fun and very effective.

So **thinker** has an impressive array of tools. The problem is to orchestrate them efficiently, particularly in a social group setting.

The Conscious Conscience

King Richard the Third
Act 5
Scene 3

On the eve of the Battle of Bosworth field, at which he will die, Richard is troubled by a dream involving the ghosts of everyone he has wronged during his rise to power.

On waking, his consciousness flits from level to level as it struggles to make a unity of all these opposing vectors within himself. A multi-headed ego dismisses his conscience as a coward, yet it can't compete with the accuracy of his conscience's observations. Another ego seeks to capitalise on the conscience's concerns about these elements within his personality. He loves himself, and in the same breath, hates certain internal elements, recognising his own pride as delusional flattery. His conscience is critical of the historical deeds carried out under the influence of his multi-headed egos, which rush in to justify their actions.

> "My conscience has a thousand several tongues, and every tongue brings in a several tale. And every tale condemns me for a villain.
> Perjury, perjury, in the highest degree;

> Murder, stern murder, in the direst degree, throng to the bar crying 'guilty! guilty!'
> I shall despair. There is no creature loves me; and if I die no soul will pity me, since I myself, find in myself, no pity for myself."

He had behaved pretty badly, but this expression of conscience marks the low end of the conscience continuum. It is self-aware, it is taking an overview, but it is all judgement, guilt, and fear of the possible consequences after death. Very much in the predominantly western, Judgement Day mould.

At the top end of the continuum we can experience a more elevated expression of conscience which looks down on the actions and intentions of the lower-level egos, from a kinder, more tolerant, more merciful, more joyous and amused perspective. As a grandparent might look upon a grandchild playing in a sand pit, struggling to mould the sand into shapes which sand cannot maintain. Eventually the child learns the limitations of the medium, and the consequences of ignoring them. The high-level conscience is always pure, uncorrupted, untainted by the deeds of the lower egos, no matter how bad. King Richard didn't get quite that high on that occasion.

The next day, Richard is back in his gang leader role, ridiculing the interventions of his conscience, as he prepares his supporters for battle.

> "Go gentlemen, every man unto his charge. Let not our babbling dreams affright our souls; Conscience is but a word that cowards use, devised at first to keep the strong in awe. Our strong arms be our conscience, swords our law."

The Role of the Conscience

The high level conscience is a very laid-back managing director. It has the option and the authority to observe, manage and orchestrate the activity of the temporary egos and the thinker. But usually it doesn't. The temporary egos are totally self-orientated, quite unaware of the existence, or the value, of the other petty egos. The conscience is the only character that can appreciate the strengths and weaknesses of all the other's roles, their intentions, their methods and the resources they have to offer.

The conscience realises that, deep down, all our different temporary egos have our best interests at heart, even though their special styles and methods can sometimes be inappropriate and counterproductive. The conscience is in a position to negotiate with the egos, to organise alliances, resolve conflicts between their different styles, and orchestrate a pleasing balanced stimulating life symphony.

The mistake we often make, is to confuse our personality (that variable collection of temporary egos), with our real self, the conscience.

At its best, the conscience is selfless, universal, forgiving. It is not interested in force, revenge, aggression, violence. It values internal growth (arrived at through personal experience, self-observation and right thinking) over a morality based on conformity to external rules and regulations.

But as Aristotle observed, we need practice in order to develop and implement our capacity to make these observations and judgements, and to exercise control over the temporary egos.

Here is a simple exercise. Imagine a cartoon-style high diver. Imagine climbing up that ladder, higher than high, and looking down, in a superficially judgemental, but inwardly rather amused way, on the concerns, the snubs, the insults, and the actions of the petty little egos and the game players far below. From on high, the conscience can see the past and the present, and can offer the multi-headed egos new and more useful interpretations of the historical events that set their pattern of behaviour in motion. Then, after a brief period of reflection, dive back down into the pool of everyday life and try again. It is a very quick exercise so you can easily find time to do it twice a day. And so it is. Like King Richard, occasionally we rise up, as far as we can, and look down, briefly. But mostly we don't.

The role and existence of conscience has been observed throughout human history. A thousand stories have been told in a thousand cultures to explain the phenomenon of conscience in terms of gods, souls, muses, guardian angels, and genetic evolutionary psychology. Each story is believed by some and disbelieved by others, but the phenomenon persists for all, and is widely regarded to be our highest, most elevated and enjoyable state of mind.

There is an ancient and very widespread idea that the conscience level is aware of the **unity in the universe** and the **harmonic and sympathetic resonances in the universal web of everything**. Of course, the fact that it is widespread doesn't necessarily make it true.

Modern science is finding that it too is forced to take account of the large-scale interconnectedness of time, space and matter, the very long-range effects of gravity and the electromagnetic phenomena that tie the entire known universe together into a deeply interactive system. The fact that the conscience level of awareness has been giving us rather similar ideas for thousands of years, doesn't necessarily validate conscience level insights in general.

One noticeable difference between the multi-headed egos and the conscience, is that the egos want to win the game, every game, any game. They are evolved to motivate us to action, to chase after desires and to run away from perceived threats and dangers. They love all that excitement, enthusiasm, pain and exhaustion. The conscience would prefer to be playing a different game altogether. A game in which everyone contributes to and benefits from the evolution of the unified whole. It is a common problem for modern working life, that we are frequently expected to commit to ego-level games, which are not at all pleasing to our conscience-level sensibilities, which would rather be playing by conscience-level values and rewards, but with ego-style fun and enthusiasm.

It is interesting that whilst most people have, at some time, personally experienced this profound conscience level of awareness, it is currently taboo in so many public domains. I could write a novel which embraced and celebrated the theme of conscience. I could write a book about the history of the idea of conscience as a defining property of the soul. But if I suggested introducing a consideration of conscience-level insights into the design of the national curriculum or our public sector housing provision, the idea would never make it onto the agenda.

This is yet another regrettable consequence of postmodernism. Because Hitler's success in manipulating public opinion was achieved, in part, by hijacking popular Germanic religious rhetoric and terminology, the postmodernists have been working (quite successfully) towards the eradication of all western indigenous 'religious' concepts from the public arena. This may well have serious perverse consequences as someone or something even worse may come along to take advantage of the vacuum.

It is of course 'true' that the flawed application of misunderstood and distorted religious spiritual concepts has a long history of disastrous consequences, but maybe we could use our brains to discriminate a little, throwing out the rubbish and keeping the good stuff.

The game of **Snakes and Ladders** is an interesting metaphor for social organisation. It was originally a Hindu game about the life journey: the ladders represent the virtues that raise you up, and the snakes are the vices that drag you down. A society based on this idea would allow its members the freedom to learn from experience, whilst letting it be known that it approves of and encourages ladders, and dislikes and discourages snakes.

Post-modern western culture seems to have been moving in a rather different direction: it doesn't recognise the journey at all, and thinks that success is measured by the flatness of the equality monitoring statistics. It celebrates snakes for their lovely colourful diversity, and is suspicious of ladders for fear they might lead to elitism or neck injuries.

I think we should put some snakes and ladders up-down conscience-orientated concepts back into the public discussion of human goals, as a matter of urgency.

Many cultures have had a roughly similar mystical view, that this elevated conscious conscience sensation arises because a holy monad (a piece of god-consciousness) has descended into the material world and taken up residence in a (genetically evolved) material body, in order to experience self-aware **existence** in the created universe as opposed to blissful **beingness**. Through the need to make choices, and the opportunity to learn from the consequences of those choices, we experience and therefore come to understand the fruits of the tree of the knowledge of relative meaning. Most people in the west, for the last 2500 years seem to have believed a story roughly similar to this. But that of course, does not make it true.

I suspect that everyone can and does occasionally experience this elevated sense of conscience (ranging from mild self-criticism to merciful joyous bliss) as their highest state of being.

This raises some important questions. Are the values we experience as 'conscience' culturally defined - or do they transcend social prescription?

We are all aware of situations where our conscience has rejected dominant cultural values, and where it holds values which our culture actively rejects. This suggests that our conscience is not entirely culturally defined, and that the social and cultural influences on it only operate through the lower level mechanisms of habit, copying, the multiple temporary egos, and the planner's externally constructed intelligences.

One could argue that the conscience's values may be evolved/inherited, as so much else about our neural networks seem to be. Perhaps the existence of the conscience can be explained as an extension of the 'altruistic gene' concept, but it is hard to see how the values and behaviours it promotes could have contributed much to our historical survival, since it is not usually one of the modes that is triggered during the urgency of most life threatening situations, either at an individual or a social group level.

Could it possibly come from some other remote source, something more in tune with the ideas of all those ancient and mystical traditions which saw the soul / conscience as a receiver, tuned in to a higher source of values and principles - a receiver of messages from a guardian angel, guiding us on our journey to theosis (when we are ready to listen), or from a meditative connection with Plato's higher realms of archetypal forms and principles?

We don't know how this thinking level came to promote the values it does, but we do know what it feels like. Most would agree that it feels like our purest, most enduring, sense of self - our highest, most integrated, most far-seeing, all-embracing, most relaxed and joyous sense of self. As such it deserves to be held in high regard, higher than it is at the moment in western culture, even if it is nothing more than just another neurochemically driven emergent property of our neural networks.

Chapter 4

Systems Thinking for Systemic Problems

Modern Problems

The modern (human) world is a complex of dynamic systems, interlocking vicious and virtuous circles, not always self regulating, not always intuitively obvious. When complex systems go wrong it can be difficult the work out what to do to correct them. Attempts to isolate and deal with any one part of the problem can make the rest of the problem even worse. Sometimes nothing can change unless everything changes, and that requires a high degree of cooperation and communication between different professions and vested interest groups. John Hoskyns' book, 'Just in Time', gives a fascinating account of his role in the late 70s and 80s, in aligning various influential groups around a shared understanding of what had gone wrong with the postwar British political economic system, and the 'stepping stones' for rectifying the problem. A recommended read for anyone interested on how to get human societies to understand and then rectify systemic problems.

Global humanity is beginning to realise that it is facing some new and very serious systemic problems. Some of which we brought upon ourselves, and others which have remote causes that are beyond our control, but which have set in motion systemic changes with serious consequences which we need to understand and plan for.

We are where we are, because of our historical thoughts and actions. It is time to acknowledge that the way we think, the way we perceive and model reality, the way we prioritize our goals and desires, and the way we make both individual and group level decisions, is the main cause of the problems we face today.

Old think is too linear for understanding our modern systemic problems. It still has its uses, but it works by isolating components, and it is not sufficiently sensitive to the rich interconnectivity of the new world. The post-modern preference for drawing attention to: fragmentation, discontinuity, ambiguity, opacity, anarchy and chaos, operates to prevent the synthesis of a holistic systemic viewpoint; although their emphasis on discord, contradiction, paradox and perversity does help to highlight systems components and processes that might otherwise have been overlooked.

If democracy is to cope with systemic problems whose solutions require us to make short-term personal sacrifices, then the media, the public, the politicians, business leaders and the fund managers and investors who finance them, are all going to have to get better at understanding and discussing systemic problems? We have to improve both our individual, and our group skills, at holistic systemic thinking.

There is not much survival value in agreeing to deny the existence of problems or pretending that we have solutions when actually we don't. Morale boosting feel-good back-slapping group-think is all very well where the problems and their consequences are trivial, but it is not a very good way to approach serious problems.

So - if we want to participate in a democratic attempt to resolve these problems, we had better start equipping ourselves with the necessary thinking and communication skills. If we don't have a healthy, well informed and systems-capable democracy, then there is a good chance that some other political mechanism will evolve to direct and contain the forces of over simplistic short-term economic greed, runaway belief systems and group-think.

We must get to know the strengths and weaknesses of human thinking, so that we can make the most of our strengths and be alert to our weaknesses. At the moment our education system places very little emphasis on teaching even old style linear/critical thinking, and almost no emphasis on holistic integrated systems thinking.

In researching this book I have looked at 55 different schemes for teaching thinking skills, and none of them made any mention of systems thinking.

Thinking Is a Natural Activity

Thinking and problem solving are very natural activities for the human brain. We don't have to learn to identify and categorise objects and concepts, on the basis of the similarities and differences in their properties and relationships. Modelling the world is an automatic pre-conscious function of our inherited neural networks. They are specifically designed to capture the (local) cause and effect connections between objects, to generalise and abstract, and to apply that knowledge when we need it.

Of course it helps if you grow up in a culture that values encourages and rewards the application of these basic abilities. It helps if you grow up around people who are role models of effective 'thinking', 'making things happen' and 'solving problems'. If you are privileged to grow up in such an environment, you will get the opportunity to copy the techniques, and absorb the attitudes and presuppositions that go with them. It will probably impede the development of these innate abilities if you belong to a group which expects you to think only in terms of its standard clichés and world models.

What we do have to do, is remember to check, consciously, if our pre-conscious brain has made a good job of **modelling** the world. This is because the pre-conscious brain is not good at **testing** its own assumptions and conclusions.

Conscious Observation and Testing

We need to check if the criteria, concepts and filters our social group habitually uses to focus our attention, and to chop the world up into objects and ideas, are still valid, if they still accurately reflect our best understanding and most up-to-date experiences, or if we are being misled by our group and culture's habitual default categories.

We need to remember to test our brain's internal models and externally communicated social explanations, to check that we have not jumped to incorrect assumptions, distorted our memories or set up too limited a frame, too small a perspective, based on too little experience.

We need to become aware of the sorts of mistakes the brain tends to make, and the problems that can arise as a result of the shoddy or manipulative use of our sometimes vague and ambiguous language.

In short, we need to become more consciously aware of how we are thinking, so that we can spot and correct these pre-conscious errors, and communicate and cooperate more effectively with others, both within and across cultures.

Understanding vs. Memory

A university academic advisor recently asked me, "Why do the dyslexic students always want to understand things, why can't they just remember stuff like the rest of us?"

Hum! This question seems to imply a model of the world in which there is only one correct way of learning, but it is clear that our neural networks can learn by making two rather different types of association:

- Static Linear Associations (remembering);
  and
- Highly Connected Dynamic Modelling (understanding).

Static Linear Association

This type of learning is based on a memory chain of stimulus-response connections linking isolated static memories and experiences together into a linear sequence. This is how we construct narratives, myths, fables, slogans and sound bites - automatic answers to standard questions. This is one of the traditional ways of passing on a culture's rich knowledge base of named categories, approved perspectives, values, interpretations, predictions and prescriptions.

This type of thinking and communication is very good for conveying narratives, accounts, lists, contracts, agreements, laws. It pretends to be able to function as a medium for conveying algorithmic type instructions for assembling flat pack furniture, installing computer software, call centre automated menus, etc., but it is usually not very good at this because it is so insensitive to the changing demands of different contexts. After the first few steps, you start to get error messages or options that are not described in the instructions, and chaos sets in.

Computer programming languages are possibly the greatest achievement, so far, of this linear instructive style of human communication. With a very restricted vocabulary and a rigid system of unambiguous meanings and grammar, it has been possible to construct enormous pyramids of instructions that produce astonishing results with amazing reliability.

They act as an interface between the thoughts in the human brain, and the yes/no digital capability of the computer, and it is interesting to observe how programming languages have evolved over the last 30 years.

At the core of the new languages we find **classes** of **objects**, carefully defined by their **essential** and **variable properties**, and by their capability to **interact** (called methods) in precisely defined ways with the properties of other objects. The languages all make great use of **looping**: chasing a **goal** by repeating an instruction over and over again, until some **condition** has been satisfied, (do this until, are we there yet, are we there yet?). This would be considered very bad style in ordinary prose. Humans interact with the system by triggering **events** which initiate **processes** that **transform** the properties of specific objects. All this happens within a frame, a **system boundary.**

This new evolution in human language can instruct machines to model the operations of a factory, a racing engine, a library or a space flight to Mars. It has been astonishingly effective and gives a glimpse of the potential of human thinking and communication. But as we know, the development of complex computer systems often goes very wrong. In my experience these failures are usually caused by distortions introduced to try to make reality comply with group-think - project managers being persuaded to adjust the design of the system in order to hide inadequacies and contradictions in policies and ideologies.

Humans are so good at this sort of perceptual monkey business that they genuinely don't realise what they have done, until the computers' inability to handle the pretense and distortion brings the system crashing to a halt.

Text/linear thinking is commonly used to define policies and procedures, and usually results in an insensitive oversimplification of the reality it purports to describe. When strings of static text are used to attempt to describe a 3D dynamic system, a complex process, a machine, a building or an environment, it fails miserably. A text-based description of a cathedral can tell you interesting things about who built it, or when, or how it was paid for, what styles influenced the design, what the author felt on entering the place... but you could not even begin to start actually building a cathedral from a text-based description. For that, we use diagrams that represent shape, form, structure, materials, scale and spatial relationships.

Understanding

Our neural networks also have the capability, and a huge capacity, to understand things - to build up highly connected dynamic mental models: hierarchical systems of mental objects, linked together by subtle patterns of cause and effect, and transformed by processes which respond to events. We can update our mental models, tuning their emergent properties to make them even more sensitive to changes in our environment and thus more effective at directing our activity, steering us towards or away from changeable goals.

In our daily lives, we interact with an increasing number of complex systems, such as: cars, traffic management systems, cookers, fridges, central-heating and air-conditioning systems, computer systems, bureaucracies, business rules and regulations, taxes and credits, geological processes and climate systems.

Complex systems are not a new experience for humans. The historical success and geographical spread of modern humans depended on our ability to understand (certain aspects of) the life cycles of the plants and animals we depended on for food and resources. Our version of the mammal brain has clearly had the ability to understand some types of complex dynamic systems for tens of thousands of years. Rather more recent examples include the building of the pyramids, Roman aqueducts and amphitheatres, medieval cathedrals, C17th sailing ships and computer chips.

Model Making

Static linear word-based association is a good way of **learning** static information like multiplication tables, historical dates and mnemonics. Rhyme, rhythm and unexpected associations make them easier to remember, but to work with dynamic systems, to **understand** them, we have to use the brain's model-making mode.

Our brains are perfectly capable of understanding large dynamic systems, it is our language that is the obstacle. Linear sequential language is very clumsy at describing complex interactive system dynamics.

Despite the fact that every building, machine, and system that we create, starts life, and is communicated as, some form of diagram, our educators continue to **value text over diagrams**, as a means of communication. Because text is so poor at modelling dynamic systems, our education system offers most people very little practice at thinking about dynamic interconnections.

Unless you choose to study something like plumbing, building, mechanics, engineering or systems analysis, you are not likely to have much contact with dynamic systems thinking, and even if you do, your teachers probably won't explain that this style of thinking is a transferable skill, which is useable in all subject domains, not just in that specific field.

So, in this increasingly systems-orientated world, with increasingly systemic problems to deal with (globalisation, culture clashes, market economies, the environment, etc.), we really do need to improve both our individual and group ability to model, understand and communicate dynamic systems.

The principles are easy, and well within our intellectual grasp, even at an early age, so start young, and if you are too old to start young, start now.

Practise on any system that interests you. It does not matter whether it is bicycle mechanics, cooking, fabric making, building, electronics, computing, gardening, DIY, sport, motor mechanics, history, mathematics, or plumbing. The principles of systems modelling are the same, and the building blocks are transferable from one domain to another.

Diagramming

Because of the limitations of text, humans have always resorted to diagrams for modelling and communicating dynamic systems. The word 'diagram' comes from the Greek for *through something written,* which illustrates that it has long been realised that text is not the only way to make a lasting written record, or to communicate ideas.

Leonardo da Vinci wrote (in referring to the detailed anatomical drawings which he made for his own research):

> 'No one could hope to convey so much true knowledge without an immense, tedious and confused length of writing and time, except through this very short way of drawing from different aspects.'

Lots of different diagramming techniques have been developed in response to the special needs of different industries (architecture, boat building, civil engineering, mechanical engineering, clothing, furniture, electronics, computing, etc.).

Graphical Thinking System

Graphical Thinking is a general-purpose entity-relationship systems diagramming technique, which can be used by individuals or groups to think through, and develop a deep understanding of, any kind of problem, and any subject on the ever changing National Curriculum.

There are only a handful of elements in this diagramming system:

- Things - and their properties and capabilities;
- Ideas / concepts – and their properties;
- Connections – (between things and or ideas) and their conditional structural transformative properties;
- Events and;
- A Frame or Boundary - and its properties. This sets the context, limits the area you need to pay attention to, and very often includes important conceptual 'values', 'filters' and 'amplifiers', telling you which aspects are important, and which aspects to ignore. It may also have properties like depth, and

scope: is this an egocentric or a whole system perception? is it client centred or officer centred? production centred, customer focussed, environmentally aware, etc?

Let's start with a simple example. Children love doing this.

Draw a circle (the size of a bottle top, near the middle of a page of A4) to represent a familiar class of object: 'Chair' for example.

Ask someone: "What are the defining properties of a Chair?" How do you know that a thing is a chair, and not a stool, or a bench, or a swing, or a table? The conversation might go like this.

Answer — Well it must have legs.
Question — How many legs?
Answer — 4
Question — Must it always be 4? If it had 3 legs, would it still be a chair?
Answer — Ok, between 3 and 10.
Question — What if it had 1 very wide leg and was still stable?
Answer — Ok, it may have 1 to 10 legs, as long as it is stable.
(Note - anything other than 3 may be unstable on an uneven floor.)

Question — What else?
Answer — A back support – definitely,
Answer — and it might have arm rests,
Answer — and it might have a cup holder,
Answer — but it must have a level area, a seat, big enough for your bottom, and comfortable.

Question — Must it be perfectly level or can it be slightly sloping or slightly contoured?
Answer — Ok, it must be close to level and maybe a little bit shaped.

Question — How high might the seat be from the ground? And what should it be made of?

Etc.

So the object chair has a number of essential and variable properties.

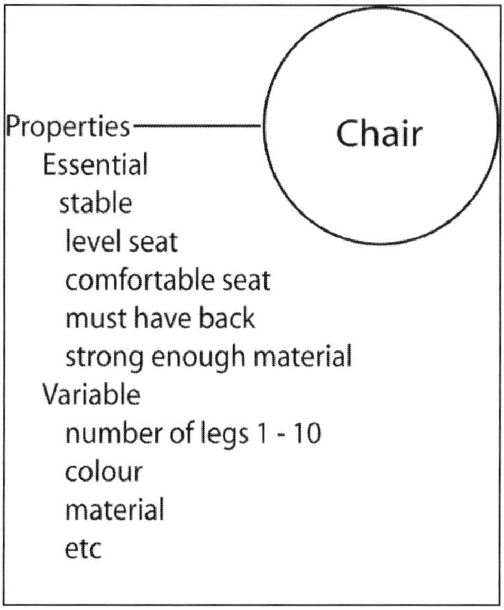

Figure 4.1 Essential and variable properties.

If you were designing a new chair, you would probably spend a lot of time thinking and discussing with others, in great detail, the essential and variable properties, and the capabilities of the chair you want to make.

In the context we are currently thinking about (our chosen frame), chairs do not exist in isolation from the rest of the universe; they interact with lots of other things. So:

Question What do chairs connect to, what do they interact with?
Answer People, the floor, tables, pets, jackets, cushions.

Question Ok - what is the nature of the relationship, the properties of the connection between chairs and tables?
Answer Well, the chair must be able to fit under the table, with you sitting on it.

Question **Must** be able to?
Answer Yes - **if** you are going to use the table and the chair together.

Question What about a coffee table, that's used with chairs

Answer	Ok - so it depends on the purpose - how you want to use them – and there are different types of tables – dinning tables, coffee tables, etc.
Question	Are all chairs designed to be used with a type of table?
Answer	No, it's optional, lots of chairs are designed to stand alone.
Question	So there are different types of chairs, **and** different types of tables?
Answer	Yes.
Question	If chairs are used together with a table, how many tables and how many chairs make up a set?
Answer	6 chairs to one table, no 8, no I have seen 20.
Etc.	

So, in this **frame**, we have chosen 7 **objects**: the floor, tables, chairs, people, pets, jackets and cushions. We can easily represent them, communicate them, by drawing a circle/blob for each one, and labelling each one with the name of the category[6].

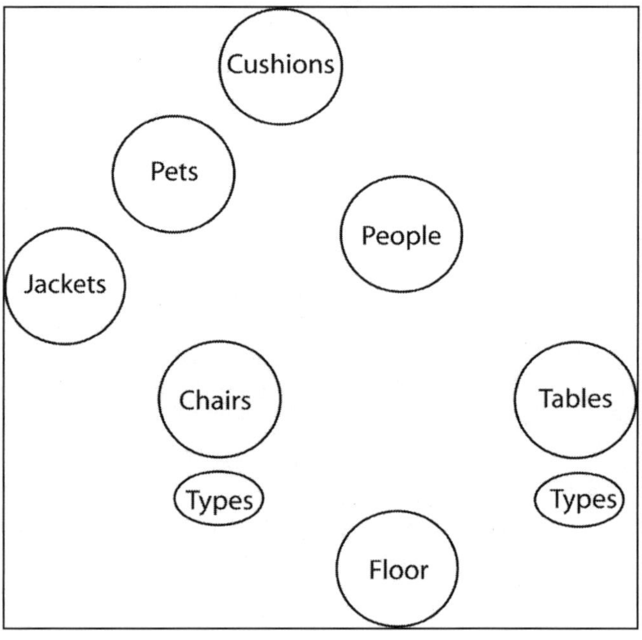

Figure 4.2 Classes of objects.

[6] Category = a class of things or ideas (from Greek for *statement*)
Class = a set of things grouped together (from Latin for *assembly*)

Relationships

How do these objects relate to each other? From our brief discussion we already know something about how chairs and tables relate to each other, so -

> draw a line connecting chairs to tables, and start thinking about the **properties of that connection.** What is important about the way chairs and tables interact? We have already thought that chairs can exist without tables and vice versa, but if they do work together as a set, then their relative heights are important, because if you want to sit at the table to eat your dinner, or to write a letter, then you have to be able to get your legs under the table, and the table top needs to be at a reasonable height for your elbows. Maybe the construction and surface materials should be coordinated so they look nice together. Maybe the chairs should be designed to stack together, and fit out of the way (under the table?) when not in use, etc.

And what do we know about the **relationships** between the other items?

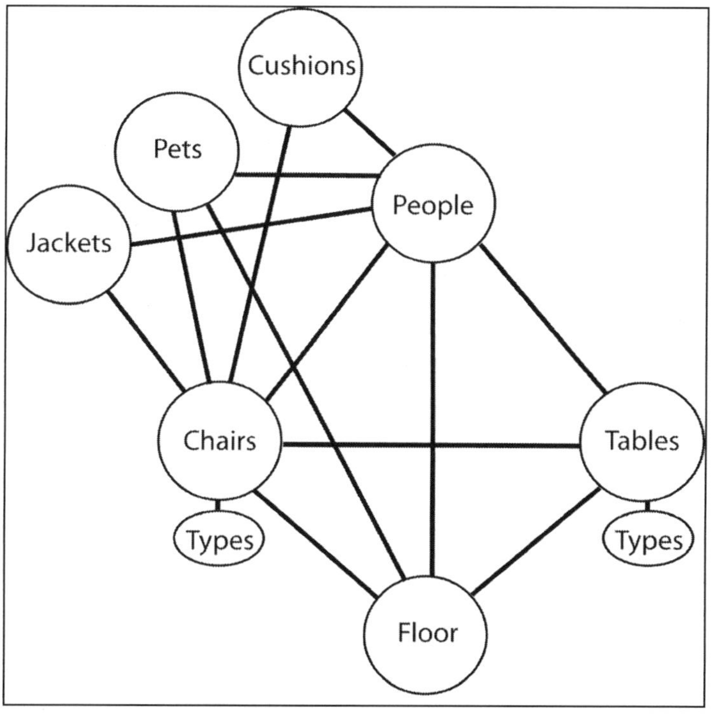

Figure 4.3 Relationships - Connections.

People may have pets. Pets may sit on chairs but in this example, pets do not sit on cushions. People have jackets which are often left on the backs of chairs. Chairs may have cushions on them, and people may sit on those cushions. This raises an interesting new point - cushions may also be on the floor and people may sit on the floor, and on cushions on the floor, but we did not discuss these ideas so I have not put them in the diagram.

In many everyday situations it is enough to simply focus our attention on the **properties** of the **objects** and **relations** in the diagram, but sometimes it is important to write them down, summarise them on the diagram, or if necessary, write them out in detail on a separate sheet of paper. If you are using diagramming software it is usually possible to add a note field to each object or relationship.

Think about the words and symbols you could use to describe your understanding of **each of these connections**. For example, people have many uses for tables. People like to sit on cushions.

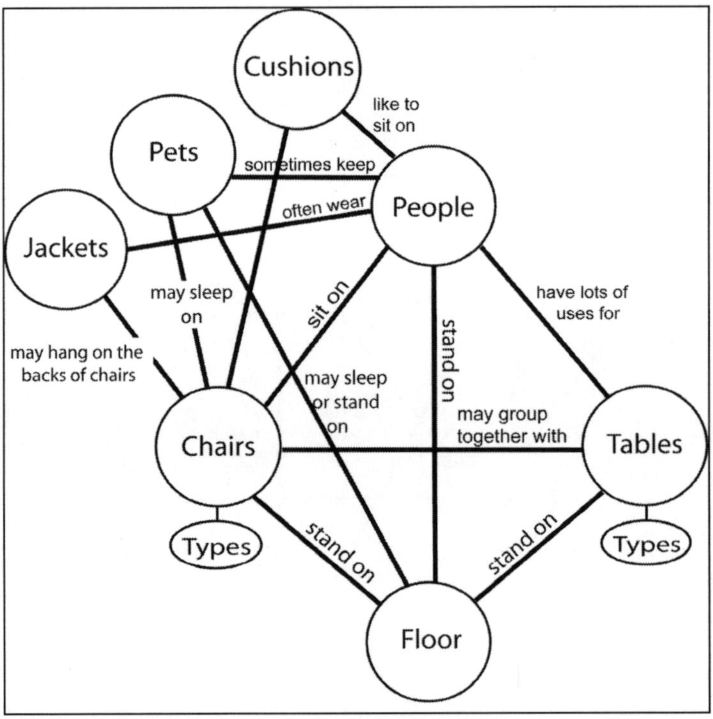

Figure 4.4 Annotating the relationships.

People may keep many pets. Pets may sleep on chairs. There are different types of tables and chairs (coffee, dining, rocking, arm, folding, etc.).

You might want to add some symbols to represent the 'structural' properties of the connections, such as:

Must;
May, its optional;
One to one;
One to many;
Many to many (for example; teachers have many students and students have many teachers).

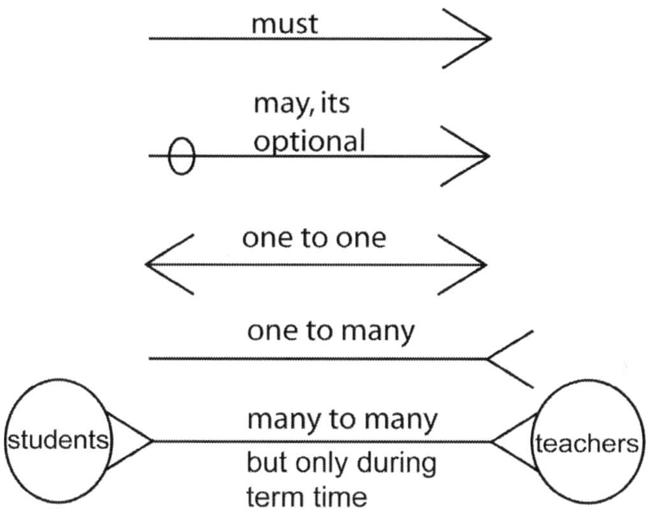

Figure 4.5 Structural relations.

Each line (relationship) must have at least one verb type word (action, cause, effect). For example, people **stand** on the floor. If it is necessary for clarity, then the direction of the arrow can be used to tell you which way to read the connection. Do people stand on the floor, or does the floor stand on people?

Less obvious, but very useful relationship labels are: is part of, feeds into, shapes our view of, is of the type, has these properties / characteristics, is an example of, leads to, causes, results in, is the same as, is similar to, can do, has the ability to perform an action or to interact in a specified way...

When you start to think in detail about the nature of the chair to table connection, you soon realise that some types of chair have a very definite relationship to tables and other types of chair (armchairs, rocking chairs) definitely don't.

Whenever you come across a situation where the different examples of a category don't seem to share the same connections with the rest of the model, it is a sure sign that the category is too general for the particular context, and needs to be broken down into different types. We have already seen this with chairs and tables. Some types of chair are designed to be stand-alone, some are designed to be used with a dining table, and some with a coffee table.

There are two ways to represent this.

> This way emphasises that there are potentially many different types of chairs and tables, and the complexity of how the different types interact with each other must be described in the single relationship between chairs and tables.

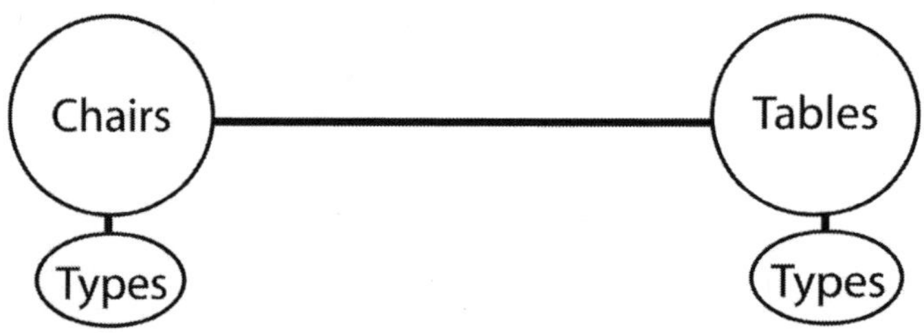

Figure 4.6 Using a "Types" blob – a high level of generalisation that leaves a lot of details to be explained in the properties of the relationship.

This second approach goes into more detail about the connections between the each different type.

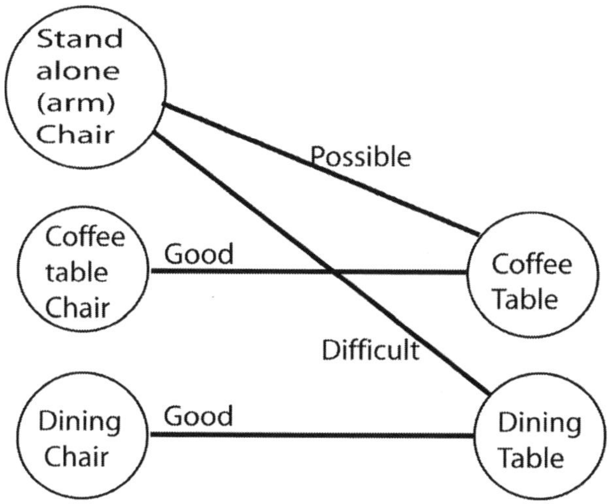

Figure 4.7 Detailing the interactions between the different types.

Be aware of the difference and use whichever is most appropriate.

Conditional Properties

Relationships often have **conditional** properties, describing when, or how many, or under which circumstances, etc. These conditions can be very specific, and might include mathematical formula, for example, the seat height of a dinning table chair should be between 5/7 and 6/7 the height of the bottom surface of the top of the dinning table.

The properties of the connections are very important in the understanding of dynamic systems. Most of the **systems information** is in the description of the **interaction between the things** - in the **properties** of the **connections.** If necessary, you can number the connections on the diagram and record all the important details on separate numbered sheets.

With these **lines** (the verbs) and **blobs** (the nouns, subjects and objects), and ideas about the **properties** of the lines and the blobs (adjectives and adverbs), you can represent the essential structure of **any** human thinking.

You could diagram your understanding of all the players and commentators in the Middle East conflict: what are their fears, what are their aspirations, what are their tactics, what are their resources, how do they frame the situation, what are their beliefs, who are they dependent on for help and support, who wants to obstruct their goals, who stands to gain what, etc?

This particular 'chairs and tables' example is not a matter of great significance or international importance, but already you can begin to see how **easily** and **efficiently** this graphical technique represents the depth and complexity of our understanding of this everyday situation.

It also has a dynamic-expansive quality which **gently challenges our assumptions.** It encourages us to think about where else the jackets and the cushions could be when they are not on chairs. Maybe it helps us realise how useful a level floor is, instead of taking it completely for granted. It gets us thinking about the different ways we use our tables during the course of a day. Maybe it suggests improvements you could make to the location, design or use of the tables in your house.

So far we have used only two of the elements of this system of diagrams:

- things and their properties;
  and
- connections between things, and their properties.

What about Concepts and Ideas?

Well in that initial brief question and answer session we thought that a chair should be **stable, comfortable**, and should have a back **support.** We talked about the importance of the **shape** of the seat, the **feel** and **appearance** of the **materials**, the **relative heights** of the chairs and the table, and the possibility of **designing** the chairs so that they can be **stacked together** to make good **use of space** when not in **use.**

There are a lot of important ideas here. Diagram them. Get them down on paper. Use a pencil and a rubber, so that you can move things around easily, or better still, use a diagramming software package. Start thinking about how these ideas relate to each other, and in ten minutes or so, you can do a lot of high quality thinking about the design, manufacture or marketing of chairs. It all depends what your **frame** is, what your point of view or interest is.

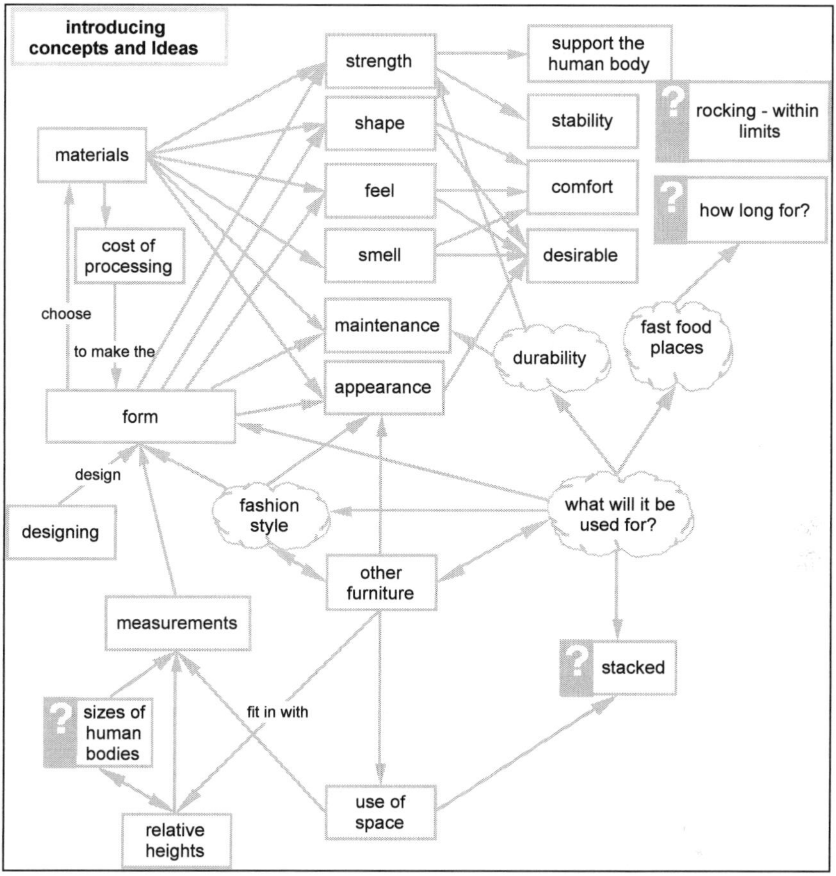

Figure 4.8 Introducing concepts and ideas.

The frame I was using when I came up with this diagram emphasised the design process. I could just as well have focussed on, the manufacturing processes and constraints, the marketing and distribution, the financing of the whole process, or the history of chair design.

In thinking how to draw this diagram, I incorporated a lot of associated knowledge and ideas from my own personal experience, but the process also generated many new connections and realisations which I had not previously been consciously aware of. It is a dynamic and creative process. Other people could easily have been incorporated into the process, and their personal/cultural experiences and new realisations could all have been included in the diagram.

Diagramming my thoughts about the deep structure of this situation also highlights questions that need further research - more thought and attention – such as:

- What size are human beings – do I want one chair to fit all sizes and ages – or do I want a range of different sizes in the same general design?
- What do I mean by stability? A rocking chair is stable within limits. A swing is stable within limits.
- What uses do I want this chair to be good for?
- Do I want it to be stackable or not?
- I need to research the size, styles and fashion of other traditional and popular furniture.
- What materials are available? What are their properties? What shapes can they support? What do they cost, etc?
- How durable do I want it to be?
- How comfortable? (If it is for a fast food restaurant or a bus station, it may need to be designed to be quite uncomfortable after 15 minutes, to encourage people to leave soon, not to sleep on them, etc.)

The fact that there are outstanding issues that need to be resolved doesn't stop the thinking process. When thinking only in a **linear** sequence of words, there is a tendency for any blockages or unknowns to stop the whole thinking process. "Well, we haven't decided on the **use** yet, or the **style**, so we can't do anything else until that is decided."

Graphical Thinking (GT) diagramming - general

Graphical Thinking diagrams represent our mental models of the world. They are works in progress. They are never completely finished. They represent current thinking within one of many possible frames.

They are a very condensed record, or map, of the thinking that has taken place. That is why they mean so much more to the people who were involved in the thinking and discussion that went into the building of the diagram than they do to a casual observer who only sees the finished diagram. Their full meaning only becomes apparent once the new observer has experienced / worked through (or been guided through) a similar thinking process for themselves. Just as looking at a map of the Lake District is not the same experience as visiting the Lake District.

So GT diagramming is a great tool for structuring and recording, dynamic thinking processes and their conclusions. It is also a very useful tool for communicating that thinking process to other people, but they are not a substitute for thinking. You can't give someone a diagram and expect them to leapfrog straight to the understanding phase – they have to work through the thinking phase first.

But as a map, a guide, prepared by someone with experience, someone who has been there before you and has some suggestions on where to go and what to avoid, they are a valuable teaching / learning tool - particularly if you are trying to pass on **dynamic systemic understanding style knowledge**, rather than simple **linear associative memory** based knowledge.

Because of the dualistic experiential nature of our learning processes, being **told** for example, that X works and Y doesn't, will not result in quite the same quality of understanding as finding it out for yourself. Being given the answer is not the same neural experience as struggling to understand a problem, hoping you have found a solution, testing it, and finding your were wrong, over and over again, and then coming up with an idea, a model, an understanding that produces results that work. Struggle, hope, disappointment, joy, elation, relief and satisfaction are all part of the neurochemical process.

From the Big Picture to the Detail

GT diagrams can operate at all levels. They can be very detailed or very big picture.

For example, here is a 'big picture' diagram I constructed during a one hour conversation with a postgraduate history student. I had never studied history, but after drawing this diagram, I felt as if I had a really powerful framework on which to start building an understanding of the subject.

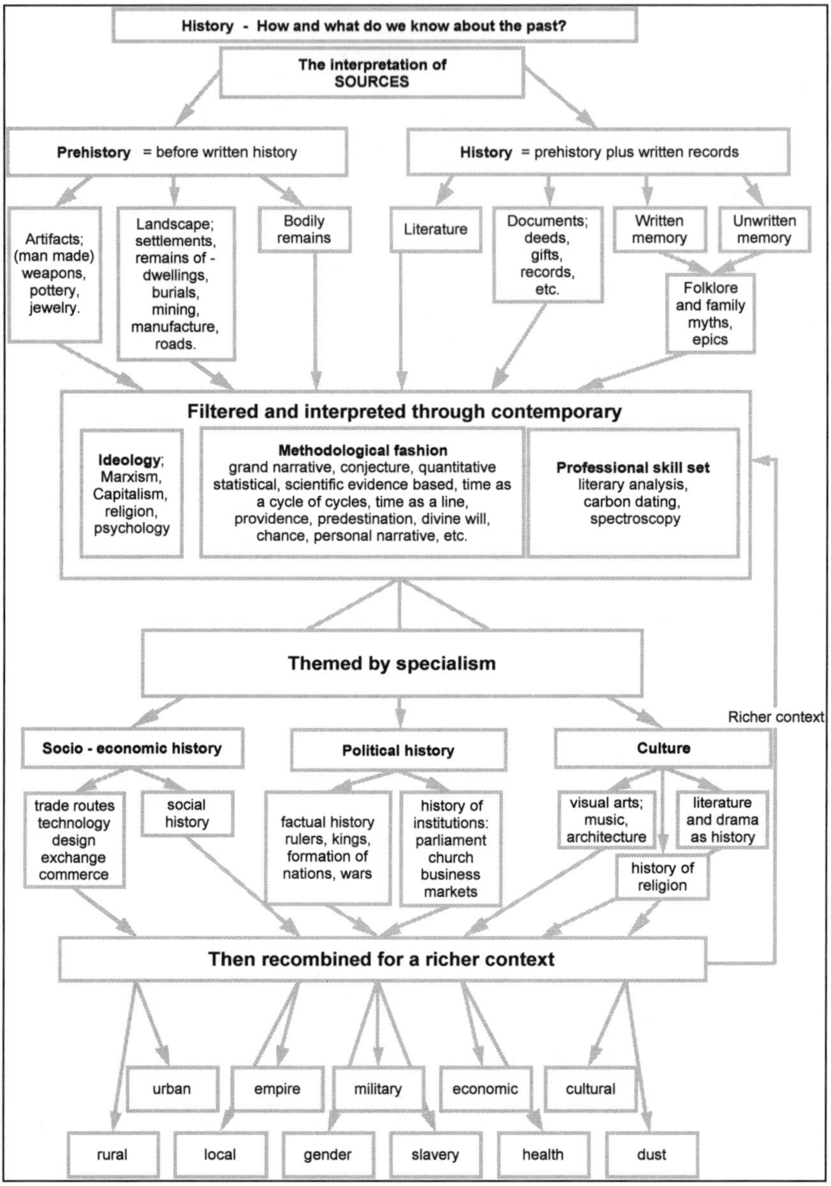

Figure 4.9 High level diagrams for curriculum subjects.

This model shows one person's current thinking on how to organise her understanding of history. It begins with the discovery of sources, which are interpreted according to the prevailing ideological, methodological and technical fashion. The material is then themed into professional /

academic specialisms and later gets recombined into more commercial themes for presentation/marketing to the public.

Of course there are many other (big picture) ways to look at history. Buckminster Fuller triggered my interest in history when he wrote that the key to understanding human history is to understand the history of transport technology and its effect on trade routes, and then to understand the various systems of land and resource ownership and control. Everything else follows from that. That is so much more interesting to me than learning the names of kings and queens without any understanding of the forces of change they were struggling with.

Some would argue that his trade routes view is too simplistic because it ignores other important ideas that we should bear in mind when organising our view of history, such as the changing religious, philosophical and social ideas that have been used to justify the use of force and taxation, in order to get control of, and profit from, trade routes.

At a more detailed level - here is a diagram produced by Tom, a 9yr old dyslexic student, which consolidates his understanding of his school history project on Tudor England.

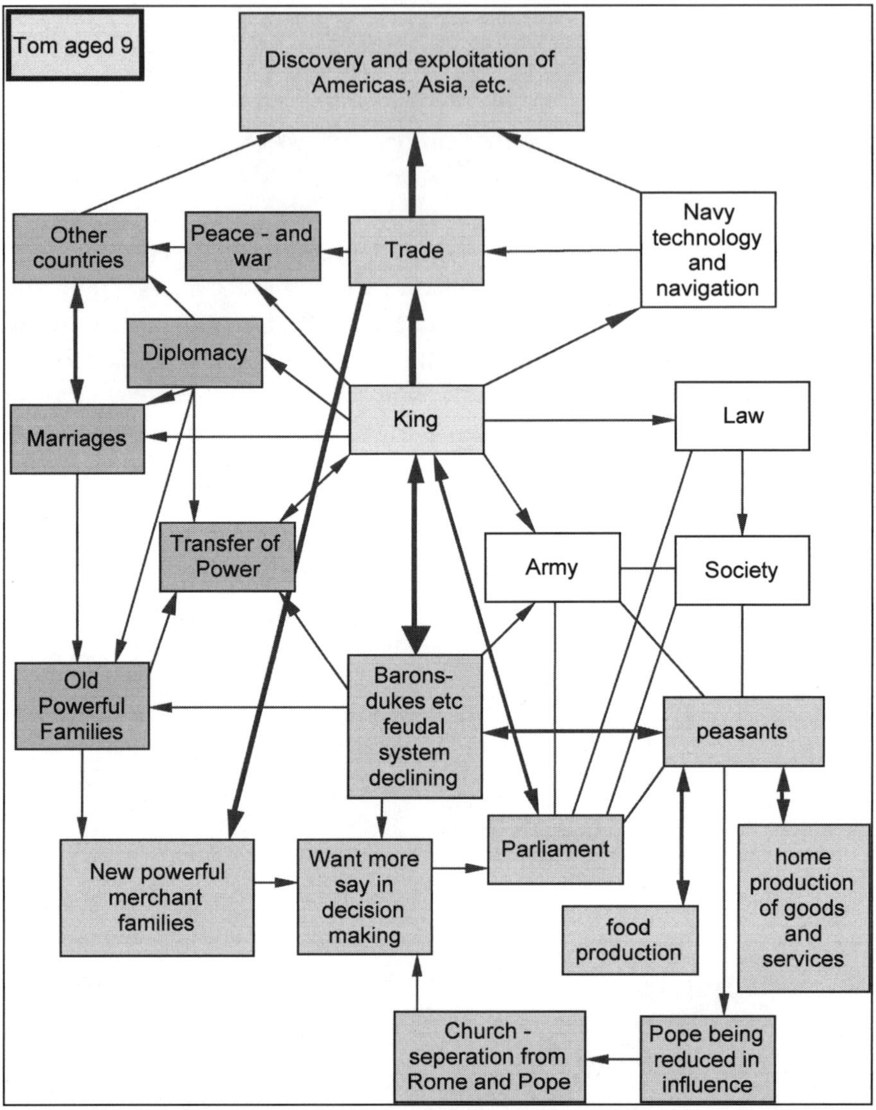

Figure 4.10 Tom's Tudor England, aged 9.

Representing Systems

Diagrams are much better than text at representing systems. That is because systems involve the simultaneous interaction of many elements. This can easily be shown in a diagram and understood by the brain, but it cannot be easily shown with linear sequential text. Text is good at **describing each element**, but it is not good at describing how they **interact.**

For example, a domestic central heating system typically has the following components:

Pipe work - copper or plastic, usual sizes, 8mm, 15mm, 22mm.

Radiators - various sizes and designs. Designed to heat the air by radiation and convection.

Thermostats - designed to open or close water valves or electrical circuits when the local temperature rises above, or falls below, a set (adjustable) level.

A boiler - where either gas or oil is burned to heat water. It has probably got a condenser to recover waste heat in the exhaust gases, and a pressure vessel to accommodate the expansion and contraction of the water as the system heats up and cools down. It has a pilot light to ignite the fuel.

Balanced flue - to bring in fresh air and get rid of the dangerous burnt gasses.

Water pump - electrically powered, to push the hot water around the piping.

Safety devices - to stop the supply of fuel if: there is no water in the system, the water returning from the radiators is still hot enough, the pilot light is not already burning, or the electricity supply fails.

The whole point of the system is to heat the air in parts of the building to specified temperatures at specified times. Main area and local area thermostatic sensors are used to measure the air temperature in different parts of the building and compare it with the desired temperature goals.

The control module - receives information about the main goal and the current air temperature (both from the main area thermostat), and gets safety information from the safety module. It makes simple decisions and controls the fuel supply, the boiler and the water pump.

It needs inputs:

- Water supply;
- Gas (or Oil) and Air supply;
- Electricity supply;
- Temperature goals (settings on the thermostats);
- Maintenance.

It has outputs:

- Burnt gas fumes;
- Distributed heat.

It operates in a context: it must comply with local quality and safety standards, rules and regulations.

It has been designed to take advantage of our understanding of the laws of physics (thermodynamics, radiation and convection), the chemistry of combustion, and the properties of different materials. Radiation and convection are two different physical processes by which the energy in the radiators heats the surrounding air, and the fabric of the building. Radiation operates by shaking atoms (remote bottom-up), and convection operates by shaking air molecules (close contact top-down).

There are many different ways to communicate the collection of ideas and material components that come together to make up a central heating system. This particular approach focuses on the high-level properties of the main components, and how they interact. It does not go into the question of how to make watertight joints in the pipe work, or how to calculate how powerful the boiler needs to be in order to heat a particular building.

It does not give the physical information that would be needed to install a central heating system in a specific building. For that we would need to know where to put the boiler, the flue, the pipes and the radiators, etc. But that can all be accurately described with a diagram as well – a different type of diagram that concentrates on describing spatial relations between physical objects. Those diagrams can tell you where to put the things, but not how the system works conceptually.

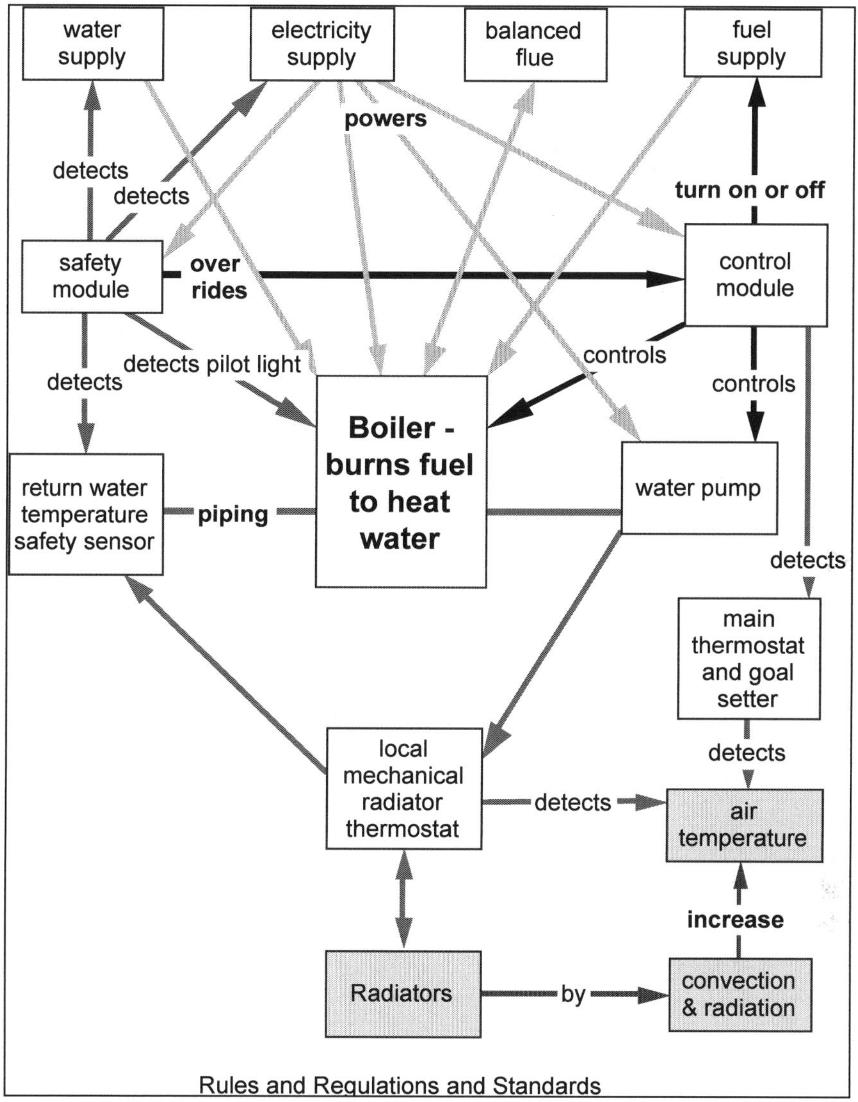

Figure 4.11 Domestic central heating concepts.

GT is to Thinking what Topology is to Geometry

Topology is a way of looking at geometry which ignores the fluff of direction and distance in order to focus more clearly on the underlying structures and connections. Graphical Thinking does the same for thinking, it ignores the fluff in order to focus on the structures, the properties of the objects and their interconnections, the frames and the emergent behaviours.

GT and Neural Networks

There is a noticeable similarity between GT's spatial modelling of our understanding of reality, and the interconnected spatial patterns in our neural networks.

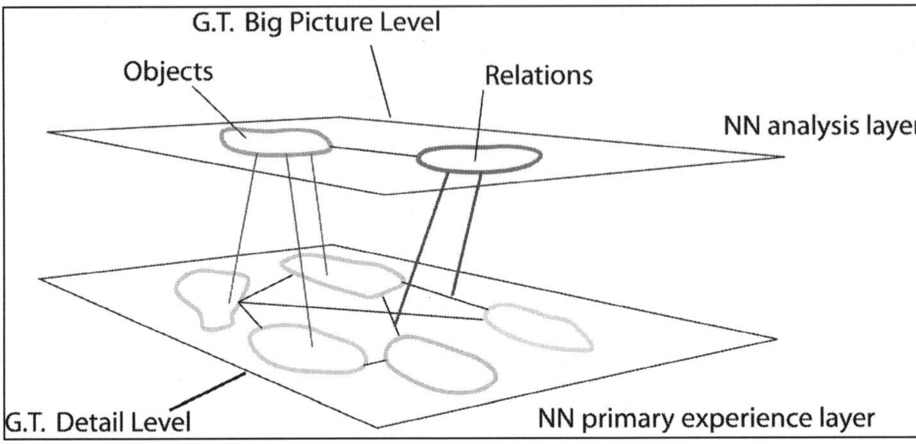

Figure 4.12 Parallels between GT and neural network representations of reality.

My guess is that GT speaks the same sort of spatial language as our neural networks, and this is what makes it such a powerful tool for communicating understanding.

Wider Uses

For Students

GT diagramming can be used to document your understanding of anything. Students can use it to maximise the amount of meaning and understanding they can extract from linear text-based materials - books, reports, plays, lectures, etc.

For example, here is a diagram I made as I read "The Long Tail", by Chris Anderson. It does not represent the entire contents of that best selling book, just the bits that jumped out at me, given the current state of my neural network.

It's an explanation of the New Economics of the Internet. In the old days, when production and distribution costs were much higher, it was difficult for new products to enter the market place. Only products that were expected to have very high sales (potential hits) were allowed in.

This is the economics of **scarcity**. A few potentially high selling products competing for scarce and very expensive shelf or broadcast space. This resulted in a bland homogenised culture in which we all had to settle for the commonality of the lowest common denominator big sellers (although it produced some very high quality products as well).

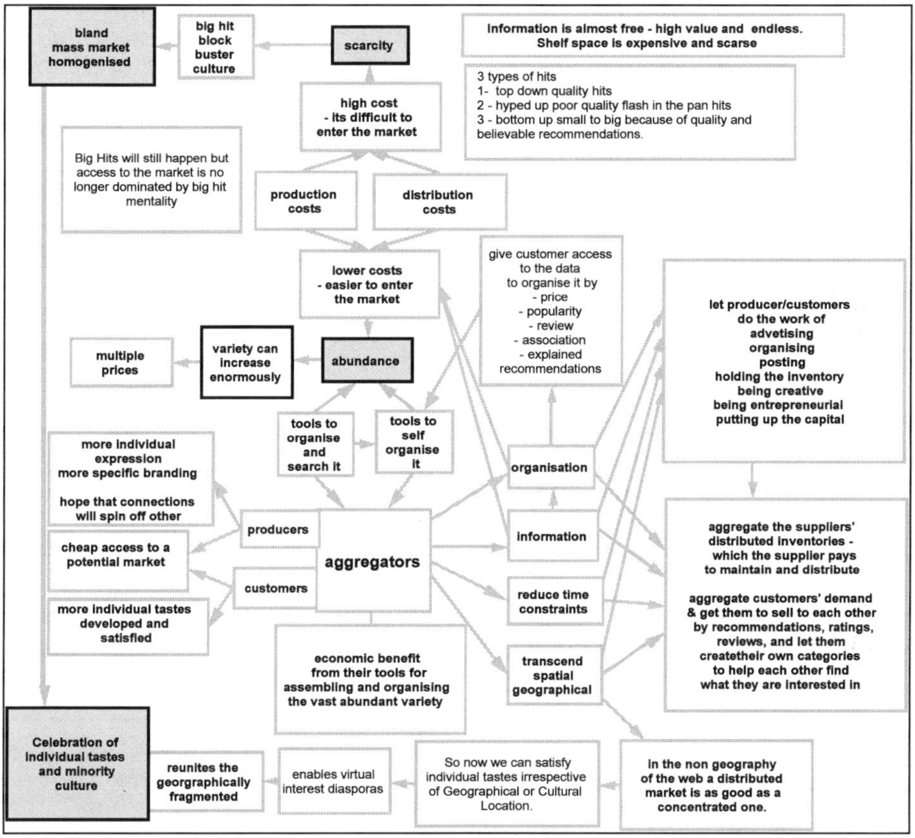

Figure 4.13 New Internet Economics.

The internet, and other computer-based technology, lowered production and distribution costs for some items, making it easier for them to enter the market. This greatly increased the variety of goods on offer, and the variety of prices for the same goods. This is the economics of **abundance**. Now the main problems are: how to find what you want (when you may not even know that you want it yet), and how to reduce the risk and hassle of it turning out to be rubbish when you get it.

The aggregators (Amazon, Google, etc.) created database driven tools to enable us to search and organise the data. That made it a bit easier for us to find stuff. But the predefined categories, keywords and genres can be a hindrance as well as a help. If I am looking for music tracks that feature a particular instrument, or a particular session musician, then the usual music industry categories are not going to help me. Now we are moving towards tools that will enable us to start self-organising the information. We can search and sort by ratings, recommendations, price, etc. We are told that customers who bought this, also bought that (associations). Believable, unbiased, reasoned recommendations turnout to be very important in driving sales – that's customers selling to other customers and the aggregator gets the commission. Very clever.

So by providing these tools to help us find what we want in the vast variety of everything, the aggregators can bring together millions of remote distributed producers and customers at very little cost. In an amazing stroke of genius, the aggregators get the customers and the producers to do almost all the work: advertising, informing, organising, posting, holding the physical inventory, being creative, being entrepreneurial, putting up the capital.

Who benefits?

- The aggregators make a lot of money on millions of small percentages.

- Both producers and consumers get cheap easy access to a huge market.

- The producers get much greater freedom of expression and more specific branding. They may not make much if any money, but they may strike a chord and create a quality driven hit on the basis of solid networked recommendations, and they hope to attract attention and respect that will spin off monetary rewards in some other field.

- The customers get to develop and satisfy more individual tastes, and benefit from variable pricing – in fact a lot of things are free in order to attract our attention to other paid services.

There are some principles at work here:

- Shelf space and physical storage is expensive.

- Information is almost free to store and distribute.

- Organising information adds value to it. It can be pre-organised and or self-organised.

- The cheap storage, organisation and distribution of information, transcends the old limitations of time and space. You don't have to travel to a book shop on the other side of the world to find out if it still exists and what they have for sale, the information can come to you for nothing.

So now:

- A distributed market is as good as a concentrated local market.

- Both the producers and the customers get cheap and easy access to a potentially huge market.

- We can create virtual distributed communities of common interest, anywhere in the world, reuniting the geographically fragmented.

- We have gone from bland mass market lowest common denominator homogeneity to revelling in individual interest and individual differences.

Old style quality based hits will still be possible but seem to be getting smaller. New style quality driven hits are definitely possible, driven by recommendation. Hyped-up poor quality hits are probably on the way out.

Fascinating. And now that I have diagrammed it, I understand it, I have consolidated it in my neural networks and I will remember it.

For News Hounds and Journalists

You can use GT to build up a deeper understanding of topical events from a number of different partial and over-focused news reports. If you experiment with this, you will find that newspapers present you with the detail that x number of people were killed in a battle at some time and place, but usually don't give much information about the big picture. Why are these people fighting? What different groups are involved? What are their different perceptions and goals? What is incompatible about their viewpoints? What is the history of the problem? What international forces have been pulling strings behind the scenes? Who is making money out of it? Who stands to gain what? Etc. When you try to diagram the information in daily news reports, you soon realise how much information is missing. Journalists could use GT style diagrams in conjunction with text, to paint a much more comprehensive picture of the deep structure of the situations they report.

From Text to Understanding

The process of extracting high-quality understanding from a piece of text is much the same, whether you are working with a science textbook, a Shakespeare play or a newspaper report. Start by highlighting the main things and concepts. Our language is good at naming things, so these will usually be fairly obvious. If it is well written it will be quite easy to extract a pretty full list of the important elements. If it is not well written you may be left wondering whether or not you have got a full list, or whether some of the elements have been referred to several times, but using different names each time to avoid repetition - which is considered good style in some publications.

Then look for information describing the **properties** of the things, and the **interactions** between them. If it is well written is should be reasonably easy to work out the character, motivation and capabilities of the players, and their relationships. If it is not well written you will be reading and rereading between the lines, trying to guess why x fired 6 rockets, why the king abdicated, why they interviewed the spokesperson from the bank, or the opposition party. It can take a while to build up a comprehensive diagram from an averagely vague and shoddy text. Stay calm - just put a temporary "?" on your diagram to show that this element has not been clearly explained yet, and concentrate on the bits that have been explained. As you read further, or look at more reports of the same event, you will hopefully be able to fill in many of the gaps, and correct some of your earlier mistaken assumptions. You may notice, and want to record, that there are conflicting interpretations being presented by different commentators. Bit by bit, you build up a richer understanding of the situation and begin to realise that each of the different observers have placed their own subtly different frames around the same events, and are therefore emphasising some aspects and ignoring others. They are reporting the same situation from different perspectives.

And finally, look for the circumstances, the events. What were the important triggers that caused the king/war lord to react in that way, the companies to merge, or the oil price to rise.

It is an interesting aspect of text-based communications that they can leave you with an initial feeling that you have been clearly told what is going on, but when you look at it diagrammatically you begin to notice significant inadequacies in that text-based information flow.

Practise. Use it frequently. Involve others. Explore its ability to embrace more than one person's view of the world.

Committee reports from your local council can be a good source of text-based materials for practicing your Graphical Thinking Skills. They read initially like a complete set of ideas. It seems somehow reassuring to know that they have carried out a risk assessment and agreed a timetable for the consultation phase of the review of the strategy and will be following best practice in the development of the action plan. But as you start to diagram the content of the report, you may discover that there are glaring omissions, vaguenesses, contradictions and inconsistencies.

Job descriptions are another fine source of practice material. I recently analysed a job description for a classroom assistant, which went on at length about facilitating relationships with parents and carers, teachers, head teachers, other professionals inside and outside the school, contributing to the development and monitoring of support programs for identified pupils, the keeping of records in accordance with policy and procedure, etc., but not once did it refer to any interaction with pupils in the classroom.

Policy Officers -

can use it to 'join up' their thinking, and work through the real world consequences of their single-department-perspective policy initiatives. What effects might a particular housing allocation policy have on the catchment area of local schools, or on community cohesion, for example?

In recent years there has been a trend towards 'partnership working' and a noticeable blurring of responsibilities. Instead of an identifiable body being responsible for a particular process, we now have partnerships in which a number of agencies are all committed to supporting each others' relationships with client groups, in pursuit of a tick box list of outcomes.

This new way of working has given rise to a new style of language and it has also given rise to a new feature in GT diagrams. In the old way of working, things had relationships with other things. Teachers taught Students. In the new way of working it is very common to find that things have relationships with the relationships between other things. Teachers, assistants and advisors all support the student's relationship with the learning resources.

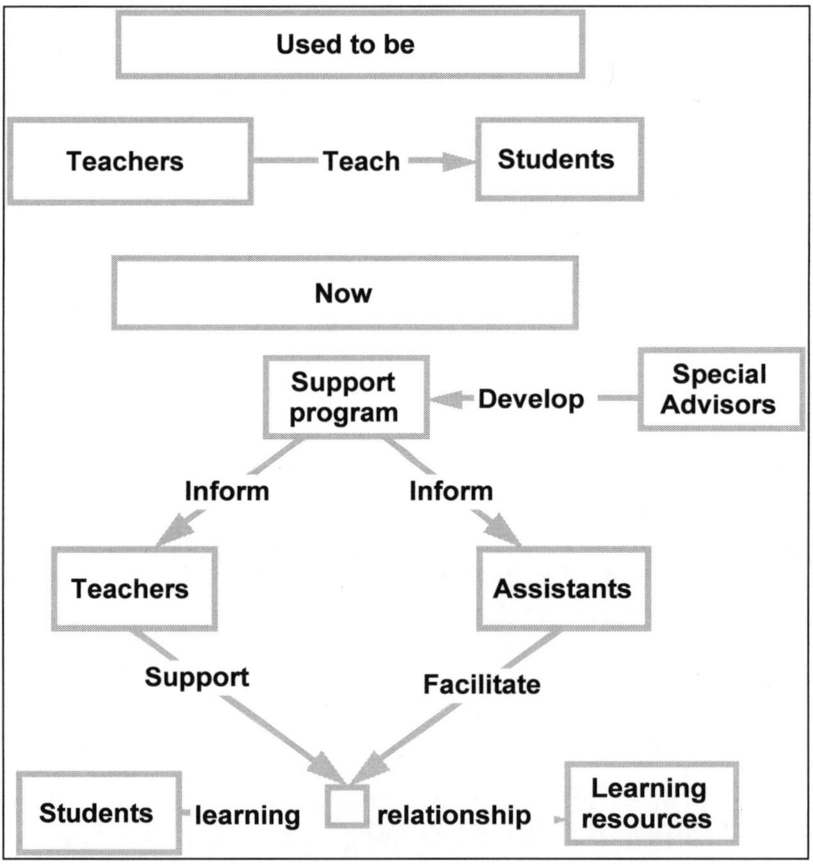

Figure 4.14 Relationships with relationships – but who is responsible?

Model Making, Problem Solving and Thinking

This book suggests that thinking and problem solving is primarily about building and maintaining useful dynamic mental models of the world.

As it is not possible to carry the whole world/universe in your head, evolution has arranged for us to carry **cut-down** mental models of reality instead. Just as a model car only represents selected aspects and approximations of a real car - so our mental models only represent selected aspects and approximations of reality. In cutting reality down to get it inside our awareness, evolution has decided which aspects of reality we can represent and which we cannot.

Our internal mental models of reality are so convincing that we forget that they are only models. We mistakenly believe that they are reality. Hence the expression, 'the map is not the territory', which is intended to remind us that our current models of the world are at best gross simplifications, probably inaccurate in many respects, and that we should always be prepared to **update** them in the light of new information, or **adjust** them to fit **changing contexts**.

Models

A business computer system is a model. It reduces real life customers to their name and address, contact details, account details, purchasing history, credit rating, socio-economic group, benefit entitlement, market segment classification, etc.

A toy car is a model, it represents certain aspects of the proportion, scale, shape, colour, and appearance of the original, it has wheels that turn, doors that open, but it is not made of the same materials, it does not have all the functionality of the real car.

Models only represent approximations of some of the features of the original, and they lose lots of other detail. What you keep and lose depends on the context, and what you want to use it for.

The fact that the brain can so easily be taken in by these cut down illusions tells us a lot about human perception, about the way our neural networks model reality. Skilled artists, sculptors and cartoonists are so accomplished at the manipulation of human perception that they can present us with experiences that seem almost more real than reality. We can build mental models of imagined realities, and they can be so convincing that we come to believe they are real. This problem is probably more common than any of us care to admit.

Modelling is automatic. Our neural networks organise themselves into models that represent our accumulated real or imagined experience of objects, ideas, their properties, their interaction, etc. Once these neural network patterns are established, we can make enquiries of the mental model just as we can make enquiries of the business computer system. How many customers? How much did they spend?

Just as an aircraft designer builds a scale model of a plane to study how it behaves in a wind tunnel, so we can explore our mental models to work out what might happen if the boss finds out about X, interest rates rise, or the other party wins the election.

Building Blocks

A child's Lego kit comes with a relatively small number of pre-existing elements, types of building blocks, which can then be assembled into a lot of different models.

Our mental model making is rather similar. We need to have pre-existing experience of a range of conceptual and experiential building blocks, before we can assemble them into mature mental models. Once we have got those building blocks we can use them in lots of different settings.

So – prior **experience** is essential to problem solving and creativity. Unless you are privileged to receive divine inspiration directly from the muses, there is no substitute for developing a deep pre-conscious exposure and conscious understanding of the fundamental building blocks needed for model making. These are the same fundamental thinking elements that were first identified long ago by the Ancient Greeks and others. They have re-emerged (through a process of evolution) as the fundamental building blocks of our computer programming languages, and have now been rediscovered at the heart of our neural network construction of human perception.

GT is specifically designed to work with these building blocks, but it is only one of many different graphical tools we can use to represent and communicate our internal mental models. We also use technical engineering style drawings, computer-aided design software, multi-dimensional graphs, artist's impressions, physical models, flow diagrams, time lines, mind maps, etc.

School-Style Problem Solving

In schools, the thinking behind a typical problem-solving session goes something like this.

From all the possible real life problems and goals that we could use to give our children experience of real world problem solving, we select a typical school-type of problem. The problem is described, usually in writing, and a **goal** is set. This will usually be one, or perhaps a combination of:

- a correct answer by a correct method;
- make something that satisfies some criteria;
- come up with a plan of action.

Learning, as in, understanding something about the structure of the problem domain, may be an accidental bonus, but is not usually the primary objective.

Perhaps this is because the educators' view of the world is framed by their need to find ways to assess the children's ability and performance. The targets they are working towards do not require them to show that the children can understand or solve real life practical, emotional, moral or commercial problems.

The Goals

There are several types of 'correct answers'. Usually the teacher is looking for a number, a formula, a proof or a statement.

Most of us know quite clearly what is expected of us when the goal is a formula, or the number of tins of paint required to paint the markings on 10,000 road humps, but when the question asked for a proof, then I for one was always very confused. It is possible that I was skiving off to avoid the weekly spelling test on the day proofs were explained, but I don't think so. As far as I know nobody ever explained to us, at school, college or university, exactly what they meant by 'proof'.

Proof

The idea of a 'proof' crops up quite a lot in real life, but it is a word which is very often misused, usually to undermine someone else's opinion (where is the proof?), or to exaggerate the benefits of the persuader's argument (blah blah blah... which clearly proves that...X! – when actually, it does not prove it at all, but it sounds good.)

It turns out that there are different types of proof, different approaches to proof. The gold standard is the **formal logical Euclidian** style of proof, so called because it was developed / written about by Euclid, who was, guess what, an ancient Greek mathematician 325 BC – 265 BC. He is best known for his treatise on geometry, *The Elements.* This work profoundly influenced the development of western mathematics for more than 2000 years. Euclid's geometrical proofs became the model for modern logical (and legal) style proofs and arguments.

This type of proof is as good as it gets. It provided a solid foundation for serious science and technology, and thus it has had a profound effect on our everyday lives.

The general idea is that if we **follow this method**, we can explore our understanding of the universe and build up a body of knowledge with a very high degree of certainty of truth.

The Euclidian Method

(expressed in modern language)

1) Start with a set of agreed **axioms**. These are very clear simple basic statements and definitions. Here are some of Euclid's axioms concerning shapes and space:

   1. A point is that which has no part.

   2. A line is breadthless length.

---

   15. A circle is a plane figure contained by one line such that all the straight lines falling upon it from one point among those lying within the figure are equal to one another.

   17. A diameter of a circle is any straight line drawn through the centre and terminated in both directions by the circumference of the circle, and such a straight line also bisects the circle.

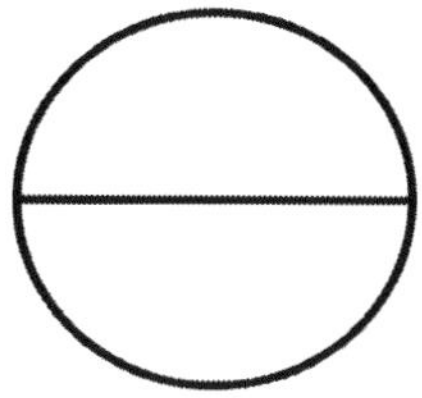

23. Parallel straight lines are straight lines which, being in the same plane and being produced indefinitely in both directions, do not meet one another in either direction.

2) Specify a list of allowable **constructions** or **transformations** that can be assembled from the axioms.

e.g. draw a straight line from any point to any point.

3) Agree a set of **symbols**, that can stand for quantities, transformations, operators and concepts e.g.: length of a line, size of an angle, middle of a line, 1, 2, 3, 2_2, 3^2, +, =, etc.

4) Define the **'Rules of Deduction'** - stating how you are allowed to combine and manipulate the axioms, and the symbols. This includes a **syntax** = an agreed set of rules for combining the symbols together, e.g.,

2x X 3b results in the same value as 3b X 2x
2x - 3b may not give the same result as 3b - 2x

At each step in a finished logical proof, the author explains what **axioms** have been used, and how they have been **transformed,** using which of the **Rules of Deduction.** The end result is called a **'Theorem'.** The process is called **'Deduction'** (= leading logically step by step according to the rules, **from** a few elemental established truths (axioms) **to** many new accepted conclusions).

The world of mathematics builds proofs in much the same way, but is less pedantic. To speed things up it assumes it is speaking to a knowledgeable audience who already accept a set of tried and tested tools and processes, binomial theory, calculus, etc. They do not seek to justify and explain every step, but they could if they had to.

It is a game. It starts with a set of axioms and definitions, which **may** be an attempt to model the real world, or they may be entirely imaginary.

It has sets of rules, a tool kit of acceptable ways to manipulate, transform and combine symbols and formulae. The game is to wind the handle and explore the world of consequences that can follow from this clearly defined starting point.

This is very similar to a game of chess. The board, the pieces and their properties are defined. It is loosely based on the idea of a battle, but it is not intended to be an accurate representation of any particular battle. There is a small set of rules (allowable transformations) describing the starting position of the pieces and legitimate moves the pieces can make. Wind the handle, and you find that an enormous number of different games can be played.

To interact with science, maths has developed a set of symbols, to enable it to refer to aspects of real or imaginary worlds - the speed of light, velocity, resting mass, relative mass, force, acceleration, etc., and to represent real and imaginary quantities. It has a well-developed syntax built up over thousands of years.

If you stick to the rules, then your conclusions are accepted within the rules of the game. In the case of maths, the rules and tools have been successfully applied and improved so many millions of times that they are considered to be a very reliable mechanism that can safely be used to explore the universe.

Science doesn't deal with proof in the Euclidian sense. It gets an idea about how some aspect of the universe appears to work, and sets up experiments designed to destructively test the idea. The more times they fail to break the idea the better the idea is considered to be, but, in theory, scientists are never sure or certain about anything. In practice, however, scientists' neural networks work much the same as everyone else's, and they have strong pre-conscious emotional commitments to their ideas, perceptions, professional groups and paymasters.

The Euclidian method and style of proof is clearly (in some respects) the best we have, but it is hardly ever applicable to the kind of problems that occur in everyday life, which are usually very short on axioms, and rich in vague language, hidden agendas, incomplete information, ambiguity, probabilistic cost benefit analysis, risk assessments, etc., and rely heavily on the brain's intuitive pre-conscious neural network style thinking.

There Are Several Other Approaches to Proof

Trial and Error

Here we look to see if something is true in all the possible (imaginable) circumstances. If there are too many, or an infinite range of, possibilities, we shrink them down to a manageable representative sample. We often use a grid or table, a database or spreadsheet, to keep track of the interaction of all the variables.

Counter Examples

This method tries to prove that X is true, by showing that lots of examples of **not** X (the counter examples) are **false.**

Double Contradiction

Archimedes made great use of this method – proving that figures A and B have equal area, by showing that contradictions would arise if A was **larger** than B, **and,** if A was **smaller** than B. So they must be the same. This is a very solid style of proof with very practical applications.

Persuasion

Would it convince others - particularly your enemy? If you look 'proof' up in a dictionary, it will probably talk about using evidence, reasoning, trials, testing, and demonstration, to establish a **fact.** This is persuasion not proof in the Euclidian logical sense of the word.

The legal (and theological) model

This relies heavily on an accumulation of transferable principles, criteria, filters, and rules of evidence, established by respected authorities in previous cases. An English law court thinks of proof as meaning 'beyond all reasonable doubt' (in criminal cases), and 'the balance of probabilities' (in civil cases).

So if someone wants you to prove something, it is a good idea to find out which game you are being asked to play.

Analysing Arguments vs. Exploring Deep Structures

In the traditional school problem-solving model, students are encouraged to **explore the problem statement** in order to make sure they have understood the **question.** Of course it is very important to be clear what you have been asked to do, but this phase in the process would be even more productive if they were also encouraged to **explore the deep structure of the problem** (including the context, the boundary, the perceptual filters and assumptions), and not limit themselves to the question as it has been presented.

The most recently proposed school level thinking skills courses focus on the analysis of manipulative texts. The students are presented with a number of different, biased and incomplete, media reports of, for example, a topical conflict somewhere in the world.

The task is to decide, or rather guess, which of the conflicting reports of the number of people killed are most believable, and give reasons for their opinion.

The students are required to:

- devise criteria for evaluating the credibility of the different articles;

- identify the claims made, the assumptions implied or relied on, possible alternative explanations, the inferences that are intended, and any factors that strengthen or weaken the claim;

- find points of corroboration and points of conflict, balance the evidence, make a reasoned judgement.

The stated learning outcome is to learn to analyse and evaluate ideas and arguments, and to construct clear, logical and coherent lines of reasoning.

This is all about learning not to be taken in by shoddy manipulative text, it is not about learning to model reality. Argument and evaluation are important but they are not enough. The students are not asked to work out the deep systemic structure of the situation: who is involved and why they are fighting?

We should be teaching students how to **understand**, how to **model** situations. That would involve scanning the documents to see what we could find out about the deep structure of the situation. This would naturally include evaluating the evidence, looking for bias, exaggeration and incompleteness, but would go much further into clarifying what exactly do we mean by phrases such as 'insurgence' and 'angry pockets of resistance', (resistance by whom, to what?). Who exactly are the 'Fedayeen guerrillas' and how would you recognise one?

This would help students develop generalised skills and techniques for **understanding** complex situations, and build up their practical experience of a wide range of transferable model-making building blocks, which could then be applied to many other real-life problem-solving situations.

Strategy

It is currently fashionable to ask very young students to come up with a 'strategy' for solving a problem.

This is idealised rationalised grown-up speak. An **experienced** adult who is very familiar with a particular domain, with the full range of available problem-solving tools, and who is consciously aware of the range of possible 'strategies', might be able to say which strategy would be most likely to lead to a good result in that particular context.

An **inexperienced** child who has not been shown all the tools, let alone had time to build up an experience based understanding of their strengths and weaknesses, their potential uses, what kinds of problems they work on, and what a strategy 'is' - has little chance of growing in their problem-solving ability, as a result of being asked to say what strategy they are going to use.

It is actually quite a strange question when you consider how many real-world grown-up group-think driven strategies get quietly thrown in the bin after about ten minutes exposure to the real world.

It often feels as if **strategy** has become more important than **understanding.** Perhaps the post-modern dislike of the notion of truth has infected the notion of understanding as well. Strategy should be used to support understanding, not as an alternative to it. All strategies should begin with the development of a shared familiarity with:

- the background - the deep structure of the problem domain: the building blocks, the language, the underlying logic and connections, the traditions, standards, theories, methods, etc.

- and the available tools: their uses and limitations, how, where, when, and why to use them.

Then you can start to think about strategies for solving problems or designing new products.

Of course it is a good idea to review problems, after they have been solved, in order to build up a shared conscious awareness of the different ways of going about solving problems - what worked, what didn't and why? - but **exploration** and **experience** come way before **strategic awareness** in our neural network learning curve. As we are exposed to, and reflect upon, a wide range of strategic successes and failures, we will naturally develop a sense of strategy.

Here are some examples of the 'tools' and 'strategies' commonly referred to in school-type problem-solving exercises.

School Tools

(all maths based)

- Use **arithmetic** - for modelling the world in terms of quantities and ratios.

- Use **geometry** - for working with space, shape, area, volumes, and angles.

- Use **graphs** - visualising formulae, ratios, data sets shown as lines on graphs, time sequence, dependencies, connections, etc.

- Use **algebra** - for rearranging arithmetic equations - useful for finding missing values - or working with the laws of physics. For example, Ohm's Law, Volts = Amps times Resistance (V = IR) can be rearranged as I =V/R or R=V/I, to express it in the most convenient form for the problem in hand.

- Use **simultaneous equations** - using algebra to find the missing value which would satisfy two or more equations, usually by using the techniques of *elimination* and *substitution*. We need to be aware of what it can and can't achieve, for example, if you have two unknown values in one equation, or three unknowns in two equations, etc., then it can't be solved by algebra.

- Use **vectors** and **matrices** - for working with three (or more) dimensional transformations.

- Use **calculus** - for quantifying the effects of change, non-linear trends, the distance travelled by an accelerating body, etc.

- Use **statistics** and **probability** - for dealing with uncertainty, trends, investigating correlations as indicators of cause and effect.

School Strategies

- Look for patterns.

- Use a table - to explore the interaction of all possibilities, or a representative sample.

- Simplify the problem - reduce it to a manageable size, or solve a simpler problem.

- Consider extreme or critical cases.

- Trial and error - estimate, check, estimate again.

- Work backwards from what you do know.

- Draw it.

- Google it.

Not enough attention is paid to everyday problem-solving tools such as: filing systems, indexes and cross indexes, brought-forward files, relational databases (great for searching for patterns in data), spreadsheets, statistical analysis packages, etc.

Not enough attention is paid to gaining experience with diagnostic equipment and techniques for measuring, length, distance, volume, angles and heights, pressure, temperature, speed, frequency, volts, amps, ohms, weight, force, types of substance (gas emissions, spectroscopy, etc.).

Not enough attention is paid to gaining experience of the properties of materials, and of the huge range of tools we have developed for manipulating the shape of materials: computer-controlled lathes and shapers, casting and injection moulding, and a vast array of hand tools and fixings (screws, bolts, rivets, glues, welding, etc.).

In science and design technology classes, students have the opportunity to encounter many of these experiences, but not usually in a diagnostic or problem-solving context.

The current school-style problem-solving model focuses mainly on just three tools: arithmetic, basic geometry and basic maths. These three tools are extremely valuable in many everyday problem-solving situations, where we very often do need to work out how much, how many, what volume, what angle, which option is best, what will it cost (per unit, in total, now, and later)? What else could we have done with the money? How many bricks do you need to build the house? How much fabric is needed to make the dress? How many dresses can be cut from one roll of fabric? What angle to cut on the end of the roof rafters? What volume of concrete is needed for the foundations? In what sequence must the materials be delivered to the building site? How much heat will be lost through the walls, windows, roof, etc. - so how powerful will the central heating boiler need to be? How much CO^2 will it produce?

The school approach seems to assume that a little bit of exposure to basic arithmetic, maths and geometry is all the preparation you need before having your (innate?) problem-solving ability tested. This ignores the many other ingredients that go into effective problem solving in the real world.

Such as:

- Practice at maintaining a productive state of mind, an attitude that is: inquisitive, observant, careful, flexible, creative, organised, calm, active, positive, persistent, realistic. What questions to ask (very important)? What to do if you start to feel overwhelmed, defeated, confused, frustrated?

- The desire to solve it, the motivation to master the situation. Developing a taste for that pleasurable neurochemical buzz that comes with effective creative problem solving and using your brain to gain control over the problems that arise in life. The idea that it is cool to be smart and effective in the world.

- A repertoire of constructive presuppositions and internal dialogue. For example:

  every problem has at least one solution;

  everything is possible if you understand the problem and have the right tools, and resources;

  there can be many workable solutions, and lots of different ways to get there;

  problems are interesting and fun (not humiliating tests designed to expose your stupidity).

  If you don't know the background or the tools, then of course it can appear very difficult – but that does not mean you are stupid, you just haven't collected the necessary understanding and knowledge, yet, or have not been shown the right tools and how to apply them, yet, *so* –

  if you are stuck, ask - find out more about the deep structure of the problem and the available tools.

- Experience of the behaviour of dynamic systems, familiarity with the amazing and often surprising world of the emergent properties of simple systems. Conscious experience of using systems modelling tools, and an understanding of a few basic systems concepts (feedback, homeostasis, teleology).

- Foundation experiences from different domains, which have been analysed and generalised to create a conscious repertoire of transferable problem-solving building blocks, concepts, tools, ideas and methods.

- Experience of using, and then consciously reflecting on, a wide range of problem-solving and diagnostic tools and techniques (not just maths).

- A level of mastery in the precise use of the necessary language and vocabulary, particularly if it is to be a group effort.

- Experience of constructive social cooperation, balancing submission to group expectations with intellectual independence, familiarity with the complexity of group dynamics and the dangers of group-think.

Formal education is not paying enough attention to these areas. Rather than focussing on whether or not a child has come up with the right answer by the right method, we should be finding out where they have got to on each of these 'dimensions', what gaps, blockages and misunderstandings need repairing, and what experiences they need next, in order to progress on their journey.

Experience

The brain has evolved to learn by experience. Work with it. Give students real problem-solving experiences, and maximise the benefit of those experiences by reviewing, analysing and generalising to build up a raft of conscious, communicable, transferable problem-solving resources.

For example, there is more to understanding shape than geometry. If you want to experience the potency of shape, take a gearbox, a motor bike engine or a dress apart. It works because of the shapes, and the choice of materials, designed into every one of its interacting components. Then look at the geometry that went into refining the design, and manufacturing the components.

For a different experience of shape, go to an exhibition of Rodin's work, or any other great sculptor, and think through the creative process of imposing a mental idea on a lump of rock. Look at the traditional tools and processes used to shape the materials. Rodin's 'Dancer', the gearbox and the dress have more in common than we realise.

The real-world values problem solvers, and creative thinkers. These transferable problem-solving building blocks are very versatile and can be used creatively and proactively, as well as reactively. They can be used to design new products, new systems.

They can be applied in all domains (social, moral, political, military, scientific, technical, commercial, etc.) and in all the professions (the law/justice, accountancy, government, business and commerce, welfare, warfare, culture, education, history...). Transferring these mental resources between domains can very often bring refreshing and productive new insights.

Perhaps the school curriculum should be expressed as hierarchical pyramids of these fundamental factual and conceptual building blocks. That would provide an excellent basis for both teaching and continually assessing the student's progress and performance. If a diagram of the route map through each of the subject pyramids was on display in every classroom, the students could monitor their own progress and ask for help on any of the stages that were causing them trouble, obstructing their progress.

Real -World Problem Solving

Let's look briefly at a very common practical example of problem solving.

Suppose your car engine is running badly. How do we go about solving the problem? Well, it rather depends on how much you know about how the engine works. If you don't know much about it then your chances of diagnosing and correcting the problem are not good, so you may have to pay someone who does understand it.

If you can, manage the environment so that you are safe, comfortable and can think clearly. If possible, remove any time pressure, as you know from experience that it is difficult to think clearly, and test what may need to be tested, if you are in a hurry or stressed. Try to imagine you are very rich and money is no object, as it can be difficult to think clearly and diagnose the real cause of the problem if your pre-conscious mind is screaming 'Please let it be a small problem, don't let it be expensive to fix'.

In something as complex as a car engine, there could potentially be many different causes of the problem. In many cases you can only directly experience the result of the problem = the **symptoms** = the **emergent properties**. The root **cause** is often hidden away from view. So first, you must look for evidence of unusual behaviour as this may be a good starting point from which to home in on the root cause.

Use your senses to look at the initial superficial symptoms: unusual noise, vibration, temperature, smells, leaks, visual appearance (discolouration due to excessive heat, a broken or detached wire, a broken belt, etc.).

Then you might contrast its static and dynamic symptoms. Do the symptoms change in particular circumstances: only when going fast, or slow, or up hill, or changing gear, or starting, or stopping, or going around sharp corners?

Then you might look for less superficial symptoms. What is the condition of the cooling water (is the level too high or low, has it got traces of oil in it)? What is the condition of the engine oil (is the level too high or low, has it got traces of water in it)? Remove the oil filler cap to check for unusual pressure or smoke in the crank case. Is there visible smoke at the exhaust? Test the exhaust pulses with a piece of thick paper or plastic (are they evenly distributed?). If you have access to the necessary the equipment, measure the exhaust gas emissions.

Now you are into invasive testing. Remove the spark plugs, test the electrical spark, does the condition of the spark plugs tell you anything? Is fuel reaching the cylinders? Is the spark happening at the right time? Is there multiple or intermittent sparking, or evidence of short circuiting? Test the cylinder compression, etc.

The general point is that you must first have an idea (knowledge, a mental model) of how it **should** be working, which you can compare with evidence of how it actually **is** working. That involves detailed observation and testing. Testing can be via your senses: vision, smell, touch, even taste (I don't recommend it); or it can be via some piece of equipment for measuring the world in ways which we can't do directly with our senses.

Electrical test meters measure volts, amps, resistance, and dwell angle, or turn invisible electric currents into a visible light or numerical displays. You might use a device to make accurate measurements of physical sizes and distances, (micrometer, feeler gauge) or other physical properties such as temperature or pressure.

Nowadays, you might plug in a laptop computer running some specialist diagnostics software, to see what that has to say about the problem.

But none of this information will be of much use to you if you do not understand how the various sub-systems of an engine interact, and that requires some knowledge of physics, the properties of materials, engineering standards and traditions. The more you know about (the better your model of) the deep structure of the situation, the more use you can make of the diagnostic observations and test results.

At some point you will get an idea, an assumption, as to the cause of the problem. If it is quick and easy to rectify the assumed cause, you just do it, and see if the engine runs properly. But if it will cost a lot of time and money to correct the assumed cause, you will probably want to do some more testing first, to be more certain that this really is the cause of the problem, and not just a symptom of some other less costly fault.

This is serious real-world problem solving, on just as high a level as in any other walk of life, but it doesn't look very much like the school model, and seldom uses much arithmetic, maths or geometry[7].

An engine is a complex system of sub-systems. Interacting symptoms can be hard to read. Background knowledge and experience has a very high value in such situations. Any experienced problem solver knows that it is not uncommon to pass through a number of very well-reasoned and convincing but false assumptions, before finding the true root cause.

How does all this relate to the notion of proof? Well, the proof of the pudding is in the eating. You can only be sure you've understood and solved the problem, when the problem has definitely gone away and everything is working, in all normal situations, as it should be.

The logician and the mathematician can be sure at every step that they are following the rules of the game, but as a problem solver, you must constantly be aware that you will be swimming in a sea of possibly false assumptions until the problem is resolved - by a combination of luck and judgement.

The logician's axioms are the mechanic's fundamental understanding of the deep structure of the situation: the design of the engine, the interaction of its subsystems, the underlying physics, computing and engineering, and the properties of the materials.

The logician's symbols and syntax are the problem solver's knowledge of all of the separate components: how they can work together, what cannot work together, and the language to describe it all.

The rules of transformation are the problem solver's knowledge of all the available tools: what they can be used for, the tests they can perform, and the transformations they can bring about; and the cost, availability, performance and interchangeability of replacement parts. If they are not available you need to know how to repair them or make new ones.

A Generalised Problem-Solving Model

Can we use GT to represent a general understanding of problem solving?

[7] It was during the design of the engine, that arithmetic, maths and geometry played a crucial role - along with knowledge of the properties of materials, the chemistry of fuels and combustion, techniques for shaping materials, etc.

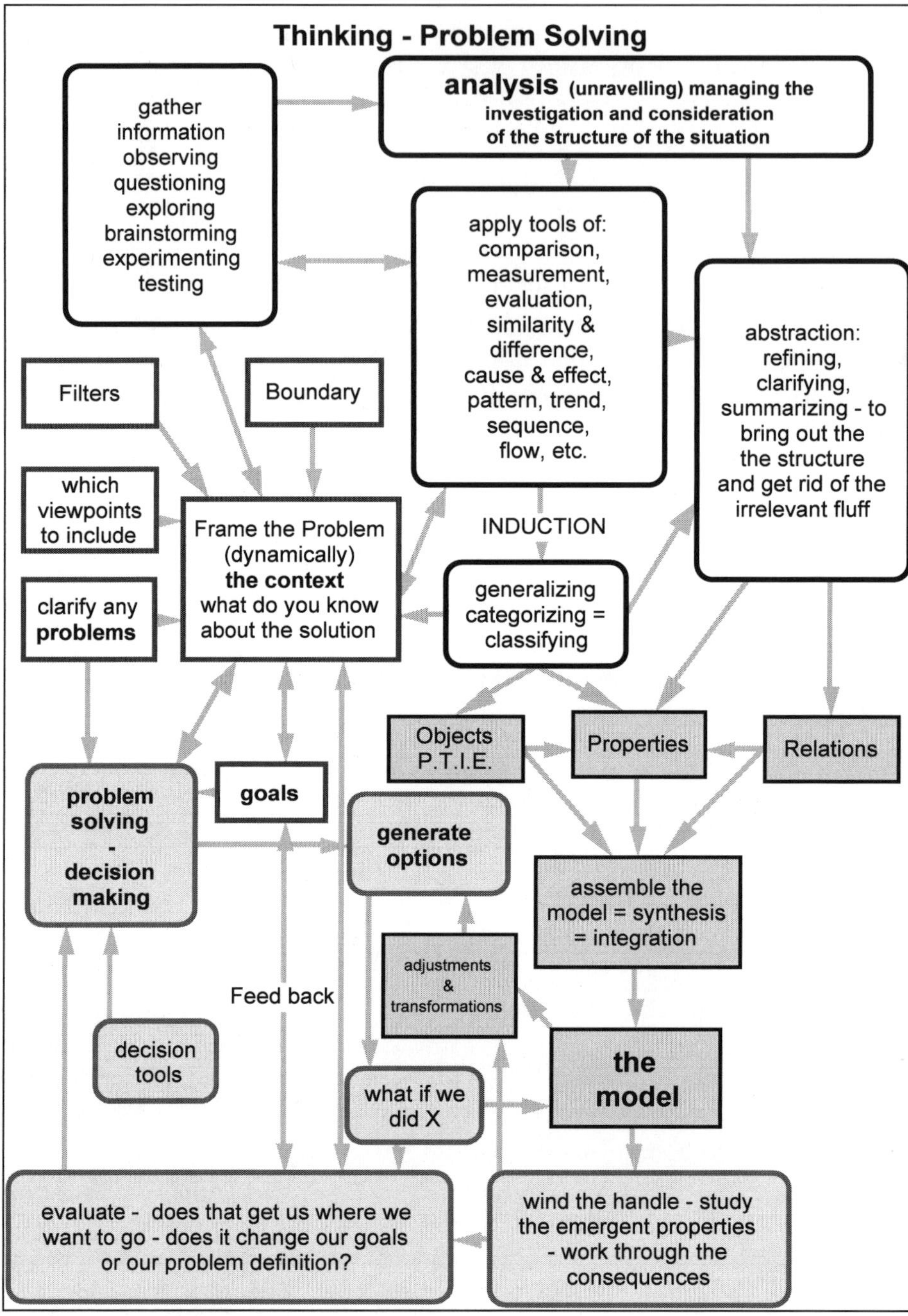

Figure 4.15 Problem-solving model.

At the top is the analysis process, the management of the investigation into the structure of the situation. We gather in information, and we look for significant stable elements. These might be People, Things, Ideas or Events (P.T.I.E.). We classify or categorise them by looking at their similarities and differences. We look at the way these things behave and interact, their capacity to affect each other, the range and circumstantial limitations of their capabilities, patterns of activity, trends, sequences, relationships of cause and effect, etc. Ever mindful that we live in a sea of false assumptions, we repeatedly test our latest understanding, taking measurements and setting up experiments to test out ideas. We know from experience that a single viewpoint can produce a flawed and incomplete perception, so we try to look at the situation from many different points of view, deliberately looking for what we may have missed, particularly when we have assumed something was obvious.

The analysed information is generalised and abstracted, and built into a GT model (centre right) that contains all our knowledge about the nature and behaviour of all the participating elements, and the subtle nuances and limitations of the relationships between them. Winding the handle, and exploring the emergent properties of the model will suggest ways in which the situation can be adjusted and transformed.

Upper centre left - we have the problem and goal framing process. What do we know about the problems we are trying to overcome and the goals we are trying to achieve? Whose viewpoints are we looking at it from? What is the boundary, how far are we prepared to go to get a solution? What filters are we imposing? What aspects of the situation are we interested in (economic, mental, spiritual, cultural, ecological, environmental, political, marketing, PR, etc.) and what are we excluding? What methods and practices will we accept and reject en route?

The framing of the problem can be dynamic and iterative[8], as it may be influenced by the information that comes to light in the analysis, or in the exploration of the consequences of possible actions. Changes in the problem definition may mean we need to adjust the scope and focus of the analysis.

Now we are into the problem-solving phase, winding the handle to generate a range of options that will hopefully have the effect of getting us to our goals without creating any more problems. The options are evaluated: what are their consequences, are they worth the effort, do

[8] Iterate - from Latin for again

they change our understanding of the problem or the framing of our goals?

The answers may be intuitively obvious. If not, we may need to employ some mathematical decision support tools to help us decide which of the model's predictions give the best solution.

Then we try the best solution in the real world. Hopefully it works just as the model predicted. If it doesn't, we have potentially got some useful information to be added to our model of reality.

The final problem is to decide when to stop. If we have worked hard but have not found a satisfactory solution, then at some point it may be sensible to stop trying. Even if we have found a satisfactory solution, we might find an even better one if we keep trying. It is not an easy judgement because it is impossible to know how much effort it would take and how much better the improved solution would be, if we find one.

Most of this activity takes place in our heads, with occasional experiments out there in reality to see if the predictions are accurate, and to test if the mental model is still an accurate representation of reality. The balance between the mental and practical depends on the nature of the problem. If you are a rocket scientist trying to get a space probe to Mars, you do most of it in your head (with the aid of computer simulations). If you are a sculptor trying to beat a piece of metal into an interesting shape you do most of it out there in reality. There is a story that the Americans designed their space rocket motors with a lot of expensive computer simulations and the Russians built theirs using a lot of cheap trial and error, (build it, fly it, see what happens, learn). The Russian rocket motors were much better, more efficient and cheaper to build. After the Soviet system collapsed the Americans bought a job lot of surplus Russian rocket motors. I don't know if it's true.

How Does This Dynamic Approach Contrast With The Usual Critical Thinking Model?

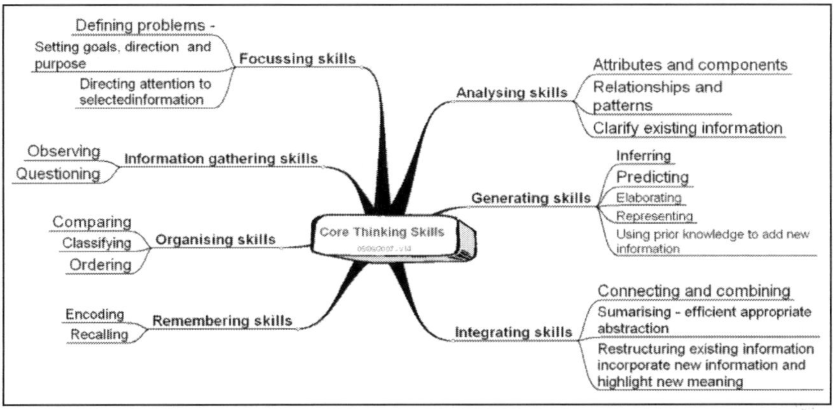

Figure 4.16 A typical critical thinking model with isolated components.

This is a mind map style diagram that represents a fairly typical 'Critical Thinking' style approach to thinking and problem solving. As you can see, it chops thinking into a number of separate isolated skills. This particular map represents the ideas in a document advising teachers to plan lessons that focus on the development of each specific thinking skill, in isolation, such as 'analysing' or 'information gathering'.

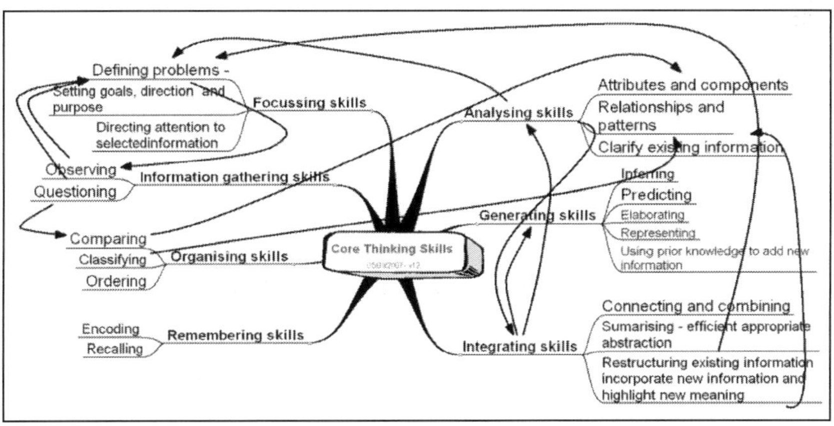

Figure 4.17 Connecting the isolated parts.

This amended version of the diagram seeks to demolish the idea of the separateness of these skills, by identifying just some of the interconnectivity that is involved in real-world problem solving. For example, in order to be able to **analyse** something into its **attributes** and **components,** we must surely get involved in **classifying, comparing, ordering,** and **integration,** before we can assemble the elements into a model that shows the **relationships** and **patterns.** If I put all the obvious interconnections onto the diagram it would become a blur.

Problems with Language

Some of our essential logical words (is, are, causes, all, some, etc.) are fundamentally vague and commonly misunderstood.

For example:

Is (and Are)

There are problems over the exact meaning of 'is' and 'are'. What do we mean when we say, 'this **is** a table'. A table (the physical object) is not exactly equal to its name 'table'. A thing is not its name, it is a collection of properties and relationships with the world. If we say, 'the table <u>**is**</u> green,' we are only describing one of its properties, one small aspect of its existence. If we say, 'it <u>**is**</u> a coffee table,' we are either describing one of its properties, or its membership of a particular class of tables. So **is** does not usually mean =, but the brain often assumes that **is** does mean =.

Is often becomes **All**

If you say, 'X is Y' – people very often assume that you meant that **ALL** Xs are Y.

Direction of Causation

We often jump to wrong assumptions about the direction of causation. This happens when our neural networks interpret 'X causes Y' as 'X and Y are associated'. **Association** is a link that works in both directions, but **causation** only works in one direction. So we jump to the assumption that 'X causes Y', also means, 'Y causes X'. This is much more likely to happen at the beginning of the learning curve, or in domains where we have no personal experience of the relationship between X and Y. If you know that sour apples cause stomach ache, you are not likely to jump to the assumption that stomach ache causes sour apples, but if I said that the movement of masons causes fluctuations in the strong nuclear force, you might well assume that variations in the strong nuclear force can cause massons to move as well. (NB I invented massons, as far as I know they do not exist.)

Causes (and is the only cause)

If you say 'X causes Y', then it is very common for people to make the assumption that X **is the only** cause of Y (it has no other causes), which may be true, but is not necessarily true.

This weakness in our language contributes to what is known as the single cause fallacy. It enables politicians (and others) to entice audiences to adopt over-simplistic single-cause models of what are actually complex problems with many interlocking causes.

You might think that the solution to these problems is simple. We just have to be very much more precise in the use of words such as: all, is, are, some, may, might, can, does, must, should, sometimes and always; and we must remember to make it clear when something is **not the only cause**, there are other causes as well. But even precise use of these words is often misunderstood. This is best demonstrated with a diagram.

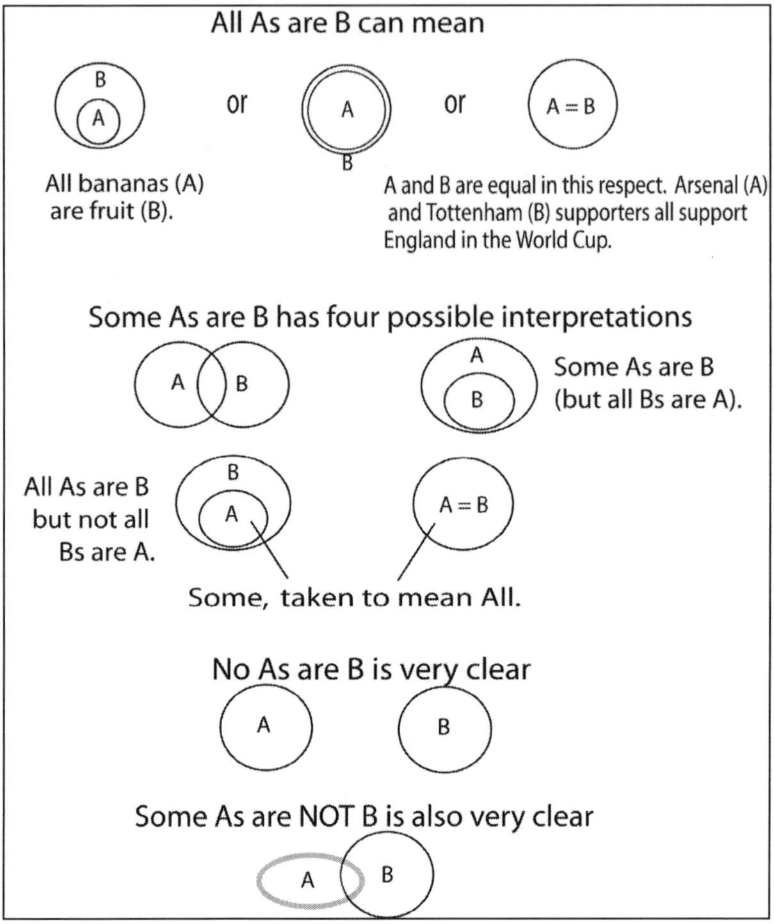

Figure 4.18 As are Bs.

So, when someone says, 'Some As are B', we have the opportunity to jump to three wrong assumptions as to what that says (if anything) about Bs relationship with A.

These tricks of the brain are not as crazy as they might seem, because our neural networks have observed that in real-life, 'all' very often does work in both directions, and 'if' very often does mean 'if and only if'. These assumptions have a probabilistic value in the real-world, and that is what our pre-conscious neural networks have evolved to deal with.

The way to reduce this kind of problem is to take care to specify these relationships in **both directions**. For example, all As are B **and** some Bs are A, and then specify exactly which Bs art A.

We Over-Generalise

In everyday speak we often say **always**, even though we know that it would be more accurate to say **sometimes,** or **occasionally.** The same distortion happens with **never** and **no one.**

We Leave Out the Quantifiers and Qualifiers

It is very common in persuasive manipulative style language, to leave the quantifiers out altogether, because the persuaders know that in the absence of a quantifier most people will assume **all.** This is a very handy way of getting around the law in situations where someone wants to imply **all** but it would not be legal to actually say **all.**

'Celebrate Diversity' seems to be an instruction to celebrate **all** aspects of diversity, even though it does not actually say so.

Group-think often encourages these media-friendly sound bite oversimplifications. The idea of 'inclusive education' began with the realisation that it was not always sensible or desirable to educate all disabled people in a specialist environment. In many cases it would be better to educate them, some or all of the time, as appropriate, in the mainstream classroom. Under the influence of group-think this good idea lost its necessary subtlety (qualifiers and quantifiers) and became over generalised. **Everyone** was to be **included** (educated) in the mainstream classroom, **all** the time, irrespective of how inappropriate it was for the individual student, or for the system as a whole.

False Opposites

Another failure of our language / brain interaction is that we jump to wrong assumptions about the opposites of statements.

> The fact that Jane likes warm weather does not necessarily mean that Jane does not like cold weather.

If someone disagrees with something, it does not necessarily mean that they hold an opposite opinion.

We Leave Out Crucial Elements of an Idea:

> Things are getting worse (which things & worse than what?);

> I am happy (about what?);

I am liking it (what and why?);

I am annoyed (about what, with whom and why?);

Things have got to change! (which things, in what way have they got to change, and why?);

It was like, so, you know, whatever ... (????) (perfectly postmodern: relative, non-discriminating, scared to commit to an opinion about properties or behaviour, and 'anything goes').

We Misuse what Linguists call Modal Operators:

I **can't** do it (when actually I am quite capable of doing it);

You **must** do X (why, is it the law, or just your preference?);

This is **necessary** (no - it's my personal choice whether I do it or not);

She **made** me so angry (she made you? Could you not have chosen to react in a number of different ways?);

I **need** X (no, you want X, which is quite different!).

And very often, we have a -

Model Mismatch – a hasty generalisation.

The brain's ability to make very quick decisions about what is going on, on the basis of a mere glimpse, a hint of sensory evidence, combined with a lot of previous experience, has saved/extended millions of human lives, but it is also the cause of one of our biggest problems. The brain gets the wrong end of the stick, jumps to the wrong assumptions and conclusions and then believes it is right. This is compounded by the mechanisms it has evolved to promote stable decision making, which cause it to commit to its existing decisions and resist change until the contradictory evidence is overwhelming.

Common Manipulative Forms of Argument

Here are some common manipulative tricks that seek to take advantage of these language problems. They are often called the **common fallacies.** There are two main ingredients to a good fallacy:

- an attempt to oversimplify, distort, exaggerate or avoid consideration of the **underlying structure of cause and effect;**

- **group-think effects** - based on an invitation to demonstrate what a good group member you are, and the threat of being expelled from the group for non-compliance. This element of the fallacy encourages us to disregard the opinions of anyone who has been declared a bad person, i.e., against the group's interest.

Most of the common fallacies have both of these components.

False Dichotomy

The persuader suggests there are only two choices - one good and one bad option - when actually there are many more options, and or, the suggested values of good and bad may not be justified. For example: either you are with us or you are against us, either you agree to us buying the company or you can kiss goodbye to your pension. Actually, there are always more than two possible options in life.

Causation Errors

The persuader suggests:

- there is a **single cause** (as above) when actually there are many other causes;

- a f**alse cause** - when it is not the cause at all;

- that we read an assumed cause in the **wrong direction** - a version of this is sometimes called **affirming the consequent,** where they say that 'X causes Y' (which may or may not be true), and then they say, 'we do have Y (affirming the consequent), **so** we must deal with X'.

This is designed to **divert our attention** away from considering whether or not X does actually cause Y, and whether there are any other significant causes.

This is similar to the -

Slippery Slope

The persuader says, 'if you accept A then it will inevitably lead to B, which we all agree is unacceptable, so, we must not start down this road' = we must not do A.

This also uses group-think conformity to discourage us from considering whether A (or X or Y) does in fact cause B.

Begging the Question and Circular Argument

Here the persuader makes a statement which pretends to be an argument (sounds like an argument in its rhythm and tone), but really it is just a re-statement of a like or dislike, usually using emotive group-think language. If we don't do X in response to this menace then our children won't be safe in their beds at night, so we must do X. No reason has actually been given for why X is the solution, just emotional pressure to conform to the group's model of the world.

Popularity

Another natural group-think twister - most people (assume everyone) agrees that X is good, which implies there is something weird about you if you don't agree with us, and we won't be your friend any more or ..., or, it must be good if so many people say so, so there must be something wrong with your judgement if you don't agree.

Appeal to Traditional Models

(Used to be called 'appeal to ignorance'.)

The typical form is, 'the reason <u>must</u> be this', what else could it be, there is nothing else it can be, and optionally, 'and it says so in our group's special book'. For example:

> Why did x happen? Its because of Z - it says so in the ***** (and there is no other possible explanation within our model of reality, and we certainly don't want you to upset our group's traditional perspective by even suggesting other possible reasons, OK).

Discredit the Person

Often called 'ad hominem' (meaning, *attack the person,* in Latin). The game here is to attack the person making the argument and thus avoid consideration of the content of their argument. The nature of the discrediting can vary to fit in with any currently fashionable ideology. Recent common forms of this have been - well you sound like a racist (communist, capitalist, socialist, ***phobic, etc.) and we don't want any of that sort of thing here. This style of fallacy relies heavily on the current group-think fashion, and very effectively diverts attention away from the real content of the argument.

Another common form of attacking the person is -

Guilt by Association

Don't listen to him, he used to be a communist, a thief, a fool, worked for the enemy, believed in x, etc. He was **associated** with an idea that went wrong, so we are invited to jump to the assumption that **ALL** his ideas will go wrong, and therefore this idea must be flawed too. Again the aim is to distract us from considering the person's opinions, observations, judgements, predictions, etc. For this style of manipulation to work well, there has to be some known or believable truth in the negative association.

Knocking Down Straw Men

The point about straw men is that they are easy to knock down, and can't fight back. This style of fallacy works by creating an entirely false, but believable, negative impression of the person's intentions, actions, affiliations, etc. - the straw man. Because the basis of the attack is not actually true, it works best if the person is not there to defend themselves. Having created this false impression, we are then invited to dismiss his arguments because of his flawed character, hidden agenda, etc.

These attacks on the person all invite us to focus on something which is not relevant to the argument. The irrelevant something is the **red herring** (the past association, the allegiances, the false rumour, etc.).

Presumably, the reason for trying to distract attention away from considering a particular argument is that it is a reasonably good argument which seems to lead to conclusions that challenge, or draw attention to defects in the group's established beliefs, values, policies, tactics, etc., and which are not in the group's currently perceived self-interest.

Linear Language vs. Diagrams

These language based problems can all be reduced in their severity by using Graphical Thinking.

In a one dimensional linear system (language, text) - to disagree **is** to say the opposite. There are no other options. Everything is either forwards **or** backwards, up **or** down, left **or** right, agree **or** disagree.

Diagramming is multidimensional, so there are infinitely more options. In a Graphical Thinking session, it is possible to question the properties of a relationship, or suggest a refinement to one of the elements, without it being taken as outright opposition.

Group-think, in its most negative expression, is intent on avoiding a shared consideration of deep structures through a balanced assessment of the detail. Even when it is well intentioned, it is hindered by the limitations of our language. It prefers oversimplifying, sloganeering and the avoidance of testing. It makes excessive use of filtering, at the same time as amplifying a few chosen aspects. It prefers to avoid thinking about complex causes and effects, consequences and perverse incentives. It is a process of group denial, which suppresses questioning and disagreement.

Graphical Thinking can cope with complexity, with the big picture and the detail. It is a tool which can be used, if a group has a mind to, to counteract these negative tendencies, and facilitate the construction of a shared inclusive understanding, which harnesses the combined experience of all its members.

The simple act of bringing a group of people together, with the intention of constructing a diagrammatic representation of the deep structure of their situation, authorises the participants to focus in detail on the fundamental elements:

- Categories – have we correctly identified **all** the relevant classes of objects, people, ideas, and their characteristics and capabilities?

- Relationships and dependencies – have we identified everything we need to know about their interactions?

- Emergent properties - have we acknowledged the relevant trends, possibilities, probabilities, incentives and consequences that may result from the dynamic interaction of these elements?

- Do the apparent obstructions actually prevent us getting to our goals, or can we find a way to work around them?

- Frames - are we allowing our usual assumptions or ideological filters to distort our perceptions? Have we considered the situation through enough different filters, have we made enough effort to consider what the situation looks like to the other players?

- Models - have we made enough effort to **learn** from our experiences and to **update** our models? Have we generalised and abstracted appropriately, or have we lost valuable information in moving from rich reality to our cut-down standard model?

Hidden Agendas

People who have a hidden agenda probably will try to distort the process in order to keep it hidden. If the group sets out with the declared aim of looking at everything that seems relevant, it will be fairly obvious if some participants start trying to limit the field of enquiry. So their tactics risk drawing attention to the possibility that something is not being fully disclosed.

In time, many participants come to realise that this holistic graphical method can accommodate and integrate everyone's perspectives, and that their goal satisfaction is best served by open and honest participation. But the reality is that political parties, companies, ideologies, religions, etc., usually think they are in a win or loose competition for scarce resources, and are therefore not happy to participate in open GT sessions, in case their true perceptions, models, values, goals and methods are exposed, thus giving an advantage to their competitors. Hey ho.

Chapter 5

The Possibility of Self-Managed Personal Change

Thinking. The brain. Human perception. What an amazing system. Pre-conscious neural networks generalising from a sequence of experiences to assemble models and meanings that enable us to understand and react to our environment. BUT - is there anything we can do to **change** those models, meanings and reactions **if** they are not getting us the results we want in life?

YES!

First lets review the -

Functions of the Pre-conscious Mind

1) It Looks After the Body, and its fundamental survival responses.

2) It Gives Us our Experience of Space and Time:

> **Space** - our mental impression of reality is organised as a vast spatial map punctuated with **objects** and **places** (and their properties) and **connections** between them (and their properties).
>
> **Time** > sequence > cause and effect.
> We experience time as a sequence of events, experiences and memories. We use this ability to sequence these elements into a story, a narrative about our life. We tend to assume, not always correctly, that things which we experience *before*, are the cause of things we experience *after* - that **causes come before effects.**

3) It Handles our Basic Emotional and Motivational Systems

The words 'emotion' and 'motivation' both derive from the Latin for *move*. Our emotional system gets us moving. There are really only two foundation emotions: towards and away from.

Towards is like gravity. It is a very long range and persistent motivator with the power to reshape the universe. **Away from** is more like magnetism, very powerful at close range but its influence fades away rapidly with distance. The motivation to move your hand **away** from a hot stove will cause you to move it 10cm very rapidly, but once it is out of the danger zone the motivation quickly fades to nothing. From a safe distance, **away from** associations can be almost invisible, but the closer we get the stronger they become.

The motivation to move **towards** things that you really want (and actually need) will carry you a very long way.

Typical Examples

Away from	**Towards**
fear, humiliation, ridicule,	love / attraction,
pain, danger,	pleasure, real needs and goals,
risk, uncertainty, the unknown,	excitement, stimulation, understanding, exploration, experimentation, development, self-expression,
responsibility (preferring submission to authority, following orders and keeping your head down)	responsibility, taking control, giving instructions,
decay, disorder.	life, order, activity.

Figure 5.1 Towards and Away From.

4) It Manages our Attention

The pre-conscious mind focuses our attention on:

- resources it thinks are relevant to our current high priority goals and desires;

- things which don't make sense yet. We pay much more attention to the unexpected, than we do to the common place: the unusual noise in the car engine, the unusually large phone bill, etc. This mechanism plays a huge role in everyday learning, motivating us to explore situations we don't fully understand yet. Maybe it plays a role in maintaining the attraction between the sexes as well.

It withdraws attention from:

- things which are now 'fully understood': established beliefs, accepted truths, rigid models.

It suppresses awareness of:

- things which are too problematic, too destabilising, too distracting.

There is an idea that these suppressed, unresolved, un-modelled, problems can be 'projected out', meaning that we are pre-consciously motivated to get into similar situations where the problem is likely to recur, so that we can find out more about it.

5) It Manages our Sense of Identity

The pre-conscious mind constructs a more or less stable sense of identity which is capable of embracing all the:

- automatic pilot and habitual reactions;
- emotional 'to' and 'away from' motivations;
- skills and abilities;
- temporary ego reaction packages;
- external cultural game playing (thinking and planning);
- moments of conscious conscience.

It creates a personal narrative, a life story which we use to explain and justify this whole variable package to ourselves and to others. If we are not careful we can become a **character in** the story (rather than the **author of** the story), distorting our perceptions and goals in order to fit in with established story lines about our own life.

6) It Traps and Accumulates Experience

Models, Meanings and Motivation

It builds up maps and models of reality, and makes meanings, emotional associations and values, which influence our choice of goals.

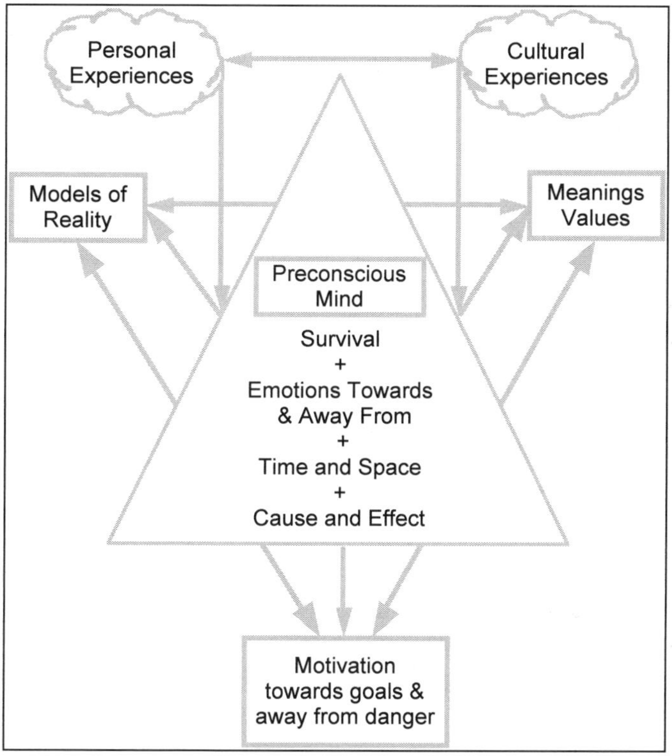

Figure 5.2 Models, Meanings and Motivation.

Passive Perception

In the early stages of the life-long learning curve, the pre-conscious is passively absorbent, soaking up our personal and cultural experiences. Bit by bit, these experiences are assembled into **models about reality** which filter and shape our perception, and influence our decisions and behaviour. The models are dynamic, giving rise to predictions, expectations, beliefs and values. Our personal experience of threats and pleasures creates a set of emotional reactions: towards or away from feelings associated with particular objects, situations, processes.

Our neural mechanisms are good at adjusting and fine tuning current models and associations, but they are not always very good at updating the deep foundations of well established models. As a result, we often get stuck with pre-conscious models and meanings that were formed a long time in the past (when we had relatively little experience of the world), and these old associations can cause us to perceive and react inappropriately to current circumstances. For example:

- if we decided at an early age that X is dangerous, then that old decision about X can become embedded in our models and emotional associations, in such a way that we continue to find X dangerous, despite numerous subsequent experiences in which X does not actually cause us any harm. Or, that original decision about the world may keep us away from X, so that we never get the opportunity to discover that it is not actually dangerous.

- Conversely, we may have decided in the distant past that Y is pleasurable and 'cool', and continue to seek out Y related experiences, despite numerous subsequent episodes which suggest Y is actually quite unpleasant, and that it would be more appropriate to move away from it, not towards it.

So, left to its own devices, the pre-conscious mind can host **out-of-date** models of the world and **inappropriate** patterns of motivation which guide us towards and way from the wrong (inappropriate) things.

Active Perception

With increasing maturity, we gradually move beyond this passive absorption mode, and start to exercise some degree of active control over our perception. If we notice that our default interpretation and reaction to some class of event is clearly not serving us well, then we **can** decide, deliberately, consciously, to change the **meanings** we have associated with that situation, and to **update our old models, reprioritise our values and rethink our goals.** We can, consciously, design new models, new meanings, new interpretations and reactions to past, and therefore, current and even future events.

Updating Old Models

Fortunately, people who study ways of improving human performance have developed a number of very effective techniques which we can use to update these old models and meanings in the light of our most up-to-date knowledge and experience. But first, we have to consciously realise that we are operating from **flawed** models, meanings and motivations.

NLP (Neuro Linguistic Programming) has developed simple techniques for 'rewriting your personal history', travelling back in the mind's pre-conscious time sequence, and deliberately inserting **new** interpretations of **old** events. The preparations may take a little while, but the transformation, the moment when those foundation neural associations are updated, is almost instantaneous. That change then ripples through the associated neural patterning, changing our understanding of that class of event and the emotions we have associated with it. These changes are no different from any other learning process. NLP also has very elegant language-based techniques that are designed to loosen up old perceptual and behavioural patterns and redirect the focus of our attention in new ways.

Graphical Thinking can also be used to bring about deep structural changes in our perceptions and reactions, but it does it **spatially.** By thinking through, and diagramming our understanding of some aspect of our world, we are **consciously examining our pre-conscious models.** If some aspects of our model don't sit well with the rest of our knowledge and experience of the world, the mismatch becomes very obvious, which makes it much easier to correct.

7) It Manages Multiple Emotional Vectors

Our brains can hold many different emotional associations at the same time. I both like and dislike different aspects of my work, where I live, etc. If I look at any topic in detail, then I can discriminate many subtle elements and many different emotional vectors. I am drawn to some elements and wish to avoid others.

Do I want a new job? Do I want to move house? In some ways 'yes', but in other ways 'no'. If all my get-a-new-job vectors are of the **towards** variety, there is a good chance that I will achieve my goal in style. If there are some critical **away-from** / no-go-areas in the package, there is a good chance that I will start out enthusiastically, but never actually reach my goal because the route to the goal is blocked by a potent but short range obstruction. When a project's emotional vectors are not harmoniously aligned, there will probably be a lot of dreaming and discussion, some activity and movement, but not much goal achievement and satisfaction.

The pre-conscious mind handles the orchestration of all these emotional vectors. Most of the time it does a fairly good job, but we all know people who repeatedly start out, with the best of intentions, on projects which (everyone else knows) they will probably not complete because they are ignoring or unaware of some crucial away-from vectors somewhere in their emotional mix.

The problem arises because away-from vectors are invisible from a safe distance and because the pre-conscious mind is not great at thinking ahead. It sets off in pursuit of a valued goal and proceeds step-by-step, handling each situation as it arises and then finds that it has an aversion to some critical step in the process and can't complete the journey. This lack of foresight can result in us going down a lot of dead ends.

If we use a more conscious strategy, map out the structure of the situation, highlight the steps involved in getting from here to there, and check what emotional vectors we have associated with each of those steps, we can see (feel) in advance where the potential motivational blockages are likely to occur.

A blockage may be caused by an inappropriate old decision that needs updating (as above), or it may be caused by conflicting emotional associations – I want to do it, but it could be dangerous = on the one hand 'yes' but on the other hand 'no'.

Parts Integration

NLP has techniques for resolving these conflicts, integrating the parts, so that we can move through the indecision. The basic principle is to acknowledge that both (all) of the vectors are intent on protecting our best interest in some way, but from different and rather limited perspectives. By rising up to a higher level, the conflicting parts can agree on common shared values (our best interest = the need to make progress in life + the need to avoid danger) making it possible to negotiate an agreement that fully recognises the holistic value of each part's contribution. Accept the challenge but take careful accounts of the risks. 'Yes' takes the helm while 'no' watches for danger from the crow's nest. It may be necessary to update some old dysfunctional meanings and interpretations before this can work effectively.

The idea behind this approach is that many of our problems stem from the way we are looking at (making sense of) the world, and that those problems could be resolved (or at least changed) by looking at the world in different ways, by updating our models, by making new meanings and emotional associations.

The mind is its own place, and in itself, can make a Heaven of Hell, a Hell of Heaven. John Milton (1608-1674), Paradise Lost[9].

Goal Setting

We have seen that our existing **models** and **values** are the result of the passive and active absorption of our **cultural** and **personal** experiences.

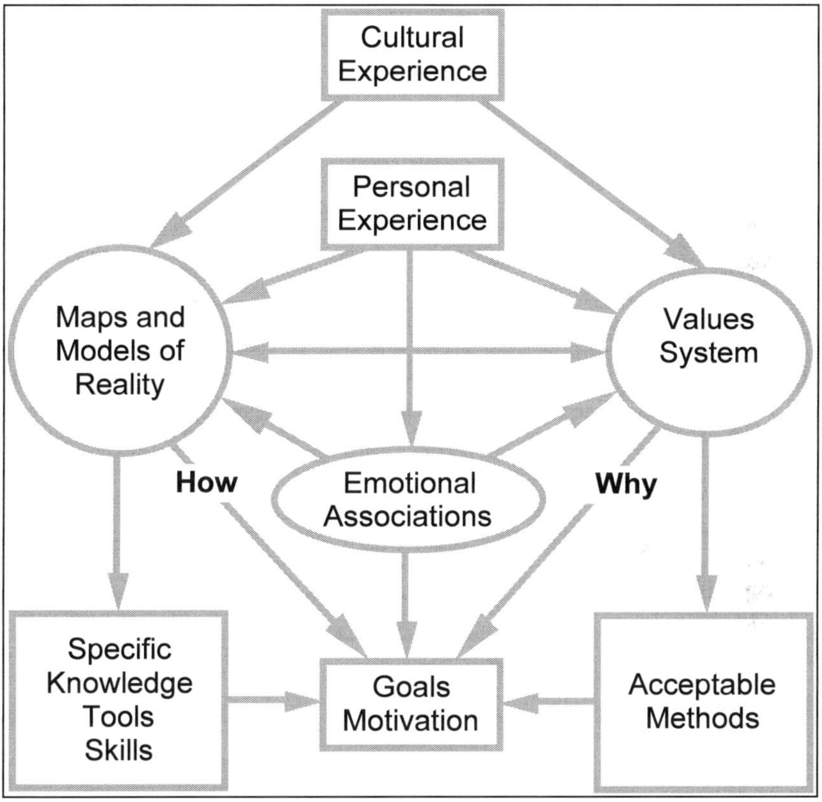

Figure 5.3 Whys, Hows and Emotional Associations.

Our **values** determine **why** we want to do things, **why** it is important for us to achieve certain goals. There are two important types of why. Towards and Away From. If your motivation is driven by a desire to get

---

[9] This widely quoted phase does not actually appear in the book. It's a summary of an idea in book 4, around line 75.

away from something which offends against your values, it will not take you far and it will run out of steam as soon as the irritant is out of range. It is much more effective, and life affirming, to motivate yourself with goals that will take you **towards** the satisfaction and celebration of your values.

Our values also tell us what **methods** we think it is acceptable to use in order to achieve our goals, what we are, and are not, prepared to do.

Our **models** tell us **how** the world is organised and what **knowledge** and **skills** we think we will need in order to achieve our goals and desires.

Our personal experiences, and the decisions we have made about what those experiences mean, leave us with **emotional associations**, likes and dislikes that move us towards and away from particular situations.

Along the way we pick up skills, knowledge and tools that help us deal more effectively with different aspects of reality.

Successful People

People who are consistently good at setting and achieving goals in their life, have clear and motivating value systems, effective models of how the world works and well orchestrated emotional vectors; they love every aspect of what they are doing and their multiheaded egos work well as a team. They either have, or know how to get hold of, the necessary knowledge, skills and resources.

Successful Projects - have the same structure.

Think of a C18th sailing ship setting off to some distant land to trade for tea, silk, spices, etc. For this to happen a lot or people have to work together to agree on a destination and a purpose that will probably provide a big enough reward to outweigh the risks, to pay for and organise the designing and building of a suitable boat, to negotiate insurance against the risks of the venture, hire and pay for a competent crew, and organise a market where they can sell the goods.

The owners, the captain and the crew have to work together as an effective team, just as the Conscience the Thinker and the Multi Headed Egos need to work together to make things happen in an individual's life.

They need a shared values system that says 'this is a worthwhile thing to do'. The WHY has to be powerful enough to motivate the whole team to keep chasing that goal despite being faced with very considerable dangers and risks.

The captain has to motivate and orchestrate the crew's activity so that all their vectors pull in the same direction when it's required. That would not be possible if they did not share a belief in the HOW and a trust that each person had the knowledge and skill to play their part in the process.

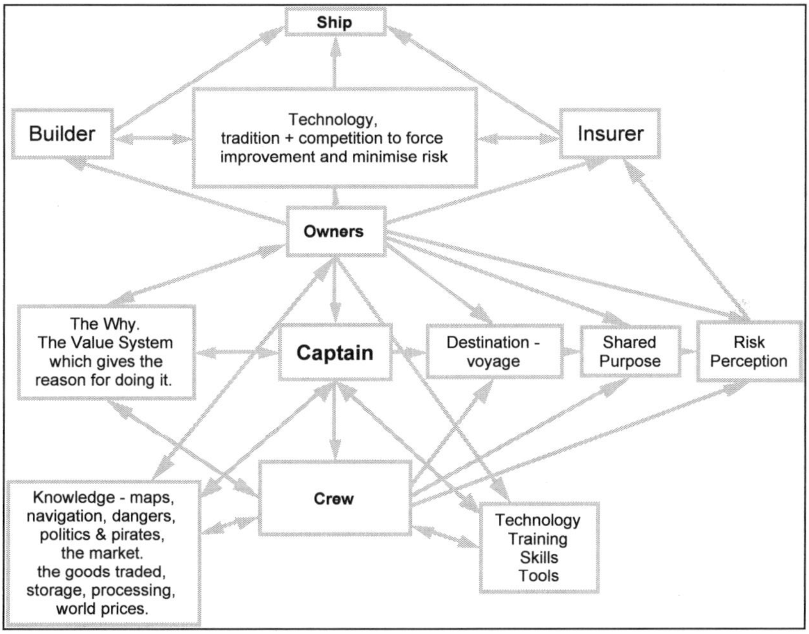

Figure 5.4 The shared models of the Owner, Captain & Crew.

To achieve that, they need:

- to develop skills, knowledge and technology;
- accurate models of the world: maps, charts and astronomical tables;
- accumulated knowledge of tides, currents, seasonal weather systems;
- organised training and qualifications;
- specialist tools: sextants, accurate clocks and mathematical tables, plus all their metal working, wood working and sail making tools;
- knowledge of how to sail the boat and how to repair any damage that might happen to the boat;

- knowledge about the goods they are trading: how to store and process them, and how much they are worth in different parts of the world;
- knowledge of how to store and prepare food and drink for the journey;
- medical knowledge to cope with illness and injuries;
- the ability to frighten off or fight off pirates, privateers and buccaneers.

The project could not happen without all these shared models, and without a harmoniously orchestrated emotional vector map.

Vector Mapping

I recently met a friend of a friend, a young Czech woman, who is making a very successful career for herself as a property developer in London. She is a very good example of a well orchestrated vector map. When she first came to London she tried working in shops but she was sacked a couple of times because her English wasn't good enough. So she decided to buy a shop. She found a freehold property for sale, with a shop at the bottom and a flat on top. She worked out the numbers - the combined rent from the shop and the flat was more than the cost of the mortgage, so she went to a bank, borrowed the money and bought the freehold. Now she has 45 shops and several flats in Mayfair.

She kindly let me spend a few days with her so that I could understand her model of the world, so I could see the world through her eyes. It was fascinating. When she walks down an urban high road she sees numerous opportunities for planning gains, buildings that could have an extra storey or two added to bring them in line with adjacent properties, buildings that could be extended sideways or backwards, separated or knocked together, groups of properties with rear access, whose back gardens could be developed, shops that could be brought up-market to attract a much higher rent, etc.

She sees an abundance of opportunities everywhere she goes, and concentrates on selecting the best of them. When she sees a good opportunity she moves fast. Her surveyor has visited by the evening. (If necessary she calls in the Architect and the Builder as well). If the resale value of the separate units is more than the overall price, and if the income is more (by a suitable margin) than the cost of borrowing the money, then next morning she sees the bank manager, and in 24 hrs the deal is done, 2 or 3 times a week. Her decision making is fast because her business model is simple. Shop keepers pay the rent because they will loose their lively hood if they don't. If they don't pay she can get rid of them very quickly (the law is on her side). With full repairing and insuring leases all the cost of any building problems are passed onto the leaseholders. Residential tenants are much more risky, so she gets full credit checks and references before they move in, and it's often better to simply sell the flats if they cause any problems.

Her knowledge of planning law, tenancy law, building regulations and building construction is not great, BUT she has a solicitor she trusts, a builder she trusts, a surveyor she trusts and an architect she trusts. None of them have ever let her down! So she doesn't focus on problems, she only sees opportunities, checks that the numbers work out and confidently leaves the problems of making it happen to her trusted crew of experts.

Her model of the world is quite similar to mine. We both have an accurate understanding of the HOW. In fact I probably know more about planning law and building regulations, and definitely know more about building construction. She knows much more about the market. I had imagined secret circles who pay a 'premium' to enjoy the first picking of any 'development potential' properties, but actually the vast majority of her projects had not come through that route.

Our **values** are quite similar. We are both active doers, and although I like making money, she is much more motivated by it than I am. I certainly enjoy turning a profit by applying a bit of creative intelligence to practical problems, such as property developing, but her value system drives her to make more and more money even though she already has more than enough, whereas mine starts to focus on other priorities.

The really significant difference between us is to be found in our emotional associations, our **emotional vectors**. For several years I had worked with property in the public sector. Because I was good at solving problems, I was often given the job of sorting out building contracts which had gone horribly wrong. So my neural networks have trapped numerous experiences of the wide range of problems that are just waiting to happen on any building project. I had also built a house with a self-build housing association, a process which turned out to be much more educational than was strictly necessary. As a result of those experiences, I currently do not find it easy to trust lawyers, architects, builders, or the inner workings of the property market. The only professionals to have left a good impression in my neural networks, were the bankers (who came up with the money when they said they would), and the quantity surveyors (whose prediction of the materials needed to build our 18 houses was very accurate indeed).

So although I have more than enough HOW, and just enough WHY, to do what she does, my experience-based emotional associations, my Vectors, make me much more focused on the potential for problems, and my aversion to trusting (and paying) the necessary professionals means that I would no longer enjoy the process, and would not be able to make decisions at the speed that she does, if at all.

This is the main difference between us. **We live in the same world but we see it differently**. That is why she is a successful property developer and I only watch from the side lines. I could only be a happy and successful property developer if I had a team of very competent solicitors, architects, builders, etc., who were bound together in a mutually beneficial, long-term, open and trustworthy relationship – like the one she has managed to create. I would have to constructively reframe my past experiences, recasting them as a valuable resource for avoiding problems and overcoming them if they do occur, as opposed to an over sensitivity to all the problems that will probably occur. But if I do decide to go back into that business, then her model is a good model to follow.

If you want to be successful at something, find people who are already successful at it and study their models, their values, their access to skills, knowledge and resources, and most important of all, find out **how they orchestrate their emotional vectors**. Then have a good honest look at your own package of strengths and weaknesses. What is holding you back? What adjustments would you like to make to your values, your models, your resources and your emotional orchestration? Are there some historical decisions that need updating and reinterpreting, some parts that need integrating? If you really want to change these things you can. It is up to you.

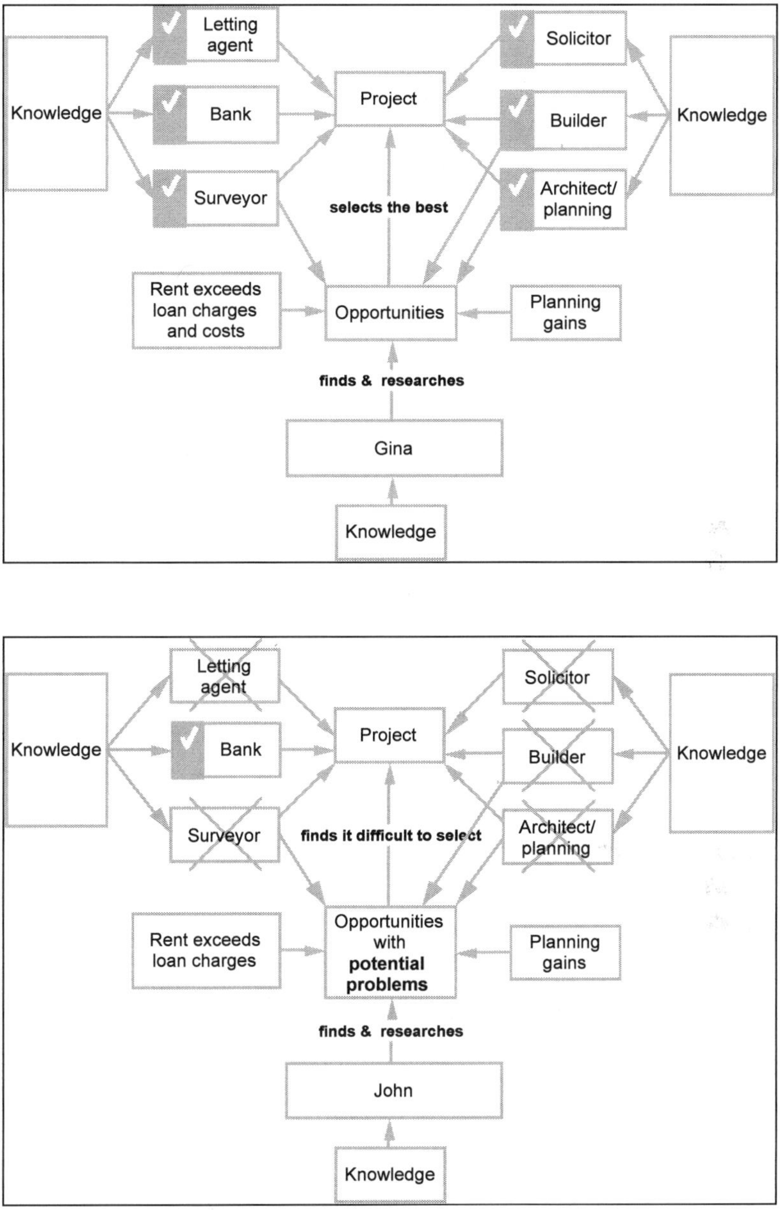

Figure 5.5 Vector Mapping - the difference between John and Gina.

Diagramming the situation is a good way to focus our conscious awareness on the values, models, skills & knowledge, and emotional vectors that are driving, or obstructing, our motivation and effectiveness in life.

If you discover out-of-date and inappropriate emotional associations, update them.

If your current value system doesn't pack a punch, doesn't motivate you, then start work on actively developing a new values system of your own, one that will get you moving.

If your model, your understanding of the external world, says that it is not possible to achieve your goals because you are dyslexic, or foreign, or not from the right social class, etc., then check it out, find out if it is actually true, research it.

Be realistic and then be flexible. It is much better to understand the problem in detail and then find a way around it, than to fall into a state of inactivity because of a vague or inaccurate assumption that something is not possible. And it is definitely a waste of precious time to chase a goal which actually is impossible.

It's OK to change your goals, particularly if it is in response to improved knowledge of how the world actually works. Your high level values can be expressed through many different (lower level) goals, so it makes good sense to morph your goals into new ones that still satisfy your values but are easier to achieve. That way you get more high level satisfaction for less effort – which sounds good to me.

Groups

The same basic vector mapping process can be used by groups, to build up a shared and inclusive map of their combined understanding of the deep structure of their situation, and of their multiple motivational vectors.

If an individual's perception and motivation seems a little bit complex, then a group's perception and motivation is at least one level more complex, because it is a collection of individuals. But there is a further level of complexity. As is so often the case, new group-level properties emerge from the interaction of many individual components. So, a human group can develop a personality of its own which is quite different from the sum total of the personalities of its members, and may not be fully shared by any of those individuals.

Groups can have their own:

- emotional triggers;
- communication styles;
- models of reality;

- value system;
- approved methods;
- approved explanations;
- taboos and no-go-areas;
- strategic allegiances;
- perception of options, risks, rewards;
- approved goals and choice of tactics.

For insiders, the tension between the individual and the group's perception and motivation is usually bridged by a system of rewards and punishments, which gives rise to a whole new set of dynamics.

To outsiders, a group's perception and framing may appear quite distorted: too limited, too simplistic, too local, over focussed, ego-centric or hypersensitive; or it may appear too large, too global, too insensitive, too habituated, etc.

The different ways that different groups model and conceptualise our shared reality is the main cause of inter-group conflict. Their behaviour is determined by their model, their way of looking at the situation.

If a group sees the possibility of a solution in which all the competitors can satisfy their goals and values (win win), it will behave very differently from a group that thinks that the only way for it to satisfy its values and goals is to destroy, consume or change its competitors.

Clearly there are many subtle graduations between 'win win' and 'win all or loose all', but it illustrates the point that inter-group behaviour is determined by their framing and conceptualisation of the situation. But that is a big subject for another book.

Do We Create Our Own Universe?

New age spirituality says we create our universe.
Neural network research says we create our **experience** of the universe.
These two viewpoints observe similar results, but explain them by different mechanisms.

I can explain the mechanism by which I actively create my perception of reality, and I can directly experience the results of any conscious changes I manage to make to the way I look at reality. But I would have to resort to a leap of faith, a belief, in order to accept that the universe actually changes in response to my thoughts about it.

Either way, the effects are much the same. The people around us appear to become even more like our opinion of them. If we focus on what we like in a person, they appear to become even more likeable. If we focus on what we dislike in a political party, our dislike increases. People who are grateful, experience abundance, people who fight against what they don't like, experience conflict and frustration. This has important implications for how we organise society.

Internal or External Causes

A lot of people get upset when they perceive social inequality. If they think that the main causes of the inequality are to be found 'out there' in external reality, then in accordance with their model of the world, they attempt to change external reality with: tax credits, minimum wages, qualifications for all, life long tenancies and the like. But this view of the world underestimates the extent to which we create our own experience of the universe, and the effect that our models, values and emotional associations have on whether our lives are chaotic or organised, impoverished or abundant.

Perhaps the reason the external-reality-interventions frequently fail to reduce the perceived inequality, is that the inequalities are actually caused by differences in the way people perceive reality, and not by reality itself. (John and Gina for example.)

Some people feel that this is a rather heartless approach to the issue of inequality. Some politicians calculate that it would be bad for votes to suggest that the way we perceive and react to the world could be a significant factor in the quality and quantity of our physical and emotional circumstances. But if it is 'true', then it could be the key to the self-improvement of many people's lives and would greatly reduce objective measures of inequality as well. So it is not heartless at all, it is just a different model of the causes of inequality, which suggests different solutions.

Clearly some problems are more 'out there in reality' than others. Dirty water, inadequate sanitation, pollution, disease, tribal warfare, gang warfare, modern slavery and feudalism, the machinery of international trade agreements, drought, starvation, earthquakes, etc., definitely contain a significant element of external reality. But even in these situations, there is a contribution from our internal perception as well. Some people choose to move away from active volcanoes, hurricane zones, war zones, political and economic oppression, etc., and others don't. Some people choose not to work for, or buy from, organisations that exploit or enslave the poor, or entice consumers to buy products with known health risks, because it does not make sense in their value system. Others see it differently. Both groups think they are doing the right thing, given their models of reality.

So

If there are ideas in your head that you think are less than constructive - diagram them, bring them up from your pre-conscious, and into the light of conscious reason. Where did these ideas come from? How much experience did you have when your brain made the decision to interpret things that way? Is there a more productive way to make sense of your personal and cultural experiences, given that you now know so much more about the world?

Wow! Have I gone all postmodern? Am I saying that it is quite OK for things to mean whatever we want them to mean - that there are no absolute meanings?

Well yes, in a way. Think about it. We make up meanings all day long. It is very difficult to think of any generalized rights or wrongs that could not change their meaning in a different context. For example, we all agree that should never ever stick knives in people - unless you are a surgeon. Only when the context is pinned down to a very specific time, place, and situation, can we say that something is good or bad in our value system. And even then some new piece of information may come along which changes our evaluation. So, act with your highest integrity in mind, from your conscience if possible, and actively design good useful productive new meanings that will work well for you, and for others, now and into the future.

Good luck.

Word List

Abstraction - the idea of moving away from the detailed physical phenomena and up towards the essence. In this book it is used to mean defluffing: removing the irrelevant or recurrent fluff to get to the generalized essence. For example, we don't need to know whether Einstein came up with the idea of relativity on a Tuesday or a Wednesday.

Action plan - a set of instructions, usually in the form of a document that specifies who is responsible for each task and when it should be completed by. It doesn't usually contain much information about why the action is required, or how it fits in to the big picture.

Algorithm - a rigid set of instructions for solving a particular type of problem. Very common in computer programming: do this, then do this until X, but if this, then do that, etc. Unfortunately the idea is often misapplied in the design of call centre scripts, and phone menu systems, which spend insufficient effort finding out exactly what type of problem they are dealing with and thus impose an inappropriate set of inflexible steps.

Analyse - exploring, examining, testing, etc. - to separate something into its parts with a view to understanding its deep structure. From Greek for *unravel* - as in unraveling a knotted ball of string.

a priori - the kind of knowledge we feel quite certain about, even though it does not seem to be based on experience and is difficult to demonstrate or test. From Latin for *from what is before* (before experience).

Argument - one or more statements that are used to provide support for a conclusion. A solid or sound argument meets three criteria:

1) 2 or more acceptable and consistent premises;
2) premises are relevant and provide support for the conclusions;
3) missing elements are identified and evaluated.

Assumptions - ideas, models, bits of models, that we automatically / habitually use in our thinking, but which we have not consciously checked or tested in this context.

Attention - our pre-conscious mind keeps a continuous and wide ranging lookout for signs of danger and possible resources, but our higher and more conscious thinking processes require that we focus our attention much more precisely.

Attribute - a property (characteristic or quality) of a thing, relationship or system (adjectives & adverbs).

Awareness - that portion of the universe that we are paying pre-conscious and or conscious attention to at any particular time.

Axioms - small precise accepted chunks of truth.

Bias - a socially unacceptable level of perceptual distortion, predisposition, prejudice (pre-judgement). It's all a question of degree because all human thinking (with a neural network) is inevitably based on these fundamental processes.

Belief - at the end of the learning curve our neural networks start to become saturated, insensitive to new information about a particular domain, and can no longer learn from new experiences.

Category = Class = Kind = Sort = Type - different words from different languages to describe a group of things with similar (but not necessarily identical) **properties** and **relations** with the world.

Categorizing - getting clear about the main essential and variable properties of each class of thing you are dealing with. Your brain has already, pre-consciously, created these categories for you, but you can check if your pre-conscious model of the world is up-to-date by drawing a GT diagram of the situation. By doing this you'll become more consciously aware of the properties and connections of the pre-conscious categories you are already using. So GT diagramming is a way of ensuring that your perception is up-to-date and appropriate to the current context.

Compare - looking for similarities and differences in properties, relationships, and cycles of probability and possibility.

Comprehend - (Latin for *seize,* or *grasp*) to make an internal mental model of something.

Concept - in this book it usually relates to a process (e.g. teaching, designing, shaping, monitoring) or a perceptual filter (e.g. socialism, capitalism, profit, investment, progress, sustainability) which tells us which aspects of reality are important and which are not.

Conclusion - in critical thinking speak we arrive at conclusions by reasoning from premises and evaluating evidence. In this book we argue that it is a more accurate reflection of how our neural networks actually work, to think in terms of trapping experiences and building mental models, which we might call a belief, an opinion, a model or a map.

Context = frame = systems boundary - sets limits on what we need to pay attention to. The system boundary usually has properties such as filters, amplifiers, and values, which tell us the relative importance of the elements within the system boundary.

Continuum - the idea of a linear sliding scale between extremes of some quality or quantity.

Correlation - a relationship between two (or more) things (variables), in which a change to one coincides with a change in the other(s), and maybe it is mutual. If they both rise and fall together it is a positive correlation, if one rises when the other falls its an inverse correlation. Maybe the correlation is an indication of a cause and effect relationship, but it maybe that they are both just the effects (results) of another cause which has not been identified yet.

Create - to bring into existence.

Critical Thinking - an academic style of thinking that focuses on the quality of the conclusions arrived at by inductive and deductive reasoning from valid premises and the evaluation of evidence.

Credible - likely to convince someone that it is true - or a useable model of reality.

Cycles of probability and possibility - during the life cycle of a tree, for example, there are a range of things that can possibly happen and there is a pattern of things that will probably happen. It will probably start as a seed, grow into a sapling and then a full grown tree of its species, and end up as either a pile of rotting wood on the forest floor or maybe a piece of furniture. It will not turn into a tree of a different species or a cow. Our categorisation of the ever changing world into stable classes of objects is based on the similarities we detect in their properties and relationships, and in the range of possibilities and probabilities they exhibit.

Decision - a more active and pragmatic version of a conclusion.

Deduction - this book sees deduction as the application of our mental models of the universe, mental models which were built up by induction, by trapping, generalising and abstracting from a series of personal and cultural experiences. (see Reasoning, for the critical thinking version.)

Dependent Variable - if two variables are correlated, then a change made to the independent variable (the one you can influence) should result in a change to the dependent variable (dependent on the state of the independent variable).

Dissertation - a detailed discourse, usually a part of an academic degree.

Distinguish = discriminate - to be consciously or pre-consciously aware of differences in the properties and relations of two things. Discrimination is the starting point for model building with a neural network. If we can't detect differences, similarities and associations, we can't learn.

Distortion - the human brain has lots of pre-conscious and conscious mechanisms which cause us to ignore, exaggerate, adjust and even imagine experiences. We do this for many different reasons: to reduce anxiety, to increase certainty, to maintain a stable perspective, to improve our social standing, to manipulate others, etc.

Epistemology – the study of knowledge (Greek *episteme* meaning *knowledge*) – thinking about how we know things.

Epitome – (see quintessential) – a perfect example of a class.

Equal (identical? similar? like?) - usually means has the same value as, but can also mean has the same properties, relationships, cycles of possibility and probability ...

Estimate (guess? predict? extrapolate?) – use your mental models to predict what is likely to happen next, or **if** x....

Evaluation - in critical thinking we weigh or balance the evidence to see how well it supports the argument. In a wider sense it means to refer to a pre-existing value system which tells us what things are worth relative to each other. Without a **value system** we cannot evaluate anything, be it evidence, actions, methods, allegiances, design quality, or financial results.

Event – a bunch of connected stuff happening in a context. Our neural networks are good at spotting connections and associations between events that are closely connected in time and or space. We are very bad at modelling things which we haven't experienced or which appear separated in time or space.

Evidence – in critical thinking, evidence is anything that establishes a fact or gives good reason for believing something (they are thinking of witness statements, test results, documents, etc,). In this book the idea of evidence is rather larger and could include any experience that stimulates activity in our neural networks.

Example (see specimen) – something that illustrates a general rule, or a thing that shows the same properties, relations, possibilities and probabilities as the other members of the class (category, group, sort, kind, type, etc.).

Examine - inspect, test, question, looking for properties, relations, emergent processes, cycles of possibility and probability, etc.

Exception - a thing that does not follow the general rule, or does not have the properties of the group or system.

Explain – tell a socially acceptable story.

Experiment – a way of exploring reality and testing the predictions or operation of a model.

Fallacy – a mistaken, faulty, misleading idea.

Fantasy (from Greek *phantasia* appearance) - too much imagination and not enough reality.

Fidelity – accuracy, truthfulness (from Latin *fides* faith).

Forgetting – an essential ingredient of learning – releasing old models to replace them with new models.

Framing (see context) – the system boundary, the extent of your interest. Get this right and it can save your resources (as you don't have to pay much attention to what is outside the frame). If the frame is too small you will ignore crucial influences on the system. The frame is the practical implementation of your priorities, your conceptual filters, and the view points you are going to consider. Our brains do so much of our context framing in pre-conscious automatic mode, that it is a very good idea to enforce the simple discipline of always consciously considering the frame.

Games - humans play lots of different thinking games. Each game has its own socially agreed rules for what to pay attention to, what to ignore, what's important and what is not, what moves and transformations are allowed, how to explain things to different audiences, rights, rituals punishments, etc.

Generalisation (see reasoning / induction) - moving from a lot of similar observations to a general understanding of how things are. For example, unsupported objects fall downwards.

Goals (aims, objectives, targets, desires) - pre-conscious goals are managed by our ancient evolved survival driven priority juggling mechanisms. Conscious goals and motivations are driven by a combination of our values, our maps and models of reality, and our emotional associations which guide us towards and away from particular types of situation.

Graph – represent an object or situation with marks, usually on paper. A line can be used in many different ways, to represent shape, form, internal and external structure, distance, the edge of a surface or a type of material, a viewpoint, ratios, relative values, intersecting sets, etc. A very versatile and precise medium for communicating human thinking.

Graphical Thinking™ is a graphical system for documenting, modeling and exploring your thinking about the dynamics and deep structure of any situation. It focuses our attention in a way that helps to bring all our valuable pre-conscious knowledge about the world up into conscious awareness, where we can deliberately check and discuss its validity, and its application to the current situation. It works in a way that complements what we know about how neural networks model our experience of the world. It also creates a situation where it is possible to think about all of the issues raised in more traditional academic thinking frameworks. You can apply it to any subject, and can use it alone or with a group.

Hierarchy – (from Greek for *sacred rule*) – a collection of elements graded by properties such as status, value, level, ownership, control, etc.

Hypothesis - (Greek *hypo* under) so it's an under thesis, the beginnings of a thesis, but not a proper thesis yet. A thesis is a proposition.

Idea – this word is used a lot, but it is often very hard to pin down what it means. In this book it means a model of reality, or a part of a model, a building block within a model.

Identical (equal?) - has exactly the same properties, relations, possibilities and probabilities as...

If x, **then** do y, **else** do z – an example of procedural logic.

Antecedent - the **if** part of an if then expression.
Consequent - the **then** part of an if then.

Illusion - what we experience via our senses.

Imagine - to invent experiences, models, events.

Induction - this book sees induction as the process of using experience to build a generalized de-fluffed mental model of how the universe works (see Reasoning).

Inference - critical thinking speak for forming or coming to a conclusion.

Intelligence - an emergent property of millions of years of neural network evolution.

Intuition - pre-conscious perception and decision making in our neural networks.

Introspection - consciously looking inside, at our thoughts, emotions, reactions, historical decisions, internal dialogue, perceptual distortions, maps, models, values, goals, motivations, etc.

Knowledge - a word we should probably redefine or break down into many different sub-types to indicate, for example, whether the sense of knowing is based on a little, a lot, or too much experience, when and how well it was tested, how new or old it is, how many people disagree, how transportable it is, etc.

Linear - in a line, a sequence in which each point connects to a maximum of two neighbours.

Logic - a branch of philosophy that explicitly states the rules for deriving valid conclusions in a particular field. **Illogical** - the conclusions are not validly derived from the premises according to the rules of that particular game frame.

Matrix - an organising framework prescribing the form of something.

Meaning – a beneficial by-product of neural network perception based on detecting associations.

Measurement – accurately observing and comparing quantities and qualities.

Metaphor (also simile and analogy) – a language tool for drawing attention to similarities in properties and relationships, and for transporting chunks of meaning from one domain to another.

Method (Greek *higher way*) - a standard way of doing something. In computer languages it is the ability of one object to transform the properties and relationships of another object.

Name – a socially agreed sound to represent a collection of properties, relationships, possibilities and probabilities.

Paradigm (see game) - a socially agree set of rules for dealing with something (from Latin and Greek).

Philosophy – Greek for the love of wisdom.

Pragmatic – down to earth, dealing with the practical uses and consequences of things.

Precision – accuracy.

Prejudice - see bias.

Premise - critical thinking speak for a proposal or suggestion.

Principle – a primary truth, law, doctrine, belief or dogma used as the basis of reasoning or action – or a non negotiable value influencing the setting of goals or the means of achieving those goals. The word is often used to try to imply moral superiority, but don't forget that Hitler had principles too. The question is, are they good principles? **Doctrine** and **Dogma** share a special property that they are used as criteria for group membership and require to be accepted without question.

Probability - looks at the statistical likelihood that something will happen by chance. If something is not behaving in accordance with random chance it suggests a cause is exerting an influence. The word comes from the Latin *probare* for prove.

Questions - who, how, which, why, what, where, when, + who **else,** how **else,...** etc. Learning to ask questions is essential to thinking and understanding.

Quintessential (epitome) - from Latin *quinta essential* - the fifth substance (the form, the matrix) underlying the four elements. It is used to mean the **essence**, the **perfect form.**

Rationalisation - this book uses it to mean a socially agreed explanation that is not necessarily a perfect match with our personal experience. In critical thinking terms it means a logically reasoned explanation.

Reasoning - in critical thinking, reasoning is evaluating evidence to see if it supports a logically structured argument, and it is considered the only valid form of thinking. In critical thinking speak there are 2 types of reasoning - **deductive** (moving from the general to the specific, or, step by step from axioms to conclusions using agreed methods at each step) and **inductive** (moving from lots of specific experiences to the general explanation, or, use knowledge of two or more premises to infer if the conclusion is valid, or, collect observations and form a hypotheses). If the premises contain quantifiers (e.g. some, many, a few) it is called either syllogistic reasoning or categorical reasoning. Clearly there are many other types of reasoning to be found in the world of human endeavour. In neural network thinking, reason is just one of the conscious external thinking games we can choose to play. We don't do it very often, and it is not the mechanism by which most of the outstanding achievements of humanity were created. In neural network thinking we build models, apply them and update them.

Reification - inventing and naming a concept or class and then treating it as if it is real.

Space and Time - our impression of space and time is created by our neural networks and seems completely believable and reliable. Ancient mystics and modern science tell us that our pre-conscious perception of space and time may be rather inaccurate.

Science - a method of approaching reality based on careful observation, creating a hypothesis that generates testable predictions, designing objective repeatable experiments to destructively test the hypothesis and its predictions. If the hypothesis stands up to the testing it is accepted as a good model, for now. The method is limited in that it is only able to work with measurable elements, and because it can only handle a very small numbers of elements at a time, and therefore needs to isolate the objects of study from the rest of their environment. As a result it is not very good at modelling the complexity of the real world.

Semantic - the meaning of words and language (Greek for *meaning*).

Specimen (example) - a small part taken to be an example of its class.

Study - Subject names ending in *ology* are from Greek *logos* meaning *word, expression,* and are understood to mean a subject of study, or talking about a subject. Subject names ending in *onomy* (astronomy, taxonomy) are from Greek for *organising, arranging*. Names ending in *ics* (physics, logistics, mathematics) are from the Greek ending used to indicate feminine abstract nouns, particularly arts and sciences.

Strategy - a plan to achieve a goal.

Symbol - something understood to represent an object, idea, function, process, etc.

Synthesis (paired with analysis) - put it back together - the recombining of separate parts or elements to form a complex whole.

Test - comes originally from the Latin *testu(m)* = an earthen pot. So to test something, originally meant, to decide which pot to put it in, which class or category it belongs to.

Theory - in critical thinking it is a set of ideas, a body of knowledge, a statement of principles, which satisfactorily thoroughly and concisely explain some aspect of the observed world. It is arrived at by investigation, observation and reasoning, and its predictions are tested by experiment. In neural network terms it is a model of reality built by the mechanism of detecting associations, probabilities, possibilities, properties and relationships and assembling them into a pre-conscious model. The model can then be brought into conscious awareness, where we can wind the handle to explore and test its predictions. The testing part is the same in both approaches but the neural network based explanation has much more to say about how the model is initially generated. The scientific model has no idea how we get those flashes of inductive inspiration in the first place.

Thinking - pre-conscious inherited neural networks trapping personal and cultural experiences, juggling priorities, managing attention, building and applying models of reality and selecting packages of reactions. This is overlaid with a more conscious ability to reflect on our actions, direct our perception, create and follow external games and strategies, and control our reactions (to some extent).

Thesis - a proposition (dissertation).

Time (see space).

Trial and Error - an ancient and very effective problem-solving strategy.

Truth - an over simplistic concept that needs updating.

Type (see class, kind, sort, category, etc.) - Greek origin.

Typical - a good example of its type.

Understand - to stand under the next level up.

Vague - (from Latin for *wandering*) ill-defined, imprecise, inexact, avoiding clarity.

Valid - strong, sound, defendable, reasoned, evidenced. A conclusion is valid if it must be true if the premises are true - if it follows from the premises.

Variable - a changeable property.

Verify - to check the truth or correctness of something, from Latin for truth *verificare* - as shown by examination or demonstration.

Word - originally considered sacred carriers of meaning and an active ingredient in the process of creation. Until recently words had always been considered the meaningful element of speech, but in the last 100 yrs or so, words have started to break free from any specific shared meaning. Maybe we could start to discriminate between the words that are still connected to their ancient shared meanings, and the ones that have broken free, and are actually just sounds that people make.

1178035

Made in the USA